I0084452

Egerton Ryerson

Canadian Methodism

Its Epochs and Characteristics

Egerton Ryerson

Canadian Methodism
Its Epochs and Characteristics

ISBN/EAN: 9783337186883

Printed in Europe, USA, Canada, Australia, Japan

Cover: Foto ©ninafisch / pixelio.de

More available books at **www.hansebooks.com**

CANADIAN METHODISM;

ITS EPOCHS AND CHARACTERISTICS.

Written at the Request of the London, Toronto, and Montreal
Conferences.

BY THE

REV. EGERTON RYERSON, D.D., LL.D.

*Reprinted, with much additional matter, from the CANADIAN
METHODIST MAGAZINE.*

TORONTO:

WILLIAM BRIGGS.

78 & 80 King St. East.

1882.

Entered according to the Act of the Parliament of Canada, in the year one thousand eight hundred and eighty-two, by WILLIAM BRIGGS, in the Office of the Minister of Agriculture, at Ottawa.

PREFACE.

By a sad necessity it falls to the lot of the present writer, as Editor of the periodical in which these essays first appeared, to prepare a preface to the volume in which they are now collected. From frequent and intimate intercourse with their lamented Author we can affirm that controversy was not the object with which they were written. Being invited thereto by the formal request of the London, Toronto, and Montreal Conferences, Dr. Ryerson desired to place on record certain documentary evidence of which he was in possession, as to the eventful history of Methodism in what is now known as Old Canada. Of those stirring events, in which he played so prominent a part, it is more than probable that the honoured writer of these essays could speak with greater fullness of information than any other man. He wrote, not to revive dead issues or buried animosities, but rather, by a calm appeal to reason and to historic facts, to allay them forever.

So anxious was Dr. Ryerson to avoid all ground of reasonable offence that he gave the

Editor of the periodical, in which these essays appeared, full authority to suppress or modify any passage that might be justly construed as offensive in tone or spirit. That Editor, however, did not feel at liberty, in essays which had been formally requested by three Annual Conferences, to do more than modify an occasional phrase, and to relegate to the volume of collected essays a considerable amount of matter for which there was not space in the *Magazine*, for which they were primarily prepared. It will be found, therefore, that this volume is not a mere reprint of the essays as they were published from month to month; but that it contains a large amount of new matter which has not heretofore appeared. It will possess also, to the many admirers of its beloved and honoured author, a melancholy interest as being the latest production of that pen which, during a long and busy life, was ever wielded in the defence of civil and religious liberty.

And yet this volume is even now incomplete. During the very last interview which the present writer had with his revered and honoured friend, shortly before his death, Dr. Ryerson strongly expressed the wish that he might be permitted, before he should depart hence, to write a concluding chapter of an entirely irenical character, that should completely remove any undesigned asperities and acerbities of those already published. We can bear witness that no rancour, no bitter memories entered into the preparation of these papers, that the heart of the writer was full of gentleness and love, of sweetness and light; and that as he drew nearer to the eternal world of light and love its radiance more and more seemed to illumine his soul.

If there be anything that is polemical in this volume, or that is calculated to excite controversy, let it be read in the light of that latest utterance of him who wrote it; in the light of the resolutions breathing only sentiments of peace and brotherhood towards the once estranged branches of Methodism, and especially seeking to consign to oblivion all the painful memories of the past, which he submitted to the last conferences which he was permitted to attend; and in the spirit of the wider sympathies and warmer love which are knitting together the hearts of a common Methodism throughout the world.

> Let us then, uniting, bury
> All our idle feuds in dust,
> And to future conflicts carry
> Mutual faith and common trust ;
> Always he who most forgiveth to his brother is most just.

W. H. W.

Toronto, April 20th, 1882.

CONTENTS.

——∽——

ESSAY I.
PAGE
Loyal Origin of Canadian Methodism.............. ...   1

ESSAY II.
Benevolent Character of Canadian Methodism..........   26

ESSAY III.
Supernatural Aspects of Canadian Methodism   72

ESSAY IV.
Phenomena and Philosophy of Early Methodist Revivals..   99

ESSAY V.
Methodism the Pioneer of Civil and Religious Liberty in
    Upper Canada 129

ESSAY VI.
The Clergy Reserve Controversy 161

ESSAY VII.
The Clergy Reserve Controversy (Continued) 199

ESSAY VIII.
The Clergy Reserve Controversy (Continued) 221

ESSAY IX.
Divisions in the Wesleyan Methodist Church 247

ESSAY X.
Episcopal Division 270

ESSAY XI.
Divisions of Methodism (Continued) 289

ESSAY XII.

PAGE

Conditions and Working of Methodist Union till 1838 .. 306

ESSAY XIII.

Separation of English and American Methodism 333

ESSAY XIV.

Separation of English and American Methodism (Cont'd). 351

ESSAY XV.

Separation of English and American Methodism (Cont'd). 370

ESSAY XVI.

Separation of English and American Methodism (Cont'd). 387

ESSAY XVII.

Separation of English and American Methodism (Cont'd). 407

ESSAY XVIII.

Reunion of British and Canadian Methodism 427

CANADIAN METHODISM.

ESSAY I.

LOYAL ORIGIN OF CANADIAN METHODISM.

METHODISM exists throughout the seven provinces of the Canadian Dominion, with its more than a thousand ministers, its more than one hundred thousand communicants, its nearly two thousand churches with half as many parsonages, its academies and colleges and periodicals, its hundred and fifty thousand dollars annual income and expenditure for missions, besides the local support of its circuit and stationed ministers. This development over a new and sparsely settled country is from less than half a dozen poor people, and in less than a century. Is such a development natural or supernatural? Is it the growth of nature or the work of grace? To these questions the following Essays contain an answer.

The birthplace of Methodism in Canada was in the bosom of loyalty and in the heart of benevolence; it was first preached by men who had borne arms in defence of their King and country.

1

As early as 1780, a Mr. Tuffey, a commissary of
the 44th Regiment, came to Quebec with the
regiment. At that time there was one clergyman
of the Church of England in Montreal and another in Quebec—none elsewhere except a chap-
lain of some regiment. There were, of course,
priests in the Roman Catholic churches. Mr.
Tuffey, who had been a Methodist local preacher
in England, seeing and lamenting the state of
the soldiery and Protestant emigrants in Quebec,
commenced preaching to them, and continued to
do so with success as long as he remained in the
country. On the restoration of peace between
Great Britain and the thirteen American colonies,
some regiments, including the 44th, were dis-
banded at Quebec, leaving it to the option of
officers and men to return to England or settle
in the country. Many remained, taking up land
and settling as farmers, or becoming traders.
Though Mr. Tuffey returned home, the good influences of his life and labours remained among
the soldiers and other Protestant emigrants forming the first scattered settlements; which were
much increased, at the close of the war, by emigrant loyalists from the valleys of the Hudson,
Susquehanna, and Mohawk rivers. Some of
them were Episcopalians, some Presbyterians,
some Lutherans, some Baptists, some Methodists.

As Mr. Tuffey, of the 44th Regiment, was the

first Methodist preacher in Lower Canada, so Mr. George Neal, of a British cavalry regiment, was the first Methodist preacher in Upper Canada. Mr. Neal was of Irish descent, born in Pennsylvania, but mostly resided in the Southern States. On the breaking out of the American revolution he joined the British army, in which he was first appointed captain, and then promoted to be a major. He was at the siege of Charleston, and only escaped being killed by the timely aid of Lord Roden. He had become religious while serving in the army. Major Neal crossed the Niagara river into Canada, at Queenston, the 7th of October, 1786. He taught school and soon began to preach on the Niagara frontier, not without opposition from some quarters, but with encouraging success.

It was thus from the British army came the first Methodist preachers in both Lower and Upper Canada—true soldiers of both an earthly and a heavenly King.

Nor was it in the first preachers alone that Methodism in Canada had a loyal origin ; it was also in the first emigrants, and in the first Missionary preachers that followed them into the wilderness, and ministered to their spiritual wants.

The exodus of Methodists from New York State, and their migration to Canada, on the ground of loyalty to the King of Great Britain, commenced with the first year of the American Revolution in 1774. Nearly ten years before— three years after Canada became a British Pro- vince, and thirteen years before the American Declaration of Independence—a small number of Methodist emigrants arrived in the city of New York from Ireland. They were called Palatines,*

* "In the year 1758 Wesley visited the County of Limerick. His Journal reports there a singular com- munity, settled in Court Mattress, and in Killiheen, Balligarrane, and Pallas, villages within four miles of Mattress. They were not native Celts, but a Teutonic population. Having been nearly half a century without pastors who could speak their language, they had become thoroughly demoralized ; noted for drunkenness, pro- fanity, and 'utter neglect of religion.' But the Methodist itinerants had penetrated to their hamlets, and they were now a reformed and devout people. They had erected a large chapel in the centre of Court Mattress. 'So did God,' said Wesley, 'at last provide for these poor strangers, who, for fifty years, had none who cared for their souls.' At later visits Wesley declares that three such towns as Court Mattress, Killiheen, and Balli- garrane were hardly to be found anywhere else in Ireland or England. There was no 'cursing or swearing, nor Sabbath breaking, nor drunkenness, nor ale-houses in any of them.' 'They had become a serious, thinking people, and their diligence had turned all their land into a garden.'

" But how came this singular people, speaking a foreign tongue, into the west of Ireland ?

" The troops of Louis XIV., under Turenne, devas-

having fled **from** the persecutions raging **against** them on the Continent, **and having** found protection and hospitality under **the** British Government, for which they **and** their descendants **have** ever cherished a grateful and loyal attachment. Among those pious Irish Palatines **who came to** the city **of New York in 1765 (some** accounts **say in** 1760) **was a family** named *Embury,* **of which**

tated, in the latter part of **the** seventeenth century, the Palatinate on the Rhine. Its population was almost entirely Protestant—the strongest **reason for** the relentless violence of the bigoted monarch and **his army. The** whole country **was laid waste** ; the Elector of Palatine could see from **the towers of** Manheim, **his capital, no** less than **two cities and** twenty-five villages **on fire at** once. **The peaceable** peasants **fled before the invaders** by **thousands to the lines** of the **English General, Marl-**borough. Queen **Anne** sent ships **to** convey **them from** Rotterdam to England. More **than** six thousand arrived **in London,** reduced to dependent poverty. **The** sympathy **of** Protestant England relieved their sufferings ; and commissioners were appointed **by** the Government to provide for them. They were encamped **and fed on** Blackheath and Camberwell Commons.

"Popish rule **and** persecution **followed** the invasion of the Palatinate, **and** thousands more **of its** virtuous **and** thrifty **peasants deserted it for** refuge **in England and** other countries. Nearly three thousand **were sent by the** British Government **to America in** 1710, **and became** valuable additions **to** the **colonies of New York, Penn-sylvania, and North Carolina. Of those who remained** there were four brothers—John, Peter, Philip and David—all pious. John and Peter preached in the German language, and died at an early age. David left his property in the United States, after the Revolution, came to Upper Canada, and settled in the township of Fredericksburg, where he

in England, about fifty families emigrated to Ireland, where they settled near Rathkeale, in the County of Limerick. They were allowed eight acres for each person, young and old, for which they were to pay a small annual rent to the proprietor, Lord Southwell. The Government paid their rents for twenty years, made them freeholders, and furnished each man with a musket, enrolling him in the free yeomanry as the 'German Fusileers.' A list of those who 'settled contiguous to each other on Lord Southwell's estates' has been published ; on it are the names of Embury, Heck, Ruckle, Switzer, Guier, and others associated with the original Methodists of New York.

"Such was the origin of the 'Irish Palatines,' and thus did the shortsighted policy of Louis XIV. scatter these sterling Protestants of the Rhine to bless other lands, as his bigoted folly in the revocation of the Edict of Nantes sent half a million of his own best subjects to enrich, by their skill and virtues, Switzerland, Germany, England, and the North American Colonies. His attempt to suppress Protestantism in the Palatinate led, through the emigration of these Irish settlers, to one of the most energetic developments of Protestantism [the M. E. Church] recorded in the modern history of religion."—*Stevens' History of the M. E. Church, vol. i. pp. 48-50.*

died in 1810. Philip Embury was a carpenter and local preacher before he left Ireland ; in 1766 he was joined by his cousin and her husband, best known as **Paul** and **Barbara Heck.** That pious and energetic woman prevailed upon her cousin Philip to commence preaching in his **own house** and **to his own** company, which **consisted on** the first Sabbath of **five persons.** These with others **were** soon **formed** into **a** class. This was the beginning **of the** Methodist Episcopal Church in America—now the largest Protestant denomination on the American continent.*

* The fact that the founders of Methodism in New York were afterwards the **founders of** Methodism in Canada, and the similarity **of circumstances, will give** peculiar interest **to** the following **statements.** It has been frequently stated **that** the first Methodist **emigrants** to New York had **so far lost** their religious **zeal and** feeling **as** to neglect their religious duty, and indulge in amusements, even card-playing, **in** which Embury himself participated ; but the most careful and minute inquiry into all the particulars of the case has shown that there **is no** foundation **for** these statements. It is true that Embury felt **much** discouraged, after **his arrival at** New York, in his isolated position, and the prevalence of religious indifference around him, and did not exercise the office **of a** preacher until 1766, **and was then** prompted to it by the appeals of Barbara Heck ; **but** that either he or his fellow-Wesleyans engaged in card-playing is an unjust imputation. The Rev. Dr. Stevens, in his " History of the M. E. Church," states that—

" One of **our best** authorities in Methodistic **anti-**

Philip Embury and his **little society soon** proceeded to erect a place of worship **in John Street,**
60 feet by 42 feet, called Wesley **Chapel, in** which
Mr. Embury **exercised the pastoral** office **for three
years.** In October, **1769, Mr.** Wesley, **in answer
to the** repeated **and** urgent applications of Mr.

quarian researches (Dr. J. B. Wakeley) says : 'The
families who accompanied Philip Embury were not all
Wesleyans—only a few of them ; the remainder were
members of the Protestant Church in Ireland, but made
no profession of an experimental knowledge of God in
the pardon of sin, and adoption. After their arrival in
.New York, with the exception of Embury and three
or four others, they all finally lost their sense of the fear
of God and became open worldlings. Some subsequently
fell into greater depths of sin than others.'

"Late in the year 1765 another vessel arrived in New
York, bringing over Paul Ruckle, Luke Rose, Jacob
Heck, Peter Barkman, and Henry Williams, with their
families. These were Palatines—some of them relatives
of Embury, and others his former friends and neighbours.
A few of them only were Wesleyans. Mrs. Barbara
Heck, who had been residing in New York since 1760,
visited them frequently. One of the company, Paul
Ruckle, was her eldest brother. It was when visiting
them on one of these occasions that she found some of
the party engaged in a game of cards ; there is no proof
that they were Wesleyans, and connected with Embury.
Her spirit was roused, and, doubtless emboldened by her
long and intimate acquaintance with them in Ireland,
she seized the cards, threw them into the fire, and then
most solemnly warned them of their danger and duty.

Embury and his friends sent to their assistance
two preachers, Messrs. Boardman and Pilmoor,
the former of whom relieved Mr. Embury of his
onerous charge.

The spiritual wants of the little society in New
York being then provided for, Mr. Embury and
some of his relatives removed in the autumn of

Leaving them, she went immediately to the dwelling of
Philip Embury, who was her cousin. It was located on
Barrack Street, now Park Place. After narrating to him
what she had seen and done, under the influence of the
Divine Spirit and with power she appealed to him to be
no longer silent—to preach the word forthwith. She
parried his excuses, and urged him to commence at once
in his own house, and to his own people. He consented,
and she went out and collected four persons, who, with
herself, constituted his audience. After singing and
prayer, he preached to them and enrolled them in a class.
He continued thereafter to meet them weekly. Embury
was not among the card-players, nor in the same house
with them."—*Wakeley's Lost Chapters, chap. 2; Dr.
Roberts to the author, quoted in Stevens' History of
the M. E. Church, vol. i. pp. 45-55.*

Dr. Stevens proceeds as follows : "The little company
soon grew too large for Embury's house ; they hired a
more commodious room in the neighbourhood [a
Rigging-Loft, 30 by 40], where he continued to conduct
their worship ; its expenses being met by voluntary
contributions. In a few months there were two ' classes '
—one of men, the other of women—including six or
seven members each. No little excitement began soon
to prevail in the city on account of these meetings, and

1769 from the city to the country, and settled at
Camden, a village in the township of Salem,
Washington County, where he continued to labour
as a local preacher, and formed a society, chiefly
of his own countrymen, at Ashgrove—the first
Methodist class within the bounds of the Troy
Conference.*

they were thronged with spectators. Three musicians of
a regiment in the neighbouring barracks, attracted prob·
ably by the peculiar charm of Methodist singing, were
converted, and became active co-workers with Embury
as exhorters. The lower classes of the people received
. the word gladly ; the interest reached the Alms-house ;
Embury was invited to preach there, and the Superintendent of the Institution and several of its inmates were
soon recorded among his converts. Thus American
Methodism, like British Methodism and primitive Christianity, of which it was a reproduction, began among the
poor, and thus was foreshadowed its honourable mission
throughout the continent and throughout the world.
With Christ it could say, as the supreme proof of its
genuineness as a dispensation of the truth, that 'the poor
have the Gospel preached unto them.'"—*Ib. pp. 55, 56.*

* "He was held in high estimation by his neighbours, and officiated among them not only as a preacher
but as a magistrate. While mowing in his field he
injured himself so severely as to die suddenly [in August,
1773, says his son], aged but forty-five years, 'greatly
beloved and much lamented,' says Asbury. He was
buried on the neighbouring farm of his Palatine friend,
Peter Switzer. After reposing fifty-seven years in his
solitary grave without a memorial, his remains were dis-

The removal of Barbara Heck and family, and the surviving members of the family of Philip Embury, to Canada, is thus stated by three different writers :—

"Barbara Heck, with her husband and all her sons (John, Jacob and Samuel), removed to Camden, N. Y. (the new home of Embury), in 1770 or 1771, and thence to Canada as early as 1774; in 1778 they were in Upper Canada, and resided in Augusta (where they formed a part of the *first* Methodist class, under the leadership of Samuel Embury, son of Philip) till their deaths—Mr. Paul Heck dying in 1792, Mrs. Barbara Heck in 1804—and they lie side by side in the burying ground of the 'Old Blue Church in the front of Augusta.'"—*Dr. Stevens, vol. i., p. 69, in a note.*

"In 1774, various persons emigrated into Canada from New York ; and among the rest Paul and

interred with solemn ceremonies, and borne by a large procession to the Ashgrove burial-ground, where their resting-place is marked by a monument recording that he was the first to set in motion a train of measures which resulted in the founding of the John Street Church, the cradle of American Methodism, and the introduction of a system which has beautified the earth with salvation, and increased the joys of heaven.' Some of his family emigrated to Upper Canada, and, with the family of Barbara Heck, were among the founders of Methodism in that province."—*Dr. Stevens's History of Methodism.*

Barbara Heck and their family (three sons, Jonn, Jacob and Samuel), who assisted in the beginning of Methodism in New York."—*Playter, pp. 5, 6.*

"In 1774, in consequence of the evidently approaching revolutionary storm, and being ardently attached to British institutions, the Heck family; John Lawrence, who had married the widow of Philip Embury; David Embury, brother to Philip; and many more of the Palatines of Ashgrove—emigrated to Lower Canada, and stopped for a time near Montreal. Not being pleased with that locality, however, in 1778 they removed to Augusta, in Upper Canada. David Embury, with several of his friends, subsequently settled along the Bay of Quinte, where many of his descendants still live."—*Webster, p. 30.* *

It is thus seen that Methodism in New York and Canada was founded by the same parties; that it was first preached in both Lower and Upper Canada by officers of the British army, and that its first societies were formed of those who

* "The first Methodist Society was formed, as nearly as can be ascertained, in 1778, and numbered among its first members Paul and Barbara Heck, their three sons, John, Jacob and Samuel, and Catharine Lawrence—formerly Mrs. Philip Embury—Samuel Embury, son of Philip, and such others as felt it a privilege to unite with the class. Mr. and Mrs. Lawrence opened their house for worship, and Mr. Samuel Embury was appointed leader."—*Ib. p. 30.*

had, on the outbreak of the American revolution, fled to Canada for peace and safety, on account of their grateful and loyal attachment to British institutions.*

Such also were the loyal feelings and devotion of the first regular Methodist ministers who volun-

* "Already since the war began, several families, influenced by feelings of loyalty and duty to the British Crown, and also to escape the distractions of the country, which appeared likely long to continue, had come to Canada, and took up their residence in or near Quebec and Montreal. But, after the disaster of Burgoyne's army in 1777, the loyalists in New York State were so discouraged that they began to look upon Canada as their only refuge. They arranged their property as well as possible, and made preparations for their departure and journey. A great number came into the Provinces each year of the continuance of the war, some by way of the sea and up the River St. Lawrence, and some through the unbroken wilderness between the inhabited parts of the New York State and those of the Province. Great privations and distresses were endured by the emigrants. Families were six weeks on the voyage to Quebec. During the war, some of the emigrants settled on land in Upper Canada, before surveying had begun. The Hecks came to Augusta in 1778, and settled on the banks of the St. Lawrence. Paul Heck was a soldier for a year or two in the royal army, and obtained his discharge in August, 1778. In 1779, some families came up in boats, and settled on the site of Kingston, and along the shores of the township of Kingston."—*Playter, p. 8.*

teered and were sent to minister to the spiritual
wants of the new settlements in Canada, in compliance with their earnest petitions. The Rev.
William Losee was the first regular preacher who
came to Canada ; he was sent by Bishop Asbury,
at the New York Conference in 1790, in compliance with an earnest request of the Canadian
people. *Losee was a loyalist,* and knew some of
the settlers in Adolphustown before they left the
United States. He desired to see them, and
preach to them the glad tidings of salvation. Had
he been on the revolutionary side, the warm
loyalists would not have received him—rather
would have driven him from the country. Having
preached a few times, he spoke of leaving (his visit
being voluntary). The people were now anxious
for a missionary to reside and labour among them,
and circulated an extensively signed petition in
the Midland District, to the New York Conference, for a missionary to labour in these new
townships. He carried the petition to Conference,
which assembled in New York, and offered to be
the first preacher in these northern climes. Bishop
Asbury* and the preachers were willing that an

---

* "In order to ensure obedience to the Government,
and to distinguish between friends and enemies, all were
called upon to take an oath of allegiance to the State
authorities in which they resided, and of course *to abjure
allegiance to the Crown of Great Britain.* To the taking

entrance should be made at this new door.
William Losee was therefore allowed to return,
with instructions to form a Circuit. · As the Con-

of this oath many of the preachers had conscientious
scruples, which exposed them to many vexations, and
obliged some of them to leave their stations. Mr.
George Shadford, whose labours had been so abundantly
blessed in the awakening and conversion of souls, after
a day of fasting and prayer, in company with Mr.
Asbury, for Divine direction, took his departure this
year for England, leaving behind him the savour of a
good name and many happy souls as seals to his ministry.

"*As Mr. Asbury could not persuade himself to take
the required oath of allegiance to the State of Maryland,*"
where he was in the first part of the year, he retired to
the State of Delaware, where he found an asylum in the
house of Judge White for nearly twelve months. While
the storm of war was raging around, and while all his
English brethren had forsaken him and the flocks entrusted to their care, he determined to wait patiently until
the tempest should subside, that he might again launch
forth upon a calmer sea in quest of immortal souls. But,
though he was secluded from the pursuit of his enemies
in the house of his friend and patron, Judge White, he
says that except for about two months, when the necessity of the case compelled him, contrary to his most
ardent wishes to be silent, it was a ' season of the most
active, most useful, and suffering part of his life.'
Though he could not appear before the congregations on
the Sabbath, he was wont to leave his retreat in the gloom
of the night, and go from house to house to enforce the
truths of the gospel ; and notwithstanding the difficulties
with which he and others had to contend in those times

ference sat so late in the year (October, 1790), he had not time to prepare, and returned to Canada before the winter.

of trouble, they were gradually laying a foundation deep and broad, by their labours and sufferings, for that success which Methodism has since had in these United States."—*Dr. Bangs' History of the Methodist Episcopal Church, vol. i. pp. 123, 124.*

But though the Methodist ministers and their societies suffered much during the Revolution, the clergy and congregations of the Protestant Episcopal Church suffered still more. The Episcopal as well as Methodist ministers were mostly Englishmen, and were loyal to the British Crown ; and both, for the most part, returned to England on the breaking out of the American Revolution. The first Legislature chosen by the people of Virginia established the Anglican Church ; and the next year there was a pastor for every six hundred of its population. The historian of their Church, the late Rev. Dr. Hawks, says that " When the colonists first resorted to arms, Virginia, in her sixty-one counties, contained ninety-five parishes, sixty-four churches and chapels and ninety-one clergymen. When the contest was over, she came out of the war with a large number of churches destroyed or injured irreparably ; with twenty-three of her ninety-five parishes extinct or forsaken, and of the remaining seventy-two, thirty-four were destitute of ministerial services ; while of her ninety-one clergymen, twenty-eight only remained, who had lived through the storm, and these, with eight who came into the State soon after the struggle terminated, supplied thirty-six of the parishes. Of these twenty-eight, fifteen only had been enabled to continue in the churches which they had supplied prior

" In 1791, however, as soon as the winter was well set in, and the ice in the St. Lawrence strong enough to allow crossing with a horse, Mr. Losee was on his journey. He went through the wilderness of the western part of New York State, in the track of the emigrants coming into Canada, suffered hardships and many privations in journeying for some weeks through a country almost without roads and nearly without inhabitants, crossed the frontier at Kingston, and appears to have been safely in Adolphustown again in the month of February.

" The good impression made by Losee on his first coming, was strengthened by his second. The people received the word with a ready mind, and a number were soon enjoying the salvation of the Gospel."*

Losee was accompanied the following year by Darius Dunham, and afterwards by other preachers who volunteered to come to Canada and labour among the sparse inhabitants, and who were of like British feelings and self-sacrificing zeal with

to the commencement of hostilities, and thirteen had been driven from their cures by violence, and went to seek safety or comfort in some one of the many vacant parishes, where they might hope to find, for a time at least, exemption from the extremity of suffering."— *Hawks' Contributions, etc., p. 153.*

* Playter's History, pp. 23, 24.

2

Losee himself. Though privations and poverty·
and hardships awaited them, the " love of Christ
constrained them,"—a true British patriotism impelled them, and they counted not even their lives
dear unto them, that they might impart to the
dispersed emigrant loyalists of Canada the instructions and consolations of our holy religion. We
know of no country the early religious history of
which presents such a stamp of loyal patriotism
as that of the Methodist Church of Canada in its
first preachers, its first Church members, and
regular missionary ministers, wholly dependent
as they were for support, or rather slender susten-
ance, upon their own exertions and upon the
voluntary contributions, mostly in articles of food
and clothing, of the widely scattered people
among whom they lived and laboured.

Yet, singular to say, and incredible as it may
appear, the chief charge against Methodism in
Canada, and the most common ground of opposition to it, during more than thirty years was that
its ministers were disaffected to the Government
and institutions of the country. Such were the
pretexts for the persecutions against Christianity
during the first three hundred years of its history,
and against Wesleyan ministers in the United
States during the Revolutionary War; * and so it

* " They had," says one of them who witnessed their
afflictions, "almost insuperable difficulties, violent oppo-

was in Canada. Some of the preachers were **interrupted and** insulted, and seized by constables while preaching—in one or two instances headed **by** the Sheriff—under the pretext that they were vagabonds—the vagabond offence of preaching **the**

sitions, **bitter** persecutions, **and grievous** sufferings to endure. So many **of** the **preachers being** Englishmen, **and** Wesley, who was the founder and chief **ruler** of the Methodist societies, being in England, and **known to** be loyal to his king, and of course unfriendly to **the American** measures, occasioned jealousies **and suspicions** that the Methodists were politically **a dangerous people.** **Also** the moral views and **conscientious scruples of the** people called **Methodists, not being favourable on general** principles to the spirit **and practice of** war, **on this** ground also, the **temper of** the times combining with **other** prejudices and passions **of the day,** excited **jealousies** which occasioned **an** evil report **or alarm that the Meth-** odists, preachers **and** people, **were opposed to the** American revolution.

" When the times **were** about **the** worst, **Asbury** and **Shadford** agreed **to make** it a matter **of fasting** and **prayer for** direction in the midst **of their** difficulties, **what to do;** whether to **stay in** the country, or return to **England.** Shadford concluded that he had an answer **to leave the** country and return to England ; but Asbury, **who** received an answer **to stay,** replied, ' **If you are called** to go, I am called to stay ; **so here we must part.'** Accordingly **they** parted to **meet no more on earth.** From that moment **Asbury made America his** country and his home. He **resolved** to abide among **us, and at the risk of** all, **even of life itself, to** continue **to labour and to**

gospel from place to place, to a spiritually destitute
people; their assailants declaring that none but
clergy of the Established Church of England
should preach in the colonies, though there were
at that time but two such in all Upper Canada.*

Amidst privations, and labours, and sufferings
—to be noted hereafter—the pioneer Methodist
preachers toiled on their vast circuits, and adding
new ones, until the war of the United States
against Great Britian from 1812 to 1815, during
the whole of which not a single Methodist was

. suffer with and for his American brethren. Oppositions,
reproaches and persecutions rushed in against them from
every quarter like a tempest. During the whole period
of conflict and danger his manner of life was irreproach-
able. His prudence and caution as a man and a citizen,
his pious and correct deportment as a Christian and a
minister, were such as to put at defiance the suspicious
mind and the tongue of slanders. He never meddled
with politics ; but in those days of suspicion and alarm,
to get a preacher or society persecuted it was only necessary to excite suspicion, sound the alarm, and cry out
'Enemies of the country !' or 'Tories !'"—*Stevens*,
vol. i. pp. 277-279.

* In one instance, in the Midland District, near Kingston, while Mr. McCarty, a Whitefield Methodist, but
recognized by the Wesleyans, " was preaching," says Mr.
Playter, " one Sunday at Robert Perry's, four armed men
came up ; and leaving their guns outside, rushed into
the house to seize the preacher, intending to carry him
off to Kingston jail. But the congregation opposing, and

found in the ranks of the invaders of their country, but very many of them were amongst its defenders.

The only shadow of pretext for the imputation against the loyalty of the first Methodist preachers was their ordination and appointment by an American bishop. As well might disaffection to the American Government have been imputed to the Episcopalian clergy, because, on the ground of

Mr. Perry agreeing to give bail for the man's appearance in Kingston on the morrow, the men went away. The next day Mr. Perry took the preacher to Kingston, and brought him to the Sheriff, who refused to have aught to do with the man. Under some false pretext he was arrested and cast into prison; but was liberated again on his friend again becoming bail, and returned home [where he had a wife and four children, among whom is Mr. John McCarty, of Cobourg]. On the expiration of the bail, Mr. McCarty repaired to Kingston. And now his enemies resolved that he should never go back to preach. [Having obtained the condemnation by Judge Cartwright of Mr. McCarty, as a vagabond, for preaching the glad tidings of the gospel from neighbourhood to neighbourhood, where his family resided,] he was seized, thrown into a boat under the care of four Frenchmen, who were directed to leave him on one of the then desolate islands of the St. Lawrence; here they landed him, left him, and he was never heard of afterwards."—"Undoubtedly McCarty was a martyr for the gospel, and so he was regarded by the early inhabitants."—*Playter, pp. 17, 18.*

ecclesiastical order, they received ordination **from**
English bishops. Besides, **for twenty** years, the
voluntary preachers for the then wilds of Canada
were accepted, ordained and appointed **by** the
venerable Asbury, who had retired into **concealment** during the American Revolutionary War
rather than abjure his oath of allegiance **to** his
King, or take an oath of allegiance to any American
State authority until after the acknowledgment
of American Independence by Great Britain.

After the close of that eventful war [1812-15],
the Clergy Reserves began to be available, and
more systematic measures were adopted for the
religious and educational institutions of the country. The "Clergy Reserves" consisted of *one-
seventh* of all the surveyed lands of Upper Canada,
set apart by the "Constitutional Act," 31st
George the Third, chapter 31, which established
the parliamentary government of Upper Canada,
for the "support of a Protestant clergy," in contradistinction to the Roman Catholic clergy of
Lower Canada, who were largely endowed by
tithes and lands. It was intended that Upper
Canada should be an English and Protestant
province, while Lower Canada should be French
and Roman Catholic. In Lower Canada there
was no legislative endowment for Protestantism
in Upper Canada there was no legislative endowment for Romanism.

It **was now** claimed **that the** Protestant clergy of the Constitutional **Act of** 1791 were the **clergy** of the **Church** of England **alone,** which, **it was** maintained, was *the* Established Church **of Upper** Canada as well as of England **and** Ireland. **Not only** was one-seventh of **the lands of the Pro-** vince claimed **as the** patrimony **of the clergy** of **that** Church, but large **English** parliamentary grants were applied for, **and a** large endowment of land was granted for a University College, in- cluding a Faculty of Theology, all under **the** direction of the authorities **of** that **Church and** based on **its** Articles of **Religion and Service of** Worship.

But even this monstrous system might not have excited **m**uch attention **or** opposition, **had it** not appeared, from the documents and papers which projected and advocated it, that the great object of the whole scheme was not merely the support of the Church of England in the country, but the extermination of other religious persua- sions, especially of the Methodists, who were represented as republicans and overrunning the country, and whose influence was represented **as** hostile to the civil and religious institut**ions** of England.

But as **this** great **and protracted controversy** will be the **subject of a** distinct **paper,** in this series **of** Essays, **I** will ónly here remark that the parties assailed combined and put forth their united efforts in vindication of their character and rights, and after a struggle of nearly a quarter of a century were completely successful in establishing those equal civil and religious rights and liberties which at this day make the inhabitants of the wide Dominion of Canada the most loyal and freest people in the vast Empire of Great Britain.

It may be added, that, in compliance with the petitions of various denominations, the Commons House of Assembly appointed a Select Com-
-mittee which examined and reported the evidence of no less than *fifty-three* witnesses, consisting of the leading men of different parties. In the address to the King, founded on this evidence, the House of Assembly (a majority of whose members were Episcopalians) employed the following language in regard to the Methodist ministers of the day, 20th March, 1828 :

" We humbly beg leave to assure your Majesty that the insinuations against the Methodist preachers in this Province do much injustice to a body of pious and deserving men, who justly enjoy the confidence and are the spiritual instructors of a large portion of your Majesty's subjects in this Province. We are convinced that the tendency of their influence and instruction is not hostile to our institutions, but, on the contrary, is eminently favourable to religion and morality; that their labours are calculated to make their people better men and better subjects; and have already produced in this Province the happiest effects."

ESSAY II.

CANADIAN Methodism is no less remarkable for its *benevolent* than for its *loyal* origin. Benevolence itself is among the first of the God-like virtues—pitying the destitute, helping the distressed, " upholding those that fall, and raising up those that are bowed down." And that benevolence never shines with a purer lustre than when it voluntarily suffers wholly for the sake of others—accompanies the lonely emigrant into the wilderness, and cheers the first months of his isolation, privations and labours, by warming and illuminating his bark-covered log-cottage with the beams of the Sun of Righteousness and the angel songs of devotion and praise. If the indigenous industry of the new settlers felled the first tree of the forest, erected the first shanty, turned the first sod, made the first enclosure, planted and gathered the first crop ; so did the first Methodist preachers follow in the footsteps of the first emigrants, traversing the same wildernesses, braving the same privations and hardships, and, like emigrants themselves, without extraneous support. Losee himself, the first itinerant minister from the United States, during his first journey through an almost interminable forest from Lake Champlain to the Bay of Quinte, came " on a warfare at his own temporal charges," and therefore endured the severe hardships of ordinary emigrants. And thus travelled and endured Losee's colleagues and successors—the Dunhams, the Colemans, the Woolseys, the Keelers, the Coates, the Jewells, the Sawyers, the Bangs, and others of that epoch of Methodism in Canada— especially Upper Canada. Through long roads, or rather roadless deserts, they came to the Canadian wilderness settlements in the faith and spirit of the first Gospel Mission established by the Saviour (Matt. x. 9, 10), provided with " neither gold, nor silver, nor scrip, nor two coats," resting with assurance and dignified confidence that now, as in ancient days, " the workman is worthy of his meat." .

The ample provision which is made nowadays to defray the travelling expenses and provide for the support of missionaries to near and distant fields of labour, was not known in the first days of Methodist Mission work in Canada, any more than the modern improvements in travel and

agriculture. With these improved facilities of
travel and support there ought to be a corresponding missionary zeal, activity and consecration.
The identity of sympathy of the first preachers
with the first settlers in their toils and wants,
invested the Divine messenger with vast power
for good in behalf of the people to whom he
ministered. Perhaps there is no one element of
moral influence more powerful in the formation
of the character of a people than blending with
their earliest forest homes the domestic and public
services of religion and the associations of Christian friendship. The educated and uneducated
alike feel the power of such an influence, which
pervades the primitive dwelling and descends from
generation to generation. We have no doubt that
the energetic, manly and Christian character
which at all times, in war as well as in peace, has
distinguished the people of Upper Canada, is the
fact that their first homes echoed to the practical
doctrines and morals of the Gospel; and though
the first generation of settlers were far from being
all religious, they were not infidels—they "feared
God and honoured the king"—there was no
infidelity among them ; and though some of them
took God's name in vain, and remembered not
the Sabbath day to keep it holy, yet the skeptics
and the scorners, who would bring religion into
contempt by attacking the motives of its ministers

and professors, have ever been compelled to admit that it was not the skeptic or the scorner that first pitied the moral destitution of the early settlers in Canada, and, amid great exposures and dangers, traversed forests, and rivers, and lakes, to assuage the sorrows, encourage the hopes, and guide the morals of the first adventurers; but it was those who had experienced the Gospel as the power of God unto salvation, had imbibed the benevolent spirit of Jesus Christ, and were animated by His love.

If the character and labours of the first preachers of Christianity demonstrated the divinity of the religion they preached; the first Methodist preachers in Canada, by their self-denials, purity of life and doctrine, and extraordinary labours, demonstrated the divinity of their mission, and produced in the public mind the conviction that they were actuated by higher than human motives and were sustained by higher than human power, while their ministrations were instrumental in creating hundreds of happy homes, and the fruits of righteousness in the lives of thousands of individuals.

We will give a few examples of the self-sacrifice and hardships of these volunteer apostles of Methodism to the first loyalist emigrants in Canada.

Losee's first visit to Canada in 1790 was

spontaneous—by **permission**, not by appointment. In **1791** he was appointed the primary missionary to the Bay of Quinte. "*Losee having* **taken** *part with the loyalists during the American Revolution*, and having acquaintances in Canada, was **not the** less acceptable **on** that account; and **a** pretty extensive **Circuit was** soon formed, where he **preached** during the year. The people were soon aroused to the subject of religion, and conversions **occurred** in various **townships, so** that 165 members were reported at the close of the year."[*]

"James Coleman volunteered and was sent to Canada in 1794. On his route to and **in** his travels in the Provinces, he endured the severest privations. While passing up the Mohawk river he was obliged **to go on shore** *fifteen nights* **in** *succession,* and kindle a fire to keep off **the** wild beasts; **and** his food **failing, he was** reduced to a cracker per day."[†]

Under date of 1801, Dr. Bangs, in his "History of the Methodist Episcopal Church," thus states the manner in which the earliest Methodist preachers prosecuted their work in Upper Canada:

"Upper Canada was at that time but sparsely populated; so that in riding from one appointment to another, the preachers sometimes had to

---

[*] Rev. Wm. Case's Jubilee Sermon, delivered at London in 1855, p. 4.

[†] Dr. Stevens' Life and Times of Dr. Bangs, p. 41.

pass through wildernesses from ten to sixty miles
distance, and not unfrequently had either to en-
camp in the woods or sleep in an Indian tent;
and sometimes, in visiting the newly settled places,
they have carried provender for their horses over-
night, when they would tie them to a tree to
prevent their straying in the woods; while the
preachers themselves had to preach, eat, and sleep
in the same room, looking at the curling smoke
ascending through an opening in the roof of the
log-cabin, which had not yet the convenience of
even a chimney.

"But in the midst of these labours and privations they seemed to be abundantly compensated
in beholding the blessed effects of their evan-
gelical efforts, and the cordiality and high gratification with which they were received and treated,
more especially by those whose hearts God had
touched by His Spirit. For though the people
were in the wilderness, and many of them poor,
they seemed to be ripe for the Gospel; and it was
no less gratifying to its messengers than it was
pleasurable to its recipients to behold its blessed
effects upon the hearts and lives of such as 'believed with the heart unto righteousness.' While
those who resisted the truth often manifested their
enmity by persecuting those who proclaimed it,
such as did 'receive it in the love of it,' evinced
their affection and gratitude to those who pub-

lished it by making them welcome to their habitations and entertaining them in the best manner they could. For these self-denying labours and sacrifices of these early Methodist preachers, thousands of immortal beings in Canada will doubtless praise God in that day when He shall come to make up His jewels."*

These statements of Dr. Bangs were, in great part, the result of his own personal observation and experience, as will appear hereafter when we give some account of his labours in Canada —he being the first Canadian preacher converted and employed as an itinerant for seven years in Canada, from 1801 to 1808. But contemporaneous with the labours of Dr. Bangs, and extending half a century beyond them, were those of the venerable William Case, "Father of Indian Missions in Canada." Mr. Case says : "In June, 1805, I was admitted as an itinerant preacher in the New York Conference, then in session at Ashgrove ; and having *volunteered* for Canada, I was appointed, with Henry Ryan, to the Bay of Quinte Circuit." (Jubilee Sermon, p. 54.) "In 1806, I lost my health by hard toils in the swamps of Canada, and for three months my strength was wasting away by fever and ague. I now thought I should receive an appointment suited to my

* History of the Methodist Episcopal Church, Vol. II., pp. 124, 125.

feeble state; but, contrary to my expectations, my appointment was to the mountains of Ulster Circuit (N. Y. State). I felt it as a disappointment, and thought I could never ascend those lofty mountains, nor endure the toils of a circuit three hundred and thirty miles round. But submitting all to God, I went forward; and I have reason to believe that it was the very circuit the best suited to my febrile state; for such was the purity of the water and salubrity of the atmosphere, that I immediately began to recover. My health was again established; so that at the next Conference I again offered myself for Canada." *

* Jubilee Sermon, pp. 57, 58.

Mr. Case gives the following graphic account of the manner of his entrance into Canada, after the acceptance of his second offer of himself for the Canadian wilderness work :

"In 1808, on my arrival at Black-Rock, the *embargo* prohibited the transport of property across the line. At first I was perplexed, and knew not what to do. So I went to the hay-loft and fell on my face in prayer. I asked the Lord, as I was engaged in *His* work, to open my way to fulfil my mission to Canada. Having committed all to God, I returned to my lodgings at the inn, when a stranger smilingly said, ' I should not wonder if the Missionary should jump into the boat, take his horse by the bridle, and *let him swim round the embargo*,' and I did so ; my horse swam the Niagara ; and I landed safely in Canada."—*Ib.*, pp. 58, 59.

In a summary review of his fifty years' perils, sufferings, and labours in Canada, Mr. Case employs the following expressive and touching words :

"Five times have I been laid low by fevers, bilious and typhus ; and although with no home of my own, I was provided for among strangers, who watched at my bedside for weeks together, faithfully administering to my recovery. The Lord reward them in 'that day !' Sometimes in those afflictions, but more afterwards, I found they 'yielded the peaceable fruits of righteousness ;' and then how sweetly could I sing—

> 'Oft from the margin of the grave,
> Thou, Lord, hast lifted up my head ;
> Sudden, I found Thee near to save :
> The fever owned Thy touch, and fled.'

"In my labours it has been my lot to be much on the waters. Once I was shipwrecked on Lake Ontario ; five times have I been through the ice with my horse on bays, rivers, and lakes of Canada. Through all these dangers the Lord in His providence delivered me, and then I have sung with delight :

> 'Oft hath the sea confessed Thy power,
> And given me back at Thy command:
> It could not, Lord, my life devour,—
> Safe in the hollow of Thy hand.'

"The Christian minister in any perplexity has abundant sources for relief ; as that of the Church,

his experience, the Bible, and his God. If the
first fail, he is sure of relief from the last. 'In
all thy ways acknowledge God, and He shall
direct thy paths.'" Prov. iii. 6.*

* Jubilee Sermon, pp. 56, 57.

In his concluding appeal to parents—especially to
mothers—Mr. Case exclaims, as follows, and states a most
affecting incident :

"Mothers ! devote your sons from their birth to the
service of God and His Church ! As an encouragement,
remember *Hannah* and her Samuel. Already two hundred young men have been converted in Canada, and
engaged in the ministry ! Hundreds more will be wanted
as the harvest-fields are enlarged !

"Who has not heard of the piety of the venerated Mrs.
Wesley ;—of the faith of ' Mother Kent,' of New England ;—of ' Mother Covel,' of the Catskill Mountains ;—
of ' Mother Ryerson,' of Canada ; and of many other
' mothers in Israel' and of their sons in the ministry?
In 1807, I came to my appointment in a small log-cottage,
in a gorge of the mountains in the Ulster Circuit, where
I met two itinerant ministers, *twin-sons* of a pious
mother. After the sermon by one of them I met the
' class,' when I congratulated the mother on having two
sons in the ministry. The reference was sufficient—it
kindled anew the ardent flame in her heart, and she
broke out in expressions like these : ' Yes, glory to God,
I know how they became ministers! On my conversion
to God my soul was so blest, and I felt such a love for
my Saviour, and for the souls He had redeemed, by His
blood, that I wanted to tell it to the whole world. I
went to the cradle where my boys were asleep ; and,
kneeling down over them, I wept and prayed, and de-

I should not omit to notice here the brief visit to Canada of the apostolic Asbury in 1811, though reduced by extreme bodily fatigue and suffering [inflammatory rheumatism in his right foot and leg]. "He had," says Mr. Case, "until this period, appointed the first and only missionaries to this country, and had long and ardently desired to visit the people for whom he had taken so deep an interest, and where the work of the Lord had been so great and so extended. In his way from the New England Conference, he crossed the Green Mountains, Lake Champlain, the swamps of the Chateauguay woods to St. Regis; then across the St. Lawrence to Cornwall.* The first place on

voted them to the service of God and the ministry of the Church. Now here they are, ministers of the Gospel. Glory to God; glory be to God in the highest.' This was 'Mother Covel.'"—*Ib.*, pp. 61, 62.

* The Rev. Henry Boehm, sixty-four years in the ministry, and Bishop Asbury's travelling companion for several years, and who died recently at the age of upwards of 100 years, gives the following description of Bishop Asbury in crossing the St. Lawrence at St. Regis:

"On entering the village of St. Regis, as Mr. Asbury was leading his horse across a bridge made of poles, the animal got his feet between them and sunk into mud and water. Away went the saddle-bags; the books and clothes were wet, and the horse was fast. We got a pole under the horse to pry him out; at the same time the horse made a leap and came out safe and sound.

"We crossed the St. Lawrence in romantic style. We

this shore at which he stopped was at the venerable
and pious Evan Royce's, in one of the oldest
Methodist societies in the Province. Thence he
proceeded along the banks of the St. Lawrence,
preaching at sundry places; in some of which he
found members from Europe, and from the first
societies in the city of New York. After preaching in Kingston, and one or two places adjacent,
he crossed from Kingston to Sackett's Harbour,
on his way to the Genesee Conference in Paris.

From Bishop Asbury's Journal we learn his
feelings and views of Canada. He says : " Our
ride has brought us through one of the finest
countries I have ever seen : the timber of noble
growth ; the cattle well-looking ; crops abundant,
had four Indians to paddle us over. They lashed three
canoes together, and put our horses into them, their fore
feet in one canoe, their hind feet in another. It was a
singular load ; three canoes, three passengers (the Bishop,
Bela Smith [the Canadian preacher], and myself), three
horses, and four Indians. They were to take us over for
three dollars. It was nearly three miles across to where
we landed. It was late in the afternoon when we started,
and we were a long time crossing, for some part was
rough, especially the rapids ; so we did not reach the
other side till late in the evening. Then the Indians
claimed an additional dollar. They said, ' Four men, four
dollar,' intimating that three dollars could' not be so
easily divided among four. We cheerfully paid the
additional dollar, and were full of gratitude for our crossing in safety."

on a most fruitful soil. To the people my soul is much united."*

We now turn to Dr. Bangs, whose statements on the condition of the country and the labours of

* Jubilee Sermon, p. 46. Of Asbury it is said—" His labours in the New World were, if possible, greater than those of Wesley in the Old ; he travelled more miles a year and preached as often. On becoming Bishop of the Church in 1784, he seemed to become ubiquitous throughout the continent. The history of Christianity since the apostolic age, affords not a more perfect example of ministerial and episcopal devotion than was presented in this great man's life. He preached almost daily for more than half a century. During most of the time he travelled over the continent, with hardly an intermission, from north to south and from east to west, directing the growing hosts of his denomination with the skill and authority of a great captain. He was ordained Bishop of the Methodist Episcopal Church, when thirty-nine years of age, at its organization in 1784, when it comprised less than fifteen thousand members and about eighty preachers ; and he fell, in 1816, in his seventy-first year, at the head of an army of more than two hundred and eleven thousand members and more than seven hundred itinerant preachers. It has been estimated that in the forty-five years of his American ministry, he preached about sixteen thousand five hundred sermons, or at least one a day, and travelled about two hundred and seventy thousand miles, or six thousand miles a year ; that he presided in two hundred and twenty-four Annual Conferences, and ordained more than four hundred preachers." " Notwithstanding his advanced age and shattered health, he continued his travels to the last, till

the preachers we quoted, page 30, at the beginning
of the century, remarking that his statements were,
in great part, the result of his own personal observation and experience. Dr. Bangs came to Canada
in 1799 as a surveyor, but for want of constant
employment in his profession he taught school.
In 1800 he was awakened and converted through
the instrumentality of the Revs. James Coleman
and Joseph Sawyer, in the neighbourhood of St.
David's, near Queenston, and commenced in 1801
as an itinerant preacher under the direction of the
presiding elder of the district, Joseph Jewell. He
was therefore a *Canadian* preacher; and he spent
the first seven years of his laborious ministerial
life in Canada, after which he entered the work
in the United States, where, his biographer says,
he was " destined to do more important services
to the Church than any other man recorded in
its history, save Asbury."*

We will give some illustrations of Dr. Bangs'

he had to be aided up the pulpit steps, and to sit while
preaching. On the 24th of March, 1816, when unable
either to walk or stand, he preached his last sermon at
Richmond, Va., and on the 31st of March died at
Spottsylvania, Va. With Wesley, Whitfield and Coke,
he ranks as one of the greatest representative men of
the Methodist movement."—Stevens' Centenary of American Methodism, pp. 93, 94.

* Stevens' History of the Methodist Episcopal Church,
Vol. II., p. 345.

own personal labours, perils, and sufferings during
his seven years' ministry in Canada, from 1801
to 1808, extracted from his *Life and Times* by Dr.
Stevens, who thus describes the scenes of Dr.
Bangs' first three years' (1801, 1802, 1803) labours
in Canada:

"His first travels on the Niagara Circuit had
extended from the Niagara River westward to
beyond Oxford—more than half the distance between Lakes Ontario and Huron—a region then
but sparsely settled. They deviated also south-
ward to Long Point, which reaches into Lake
Erie, and eastward to Little York, or Toronto,
on the northern shore of Lake Ontario. His
second Circuit, called the Bay of Quinte, was an
immense range on the north-east of Lake Ontario.
He had thus gone over most of the region immediately north of the two great lakes, or rather
inland seas, of Ontario and Erie. We have witnessed the severity of his trials in these new
countries; he had endured them 'as a good soldier
of the Lord Jesus,' and he would have appeared
justified had he, in retracing his steps to his
paternal home, and to the Conference in New
York city, asked for an appointment nearer his
kindred, and in a more genial climate, especially
as he went to the Conference almost wrecked in
health. But he went hither for the express purpose of soliciting permission to throw himself

into a still more westward and more desolate region in Upper Canada—a region noted, at the time, for pestilential disease and religious destitution—the then recent settlement on the River Thames, a stream which enters the St. Clair, opposite Detroit, beyond the north-western shore of Lake Erie.

"While he was struggling and triumphing through the first year of his itinerancy (in the Niagara and Long Point country), he received a letter at Oxford, from a German Baptist [Mr. Messmore, father of the late Rev. Joseph Messmore], who lived on the River Thames, about sixty miles from Detroit, urging him to come over and proclaim his message in that country, then almost totally without religious provision. He knew nothing of the writer, but the call seemed like that of the Macedonian vision to Paul, and it followed him continually. He repeatedly offered his services for this new field to his presiding elder; but the latter deemed the wants of the nearer fields too urgent, and his health too feeble, to justify the mission. For his second year he was sent in the opposite direction, to the Bay of Quinte Circuit; but while he there lay, languishing as we have seen, with fever, and his brethren gathering around his bed to see him die, he still saw the beckoning vision in the further west, and, · expecting to rise no more, he actually made his will, bequeathing his horse and watch—all the property he had except his thoroughly-worn raiment—to any preacher who would go to that suffering people. He had prayed for them incessantly in secret, ever since the receipt of the letter which called him to them.

"After his ordination as deacon at the Conference (1803), he requested an interview with Bishop Asbury, and made known to him his conviction of a providential call to this mission [in the western district of Upper Canada]. The keen eye of the veteran leader lighted up as he gazed on the young evangelist. 'He unhesitatingly replied,' writes the latter, 'as if catching the inspiration with which my own heart was kindled, " *You shall go, my son.*"' The Bishop presented the case before the Conference, and ordained him a presbyter, that he might go with full powers to administer the sacraments.

"'No sooner,' he writes, 'was my way thus opened, than a host of difficulties rallied to prevent my going; suggestions about my youth, my want of health, want of money, the distance—it being, by the route I must go, about six hundred miles—and a thousand other obstacles; but I resolved, by the help of God, to press through them and fulfil my mission. With but fifteen dollars in my pocket I set off, in company with William Anson and Daniel Pickett—the former

being appointed to Yonge-street, the latter to
Niagara. We entered Canada by way of Kingston, then went up the shore of Lake Ontario,
passing through the settlements where I had before
laboured; stopping on the way and preaching to
the people until we finally arrived at the head of
the lake, on the Niagara Circuit, near the place
where I had preached my first sermon. Here I
was to part with my travelling companions, and
proceed alone. My money was all expended, and
I had eighty miles still to travel before I could
reach my destined field. New difficulties presented themselves, and I knew not how I could
advance any further. I went into the woods,
kneeled down, and wept and prayed. Finally the
words came forcibly to my mind, 'The earth is the
Lord's, and the fulness thereof.' I arose with renewed courage, saying, ' I will go in the name of
the Lord; for He has the hearts of all men, and
He can turn them which way soever He will.'
Before I left these parts, one friend and another
put into my hands money amounting to eleven
dollars—enough for my journey.

" Before proceeding further, I visited my sister,
with whom I boarded when I experienced religion.
She was a pious, humble follower of the Lord
Jesus. Having heard that I had died in my
severe illness at the Bay of Quinte, and having
received word of my recovery only about a week

before my arrival, she was no less surprised than delighted to see me. This beloved sister was often a comfort to me in that distant land, and I loved her tenderly. After spending a day or two with her, I resumed my journey. Unexpectedly, a young man offered to accompany me, and we set off together. August 4th and 5th we attended a Quarterly Meeting at Oxford, where I was refreshed amongst my old friends, the first-fruits of my ministry, with whom I now took sweet counsel about the labours and trials before me. Departing with their prayers, we journeyed about thirty miles to Delaware town, where I preached and lodged in the last house of the settlement. My bed was a bundle of straw; my supper, 'mush and milk.'

"August 10th we rose at break of day, took a little food, and started for a ride through the wilderness [Long Woods], forty miles long, with no roads, and only 'blazed' or marked trees to guide us. There being not even a beaten path, we were often at a loss to know whether we were right or wrong; but we got safely through at last. The flies and mosquitoes were so troublesome that our horses could not stand to eat, though we stopped in a shady meadow for that purpose; we therefore rode through the woods without any other refreshment for them than what they nibbled as we passed along. As for ourselves, we had a little Indian bread and dried beef in our pockets, of which we partook; but the water we occasionally met looked so black that we dare not drink it. Our horses seemed as eager as ourselves to get through; for whenever practicable, they would trot on with all their speed.

"We arrived about sunset, weary, hungry, and thirsty, at a small log-hut inhabited by a Frenchman. My tired horse lay down as soon as the saddle and bridle were taken off. I asked the woman of the cabin if she could give me a drink of tea, but she had none. Being almost famished, I requested the woman to procure us some water, which we sipped a little at a time, as if it were nectar; we then ate some Indian pudding and milk, the best food we could obtain. After praying with the family, we lay down on a bundle of straw, slept sweetly, and rose in the morning much refreshed and invigorated in body and mind. The poor woman was so kind as to send early to a distant neighbour, to beg some tea for us; but she had neither tea-kettle, tea-pot, nor tea-cup; she therefore boiled it in a 'dish-kettle,' and then poured it into a tin-cup, from which we drank it with more relish than ever king drank wine from a golden goblet. I thought it was the most refreshing beverage I had ever drunk. We allowed our horses to rest till about ten o'clock, and then rode above seven miles to the Moravian Mission,

a small Indian village on the River Thames. We
dined with one of the missionaries, two of whom
were stationed here. I had considerable conversation with him respecting their doctrines and
usages, as well as their labours among the Indians.
He was sociable, and seemed to possess much of
the simplicity of the Gospel. These good men had
much trouble in their work, from the corrupting
influence of the neighbouring white settlers upon
the Indians, and it was hoped by them that our
labours among the former would help their mission. The missionaries and Indians treated us
with great respect, and seemed to rejoice in the
prospect of having the Gospel preached to the
white settlements on the banks of the river
below."

Dr. Bangs' First Reception on his New Circuit.—
"After this interview with the Moravian missionaries, the itinerant and his companion resumed
their route, and early in the afternoon reached
the first house in the white settlement. 'Turning
my horse,' he says, 'toward the fence before the
door, I saw a man in the yard, and after the cus-
tomary salutations, I said, 'Do you want the
Gospel preached here?' After looking at me,
with curious earnestness, he replied, 'Yes, that
we do: do you preach the Gospel?' 'Yes,' I
answered. 'Well, then,' said he, 'get down and
come in.' I replied, 'I have come a great distance

to preach the Gospel in this region; it is now Saturday afternoon; to-morrow being the Sabbath, I must have a place to preach in before I alight from my horse.' He deliberated a few moments, and then said, 'I have a house for you to preach in, victuals and lodging for yourself, and provender for your horse, and you shall be welcome to them all if you will come in.' I remarked, 'I have one more request to make. There is a young man a little behind me, who has accompanied me through the woods : will you entertain him too ?' 'By all means,' he answered.

"This first interview in my new sphere of labour pleased me much. 'God has made my way very plain thus far,' I said to myself, 'and therefore I will praise Him.'

"This man took his horse and rode through the settlement for ten miles, notifying the people that there would be preaching at his house on Sunday morning, at ten o'clock. At the appointed hour the house was crowded. I commenced the service by remarking, that 'When a stranger appears in these new countries the people are usually curious to know his name, whence he comes, whither he is bound, and what is his errand. I will try to satisfy you in brief. My name is Nathan Bangs. I was born in Connecticut, May 2, 1778. I was born again in this Province, May, 1800. I commenced itinerating as a preacher of the Gospel in the month of September, 1801. On the 18th of June, the present year, I left New York for the purpose of visiting you, of whom I heard about two years ago, and after a long and tedious journey I am here. I am bound for the heavenly city, and my errand among you is to persuade as many of you as I can to go with me. I am a Methodist preacher; and my manner of worship is to stand while singing, kneel while praying, and then I stand while I preach, the people meanwhile sitting. As many of you as see fit to join me in this way can do so, and others may choose their own method.' I then read a chapter in the Bible, after which I gave out a hymn. When the young man who accompanied me stood up to sing, they all rose, men, women, and children. When I kneeled in prayer, they all kneeled down. Such a sight I never witnessed before. I then read my text, ' Repent ye therefore, and be converted, that your sins may be blotted out, when the times of refreshing shall come from the presence of the Lord.' In explaining and enforcing these words, I felt that my Divine Master was with me in truth and power; every cloud was dispelled from my mind, and my heart overflowed with love for these people. I believe I preached with ' the Holy Ghost sent down from heaven.' When I had concluded, I informed them of our manner of preaching, the amount of quarterage we received, and the way in which it was collected. I then said, ' All of you who wish to hear more such preaching, rise up.' They all rose, every man, woman, and child. I then notified them that in two weeks, God willing, they might expect preaching again, and closed the meeting. Thus was my circuit begun."

" *Salutations.*—' After seating myself, an elderly man approached, and offering his hand with much affection, asked me if I knew Bishop Asbury. I said ' Yes,' and then asked him if he knew Bishop Asbury, to which he replied in the affirmative. He was from the State of New Jersey, had been there a member of our Church, had frequently entertained the preachers, and among others the Bishop; but he had been in this country about seven years, totally destitute of the ordinances of the Gospel, for there was no minister of any order in all this region. I asked him how far he lived from that place. He replied, ' Ten miles, down the river.' I asked, ' Will you allow me to preach in your house ?' He joyfully replied in the affirmative. I asked, ' Have you any sons here with you ?' ' I have one,' said he. I then said, ' Let him mount his horse, ride immediately home, and notify the people that I will preach at your house at three o'clock this afternoon : you stay and dine with me, and then we will ride on together. He did so, and when we arrived the

4

house and yard were full of people, to whom I preached with lively satisfaction. Among others present, I observed a veteran man with a long beard. At the close of the meeting he was introduced as *Mr. Messmore*, a German Baptist. He was the person who had written to me the letter about two years before, inviting me to come into this neglected country. The next day I preached at his house, about twenty-one miles distant. Thus did God help me, and open my way. I felt that I was in the order of His providence. Such a sweetness of soul I enjoyed, such a liberty and unction in preaching, as plainly indicated that I was under His guidance, and His smile seemed to light up the wilderness before me.

" ' The next day, in company with Mr. Messmore, I rode ten miles and preached in the house of an Indian woman, the widow of a French Canadian, who had left her considerable property. She was a good, simple-hearted, earnest creature, and reminded me of the Shunamite, for she prepared for me, in an upper room, a bed, a table, a chair, and a candlestick. In this room I preached, and ate, and slept, and no one was allowed to enter it in my absence, except to keep it in order. She never asked me to sit at the table with her, deeming herself unworthy, but prepared my food, and put it on the table in my room. She considered herself highly honoured by having the

Gospel preached in her house, and she treated me in this way during all my stay in this country. When I parted with her next day after my first visit, in shaking hands she left a dollar in my palm. It was much needed, for I was nearly out of money.

"'The next day we travelled, partly through a scattered French settlement and partly through a prairie, fifty miles, to Sandwich, a small village opposite Detroit, where I preached in the evening.'

"From Detroit he went to Fort Malden, and down the shore of Lake Erie, among settlements of Americans, English, Scotch, Irish and Dutch emigrants. He thus completed his circuit. A more destitute region, he says, he had never seen. Young people had arrived at the age of sixteen who had never heard preaching, and he found a Methodist who had lived in the country seven years without hearing a sermon. 'But,' he adds, 'although the people were generally extremely ignorant of spiritual things, and very loose in their morals, they seemed ripe for the Gospel, and received and treated God's messenger with great attention and kindness. They treated me as an angel of God; and as St. Paul said respecting the Galatians, it seemed as if they would willingly have plucked out their own eyes and given them to me if it could have added to my comfort.'"

In this *Life and Times* of Dr. Bangs, many
incidents of thrilling interest are given besides
those quoted above—of his successes, his hardships, his perils by water in crossing rivers, his
perils in the wilderness. We will add one example of the latter, during his coming from the
western to the eastern part of his work, about
the middle of November. He says " He paused
at the Moravian Mission, and had a day of profit-
able communion with its labourers. Resuming
his route, he reached the last house—a log hut
—beyond which his way stretched forty miles
through the primeval forest to Delaware town.
Providentially he found in this cabin a traveller,
bound on the same course. Mounting their horses
early in the morning, they entered the woods.
There was snow two inches deep on the ground ;
the streams were high and still open ; the mud
was often up to the knees of their horses ; they
frequently had to strip them of saddle and bridle,
and drive them over the creeks, and then pass
over themselves on logs. The route was sombre
in its winter desolation. Night overtook them
on the banks of a stream, and it was impossible
to continue their course after dark. They resigned
themselves, therefore, to sleep in the woods. They
had ' carried with them some food for themselves
and their horses, and flint and steel, and an Indian
tomahawk for use as they might have need.' ' We

constructed,' he says, ' a small wigwam of branches
of trees and shrubs. My companion attempted
to strike fire for us, but his hands were so stiffened
with cold that he failed. I succeeded with the
flint, steel and a piece of " punk," and we kindled
a roaring flame, heaping on brush and logs. It
melted the snow, and soon dried the ground some
distance around. We tied our horses to trees, gave
them some oats, ate some food ourselves, went to
the creek and drank, and then, having prayed, lay
down to sleep in our berth, the stars shining
brightly above us, and the winds moaning through
the solemn woods.' After three hours I awoke,
and found my fellow-traveller up and shivering
over the fire, which had nearly burned out. 'Come,'
said I, ' let us get more fuel and rouse up again.'
We did so, and soon were comfortable. We then
sat down by it, and spent the remainder of the
night in conversation. It was a wild and pic-
turesque scene, and the hours passed agreeably as
well as profitably.

"At break of day we mounted our horses and
went onward. We arrived at the first house
about three o'clock in the afternoon, hungry,
thirsty, and exhausted. I had no sooner warmed
myself by the fire than I fell asleep. After supper
I prayed with the family and went to bed, truly
thankful that the Lord had preserved my life and
health through all these fatigues and dangers.

I slept sweetly that night, and the next morning went on my way to Oxford. The snow had fallen in the night, and was so deep that the travelling was difficult ; but my horse, which seemed as glad as myself to get safely through the woods and swamps, trotted on with a brave heart, so that I arrived at Oxford before night, and took ' sweet counsel' with my old friends and spiritual children. I remained there a few days to rest and preach, and then passed on twenty-five miles further to Burford, where I was received as one risen from the dead, for the man who accompanied me through the wilderness had gone on before me, and had magnified my sufferings so much that my friends had almost given me up for lost. We praised God together for his loving kindness and tender mercies." *

We have given these lengthened extracts from

* Stevens' Life and Times of Nathan Bangs, D.D., pp. 131-147. The remaining years of Dr. Bangs' ministry in Canada were spent mostly in Lower Canada, chiefly in Montreal and Quebec, where he encountered great difficulties and hardships.

" He had now," says his biographer, " been about seven years in Canada as a travelling preacher, and ' had visited,' he says, ' every city, town and village, in almost every settlement in it.' It was thought, both by himself and his ministerial advisers, that the time had come for his return to the States. He had done faithfully the work of a missionary evangelist ; he had endured his full

Dr. Bangs' Life, not merely to illustrate the state of the country and the mode and perils of travelling, and the Christian heroism of the man—the first preacher raised up in Canada—but as a sample of the manner in which the Methodist preachers of that day, and for a quarter of a century afterwards, travelled and toiled and suffered, to preach the Word of Life, and to establish societies and congregations among the early settlers of Canada, from one end of the province to the other, and in its remotest interior settlements. The former part of this paper presents examples of the sacrifices and labours of the preachers during the first decade of the work in Canada; and the majority, if not nine-tenths, of the preachers for thirty years were scarcely ex-

share of the hardships of the frontier ministry, and had achieved no small success. He had traversed Upper Canada, thundering—a Boanerges—through its forests and along its scattered settlements. He was the founder of Methodism in many of its localities where it has continued to flourish, and where, before his death, it had become the dominant form of religion, and had entrenched itself in commodious—in some instances, in stately chapels. Canadian Methodism must ever recognize Nathan Bangs as among its chief founders, and the flourishing Methodist communities of Quebec and Montreal, as they catch the glimpses of their incipient history from the record of his sufferings and struggles, may well exclaim, 'What hath God wrought !'"—Stevens' Life and Times of Nathan Bangs, D.D., pp. 163, 164.

ceeded by Dr. Bangs himself in the severity of
their privations and sufferings, the activity and
hardships of their labours. Autobiographical and
other accounts of many of these preachers have
been published; we will add an illustration from
a paper which has never been published—the
Journal of the late Rev. John Ryerson during
the first six years of his ministry, before his
marriage, from 1820 to 1826—his whole ministry
extending over a period of fifty·seven years, in the
course of which lengthened period he filled, with
diligence, ability, and success, the highest posi-
tions in the Church of which he was confessedly
the ablest legislator.

The writer, as did also the Rev. Dr. Harper,
pressed him, in his latter years, to write out his
reminiscences of his earlier years and his views
on the principal questions of Church agitation,
discussion and action during the previous half
century, and the origin of the benevolent institutions of the Church. He did so, and in 1877
placed the result in the writer's hands, for his
use and disposal. These papers, or extracts from
them, may some day see the light. Among the
various documents and papers thus placed at the
writer's disposal is the Journal referred to, of the
first six years of Mr. Ryerson's itinerant labours.
Only a few sentences in regard to each year can
here be given. Mr. Ryerson says:—

"My itinerant ministry commenced on the Long Point Circuit [his native circuit], which extended from Port Dover to Port Talbot, along the shore of Lake Erie, and some distance into the interior of the second row of townships. We [my colleague and myself] had twenty-five appointments, at each of which we preached every two weeks. These appointments were scattered over ten townships. We always met the class after preaching. This year I received nothing by way of support, except what I ate and drank, and money enough to keep my horse shod. I received no salary or presents, but worked hard—with what success I know not. At the close of the year I was sent by Elder Case to the Ancaster Circuit, during the absence of the preachers at Conference, and was appointed to the same circuit the following year —1821-1822. The Ancaster Circuit extended over the area of country (nine-tenths of which was a wilderness) now embraced in the Hamilton District. We had twenty-eight appointments. On about half the Sabbaths, we preached three times each; on the other half, twice each Sabbath. We always met the class after preaching, and, between us, visited most of the families each time around the circuit. Our plan was, in crossing each other's track, to meet every fortnight, when we talked over all that we had done, and especially the families we had visited. Then he who

followed would try and see the families not called
upon by his colleague in his previous route."
[Mr. Ryerson then narrates the means employed
to obtain subscriptions for building the first old
King Street chapel, then near Hamilton; the
giving of the land by the late Colonel Land, of
the English Church; the opening of the chapel
(then the most commodious in Upper Canada)
by Messrs. Case and Ryan; the absence of any
town now called Hamilton, more than half the
site of which was then owned by Methodists—
the names and property of each given—but one
village (that of Ancaster, of fifteen or sixteen
houses all told) in that whole region of country.
Mr. Ryerson proceeds :] "My support was *sixty-
five dollars;* besides, I lost my horse, and had to
buy another, which cost *seventy dollars;* and
although part of that sum was raised by subscriptions on the circuit, yet the balance which
had to be provided for took away most of my
salary, and left me, at the close of the year,
very poor, and quite destitute of suitable clothes.

"At the close of the year I was sent by my
Presiding Elder to supply York during the Conference which was held in the State of New York,
after which the Rev. F. Reed, stationed minister,
remaining some time to visit his relations and
friends, I was detained in York for five weeks.
When I arrived on the Niagara Circuit, to which

I had been appointed at the Conference, the leading members were much dissatisfied at my detention; but still they did not attach any blame to me.

"I had for my superintendent this year that good man and true, the late Ezra Adams. This was my last year of holding a subordinate position on a circuit or station—ever after being either Superintendent of a circuit or station, or Presiding Elder or Chairman of a District, and consequently a member of the Stationing Committee for more than thirty years; eight years of which I was co-delegate.

"The Niagara Circuit at that time embraced the whole of the Niagara peninsula east of Hamilton, except the township of Bertie." [Here follows a description of the state and extent of the country; the successful measures adopted to build a commodious church in the small village of St. Catharines, aided liberally by the old loyalist officers, who had been colleagues with Mr. Ryerson's uncle and father as officers in the British army during the American Revolution, and claimed a sort of relationship with him; revivals of religion in different parts of the circuit, and the accession of members who, with their descendants, have remained faithful and useful for more than half a century. He says :] "I left the circuit with regret, and the society of my kind Superintendent. I felt as if I were going from home.

"In 1823 I was appointed in charge, or as Superintendent, of the Yonge Street Circuit, with the late Rev. William Slater as my colleague, than whom a more honourable and upright man never lived; we were fellow-labourers two years—the second year on the Bay of Quinte Circuit; and when he died three years afterwards, I mourned for him as a brother indeed.* The Yonge Street Circuit was more laborious and harder to work than any one I had yet travelled; but my faithful and devoted colleague was a help-meet to me

* The year of Mr. Slater's death, he was the senior colleague and Superintendent of the writer of these papers, on the Ancaster Circuit, 1828-1829; he died about the middle of the circuit year—illustrating the last text on which he preached, Psalm xxxvii. 37, a few days before his death—by cold and congestion of the lungs. The duty of preaching his funeral sermon, and taking charge of the circuit the rest of the year, devolved on his junior colleague—a circuit extending at that time from Stoney Creek and the township of Binbrook on the east, Glanford and through the Grand River Swamp to within five miles of Brantford on the south and west —then to Jersey settlements, Copetown, Waterdown, including the villages of Ancaster, Hamilton and Dundas —thence down Dundas Street to Nelson, thence ten miles north, and through a mountainous wilderness to where the town of Milton now stands—thence south, embracing Dundas Street and all south (including Oakville) up the shore of Lake Ontario, to Stoney Creek, the place of beginning.

indeed. His never-failing cheerfulness and un-
tiring industry was a source of great comfort and
encouragement to me. Our circuit extended from
York (including the town) to Lake Simcoe, embracing the series of townships west of Yonge
Street to Holland Landing, thence along the shore
twelve miles, through woods without a house to
North Gwillimbury, thence through Whitchurch,
Markham, Pickering, Whitby and Darlington, as
far as Major Wilmot's, some miles east of where
Bowmanville now stands. Major Wilmot fitted
up a large room in his tannery for our services;
for though neither he nor Mrs. Wilmot were
members of our Church, yet were they very
friendly, and treated me with the kindness of
parents.

"In those days an unmarried preacher had no
home except that of the Indian who, in reply to
the question as to where was his home, said, 'I
live, and my home is all along shore.' This 'all-
along shore' home was my lot during the first
six years of my ministry, in single life. Yet I
usually had some place on the Circuit where I
left my few clothes, books, etc., and which I desig-
nated by the endearing name of home. On the
Yonge Street Circuit, this was the house of Mr.
William P. Patrick, with whom and his friendly
and pious wife, and most amiable family, I passed
many pleasant and happy hours. Mr. Patrick

was a most devoted and generous man—a scientific and beautiful singer, whose sweetness of voice and melody thrilled through my whole being when I have heard him sing 'Rock of Ages,' 'Lo! He comes with clouds descending,' and on New Year, 'Come let us anew,' etc. [Mr. Ryerson describes at some length the devout habits and kindness of Mr. Patrick and his lovely household; his perils, escapes, etc., in travelling around the Circuit. He says:]

"At our first Canada Conference held at Hallowell (Picton), 1824, I was appointed to the Bay of Quinte Circuit, embracing the town of Kingston, as well as the whole of the Bay of Quinte country, north of the Bay, to the head of it. This Bay of Quinte Circuit was the most extensive and laborious of any on which I had travelled, and many circumstances connected with its state at that time added greatly to the onerousness and painfulness of the work." [At the Conference of 1823, delegates were elected to the American General Conference, and, for the first time, Mr. Ryan was not elected, but Mr. Wyatt Chamberlain, who was travelling the Bay of Quinte Circuit, was elected to the General Conference instead of Mr. Ryan. He, to punish Mr. Chamberlain for his temerity, sought to injure him as much as possible on his circuit—sent a belligerent local preacher to beard and oppose him at his appointments—

resulting in dividing most of the congregations, loss of the class-papers and scattering of the classes. Mr. Ryan himself disturbed the troubled waters still more by professing to forbid Mr. Chamberlain from preaching, and seeking to get himself elected to the General Conference by a convention of local preachers and laymen. Such was the state of things on the Bay of Quinte Circuit when Messrs. Ryerson and Slater were appointed to its oversight and management in 1824. Mr. Ryerson says :]

" At each appointment there were more or less friends of both parties, the consequence of which was that the whole Circuit was thrown into a state of confusion, and torn to pieces from one end to the other. I arrived there about two weeks before my colleague. Mr. Case, my Presiding Elder, informed me at Hallowell that a good deal of uneasiness existed on the Circuit, but what he said did not convey to me the idea of a tithe of the sad state of things there; he, however, urged me to go on the Circuit as soon as possible. So I did not return,—I cannot say to my home, for I had none,—but I did not return to my late Circuit to get my few books and clothes, which were sent to me. Immediately after the Conference closed, I crossed the bay to Adolphus-town, preached at two places, and met the classes, if classes they could be called ; for there was not an organized class on the Circuit; not a class-paper (we had no printed class-books in those days) to be found; so we had no means from any Church record of ascertaining the membership. By whom, or for what purpose, the class-papers and Church records were destroyed or taken away, I could never find out. The party strife and heart-burnings were dreadful and painful in the extreme. The different parties asked, and sometimes tried to get us preachers on their side; but this we studiously avoided, and especially where the differences had degenerated into personal feeling and family strifes. This was the case in many instances.

"Mr. Slater and I had the misfortune of being young men; it was with both of us the fifth year of our ministry, and neither of us had been ordained Elder, though we had been ordained Deacons. This authorised us to baptize and assist in administering the Lord's Supper, but not to consecrate the elements. This impediment was very embarrassing to us, as the Circuit was very large, and Mr. Case was able to visit us only four times during the year; and part of the Quarterly Meetings were held in Kingston, where few of the country members were able to go. But in our extra quarterly meetings and sacramental services, we were greatly aided by the assistance of old Mr. Dunham, who with Mr. Losee were, under God, the founders of Methodism in the Bay of Quinte country. The good old, but rather eccentric man and able minister, was always ready to help us in time of need; although he sometimes declined preaching for me, which I always requested, much preferring to hear him than to preach myself. We young men of that day did not think ourselves wiser and more clever than our fathers.

"I have said that our youthfulness in the ministry seemed to make much against us. There were many members in this oldest Circuit in the province who were Methodists before I was born; and they seemed to think it strange that one so young in the ministry should be appointed to superintend a Circuit so old, in such perilous and difficult circumstances. Indeed I thought the same myself; and the oppositions, mistrusts, etc., quite overwhelmed me, and often deprived me of both appetite and sleep. 'Wearisome and painful days and sleepless nights were appointed unto me.' My flesh seemed to run off me like water, and I became little else than a walking skeleton; so that at the close of the year, when I came to the Fifty Conference [near Grimsby], my old friends said that by my appearance they would not have known me; but still my identity and soul were there, whatever had become of most of my poor body.

"We had thirty-one appointments; and I went

5

twelve times around the Circuit—once every four weeks—preaching and meeting the scattered remains of classes at each appointment. Mr. Slater and I, at the close of each public service, had requested the members of the society to remain for class-meeting, and accordingly met those who did so; but having no class record, we knew not who were really members from those who were not. Towards the close of our second tour around the Circuit, we commenced in each class-meeting the inquiry of each person as to his or her membership, and took down the names of all who declared themselves members of the Church; we got the names also of such as had been *Leaders*, and who desired to remain with us. From these minutes, we prepared class-papers for all the classes. The entire membership of the Church on the Circuit, as thus ascertained, amounted to more than four hundred. During the last half of the year, prospects began to brighten; interesting revivals took place at several appointments, and a number joined the Church. The following year there was a wonderful revival, not only throughout the Circuit, but it spread over a great extent of the surrounding country, in the progress of which hundreds professed to be saved, and the fruits of which remain to this day.

"About the month of April, a number of the members of the Church in what was called, and

I believe is still called, the Switzer neighbourhood, requested me to meet them to consult about building a meeting-house; the result of which was the erection of what was called the Switzer Meeting-house or Church. This commodious place of worship was not completed and opened until after I left the Circuit; but subsequently, during my four years' Presiding Eldership in the Bay of Quinte District, I held many quarterly meetings and preached many sermons in this house, and with me scores and hundreds experienced times of great refreshing from the presence of the Lord. How many times did I hear our old and well-tried friends, the Shorys, Switzers, Millars, Empies, and others, in the Love-feasts, speak in glowing and moving terms of their unity, happiness, and prosperity, compared with the dark and desponding times of bygone days.

"During this year I travelled on horseback two thousand four hundred miles, preached three hundred and fifty sermons, and met about half as many classes; received for my support as salary one hundred dollars, and no more; no presents— no, not a dollar. Then I was allowed my travelling expenses, which, however, did not exceed five or six dollars.

"At the Fifty Mile Creek Conference (1825), where I was ordained Elder by Bishop Hedding, I was appointed to the Perth Circuit [County of

Lanark], and the Rev. S. Belton as missionary to the Mississippi, with the understanding that we should interchange our labours, which we arranged to do.

"A number of the leading friends on the Niagara Circuit petitioned for me to be appointed to that Circuit; but Mr. Case was unyielding, and insisted upon my going to the Perth Circuit. He spoke to me on the subject; I told him that I had nothing whatever to do with the request for my appointment to the Niagara Circuit, and was content to go where the Stationing Committee, or Conference, or Bishop, as the case might be, should see fit to send me.

"Mr. Belton and I, about the 25th of September, started on horseback for our field of labour, and after a hard eight days' ride of three hundred miles, we arrived at our place of toil for the year, much fatigued, and not a little cast down on witnessing the state at least of temporal things at Perth. We had much difficulty in finding places for our horses, and scarcely less difficulty in obtaining lodgings for ourselves. Indeed, the Methodists then in Perth were few in number and very poor. I stopped at Doctor O'Hare's; he and his wife left their own bed and made what they called a 'shake-down' on the floor, in order to provide a bed for me, which, however, was dreadfully poor and very uncomfortable. This very gloomy introduction rather put our faith to the test; yet we could say,

> 'Come what will, come what may,
> Time and the hour run through the roughest day.'

"Mr. Belton first visited what was called the Mission, although I do not know how any part of our field of labour could be called anything else than a mission, considering the newness and roughness of the country and poverty of the people. We, however, broke up a good deal of new ground and formed several small societies; we went up the Mississippi river, into the township of Dummer (I think that was its name), to visit a Scotch settlement, and preached in a little log schoolhouse, in which a school was taught by a little rough-looking young man, or lad, by the name of Wilson, whose father, with a large family, lived in the neighbourhood. This young Wilson afterwards studied law, and became the Honourable Judge John Wilson, who lived and died a few years since in the city of London, Upper Canada. We lodged in old Mr. Wilson's house, which contained one large room used by him and his family for kitchen, dining-room, and dormitory. Fixtures or beds were fastened against the walls on different sides around, and in front of some of them were curtains suspended. The family was very intelligent and very kind, and to their

utmost ability they provided for our comfort.
They were Presbyterians.

"We went down the Mississippi to Packenham,
and then twelve miles further down to the mouth
of the river, where its waters empty into the
Ottawa river. At Packenham there was a lum-
bering establishment, and a number of lumbermen at work. I preached in their shanty, and
laid down in it as one of the lumbermen, sleeping
on a 'shake-down' of straw. This place, I am
told, is now a nice little town, with a neat Methodist church, and several other places of worship
belonging to different religious persuasions."
[After describing several narrow escapes in traversing swamps and creeks, and much suffering
in travelling this Circuit, he says:] "This year,
though one of hard work and much peril, was one
of considerable prosperity; there were a good
many professed conversions, and additions made
to the Church, among whom were many Roman
Catholics.

"After the close of this year, on the 8th of
August, 1826, I was married to Miss Mary Lewis,
of Saltfleet; so it will be fifty-one years the 8th
of August this year, 1877, that we have lived
together in married life. Of our mercies, labours,
toils, sufferings during this long period, I cannot
begin to say anything.

"During the six years of my single or unmarried life, everything I received, quarterage or salary, except travelling expenses—which were, however, a mere trifle—amounted to four hundred and forty dollars, and not ten dollars of everything in the way of presents. And during the many years of my ministry as a married man—with the exception of a house—my annual salary never exceeded five hundred and fifty dollars, and during most of the time, it was very short of that sum ; besides (with the exception of some rough furniture in Kingston and Quebec), we always furnished our own house. Under the terms, Quarterage,' or ' Salary,' were included table expenses, fuel, etc."

ESSAY III.

THE SUPERNATURAL CHARACTER OF CANADIAN METHODISM.

BY the " supernatural," we mean that which is above the powers or laws of nature ; we mean that which is produced by a Divine agency .—the immediate power of God. But in affirming the " supernatural character of Canadian Methodism," we are far from denying or ignoring the " supernatural " in other religious persuasions who hold the doctrines of the Triune Godhead, the atonement of Jesus Christ, and the resultant work of the Holy Ghost, and who practically and experimentally incorporate these doctrines with the pardon of penitent sinners, their regeneration and adoption into the Church, or family, of the living God. These doctrines are embraced in the creed of all Protestant denominations, except the Unitarians and Pelagians ; but though these doctrines were in Protestant creeds, they were not always in Protestant pulpits or in Protestant congregations. In the commencement of Methodism in England, few of the clergy of the Established

Church and few of the Dissenters preached, much less exemplified, these doctrines, though they were prominent in their creeds. But Methodism, from the beginning, in England, the United States, and Canada, gave a supreme significance and practical application to these doctrines, which have constituted the *supernatural character* of Methodism throughout the world. This is specially true of Canadian Methodism, with which we have chiefly to do in these Essays. Though the first ministers were "few and far between," there was perfect unity in the doctrines of faith and experience which they preached, and everywhere, by the river side or in the remote wilderness, there was but one doctrine, one faith, one experience, one joy, one fellowship, among the isolated preachers and societies, from Quebec to Detroit.

The summary of the doctrines which they preached was the natural depravity of the human heart; the atonement made by Jesus Christ as a full and sufficient sacrifice for the sins of the whole world; the offering of salvation to every individual, on the condition of repentance towards God and faith in our Lord Jesus Christ; justification by faith alone; but from the faith which justifies, good works proceed; the witness of the Spirit, which may be enjoyed by every believer attesting his sonship; and the pressing after "holiness, without which no man can see the

Lord,"—followed by the doctrines of future re-
wards and punishments, together with the immortality of the soul and the resurrection of the body.
It will be seen that these doctrines are but the
echoes of the doctrines of the apostles and of
the Protestant Reformation as embodied in the
Articles of the Church of England, except the
17th Article, on Predestination and Election,
which means Arminianism as contended by
Wesley and Fletcher, or Calvinism as argued by
Toplady and Shirley. These doctrines differ from
those of the Calvinistic Churches, in rejecting the
doctrines of absolute election and reprobation,
and of the impossibility of falling from grace; *
they differ from the Unitarians and Socinians,
by proclaiming the supreme divinity and atonement of the Lord Jesus Christ; and from the
Pelagians, by holding the doctrine of human
depravity—the natural corruption of the human
heart, and human inability, without Divine grace,
to turn from sin to holiness—teaching at the

---

* The earliest embodiment of the doctrines of the
Reformation is contained in the *Prayer Book and Homilies of the Church of England*, compiled by Latimer,
Cranmer, and Ridley, and their immediate associates and
fellow-sufferers, and existing at this day, with a few
verbal alterations, as they were originally prepared and
sanctioned. The Westminster Calvinistic Confession
of Faith was compiled and adopted a hundred years
later than the Common Prayer Book and Homilies.

same time, that a sufficient measure of grace is given to every man to profit withal, and that through the merits of Christ's atonement full salvation is the privilege of every individual.*

The doctrines insisted upon by the first preachers in Canada, as also by Mr. Wesley himself, and by his true and faithful successors of the present day, were few, in each of which the presence and exercise of Divine power was recognized and prayed for. Mr. Wesley says—" I have again and again, with all the plainness I could, declared what our constant doctrines are ; whereby we are distinguished only from heathens or nominal Christians ; not from any that worship God in spirit and in truth. Our main doctrines, which include all the rest, are three—that of repentance, of faith, and of holiness. The first of these we account, as it were, the porch of religion ; the next, the door ; the third, religion itself."†

* See Bishop Simpson on *A Hundred Years of Methodism*, Chapter xv.

† *Principles of a Methodist Further Explained.* Works, Vol. V., p. 333, Am. Ed.

In another place, in answer to the objection to Mr. Wesley and his preachers, that "they make it their principal employ, wherever they go, to instil into the people a few tenets of their own, and this with such diligence and zeal as if the whole of Christianity depended upon them, and all efforts toward the true Christian life, with-

If we consider separately and successively the doctrines preached by the ministers of Methodism in Canada, and the manner in which they were preached, we will see at once the supernatural

out belief of these tenets, were vain and ineffectual," Mr. Wesley answers :

"I plead guilty to this charge. I do make it my principal, nay, my whole employ, and that wherever I go, to instil into the people a few favourite tenets ;—only, be it observed, they are not mine, but His who sent me. And it is undoubtedly true that this I do (though deeply conscious of my own want both of zeal and diligence) as if the whole of Christianity depended upon them, and all efforts without them were void and vain. I frequently sum them all up in one : 'In Christ Jesus' (that is, according to the Gospel) 'neither circumcision availeth anything, nor uncircumcision, but faith which worketh by love.' But many times I instil them one by one under these or like expressions : 'Thou shalt love the Lord thy God with all thy heart, and with all thy mind, and with all thy soul, and with all thy strength ; thou shalt love thy neighbour as thyself ;' as thy own soul ; as Christ loved us. 'God is love ; and he that dwelleth in love, dwelleth in God, and God dwelleth in him.' 'Love worketh no ill to his neighbour ; therefore love is the fulfilling of the law.' 'As we have therefore opportunity, let us do good unto all men ; especially unto them who are of the household of faith.' 'Whatsoever ye would that men should do unto you, even so do unto them.'

"These are my favourite tenets, and have been for many years. O that I could instil them into every soul throughout the land ! Ought they not to be instilled

CANADIAN METHODISM. **77**

character of Canadian Methodism, its agreement
with the doctrines and spirit of the Protestant
Reformation, and with those of our Lord and
His apostles. When the voice of John the
Baptist crying in the wilderness, "*Repent* ye,
for the kingdom of heaven is at hand," was silenced
by his death of martyrdom, then "from that time
Jesus began to preach and to say, *Repent,* for the
kingdom of heaven is at hand." And in the first
great mixed assembly on the day of Pentecost, in
answer to the inquiry of the multitude, "pricked
to the heart," "Men and brethren, what shall we
do?" the Apostle Peter said "*Repent* and be
baptized, every one of you, in the name of Jesus
Christ for the remission of sins, and ye shall
receive the gift of the Holy Ghost." And in the
preaching of the Apostle Paul, who on reviewing
his ministry, declares to his brethren of Ephesus
that he had "taught publicly and from house
to house," "both to the Jews and Greeks, *repentance* toward God, and faith toward our Lord Jesus
Christ;" so the first of Wesley's "favourite doc-

with such diligence and zeal, as if the whole of Christianity depended upon them? For who can deny that
all efforts toward a Christian life, without more than a
bare belief, without a thorough experience and practice
of these, are utterly vain and ineffectual?"—*Further
Appeals to Men of Reason and Religion*, Part I. Works,
Vol. V., pp. 48, 49, Am. Ed.

trines " was *repentance;* and thus did Dr. Bangs, in opening his mission to the destitute Canadian settlers of the western district of Upper Canada, take for his text Acts iii. 19, " *Repent* ye, therefore, and be converted, that your sins may be blotted out, when the times of refreshing shall come from the presence of the Lord." So also did every Methodist preacher of that day commence his mission of love and compassion to the destitute settlers. The first race of Methodist preachers in Canada were rightly called *legio tonans*—the thundering legion ; for the thunder trumpet of their voice sounded throughout the wilderness settlements of Canada, " *Repent and be converted.*"

And the *repentance,* or conviction of sin, thus taught at the very threshold of their ministrations—a repentance consisting not merely of regret and remorse for past misdeeds, and a desire and determination to forsake them, but a repentance involving a consciousness of the sinfulness of the heart, the guilt and condemnation of sin, its burden and misery, dread of its punishment, and struggles to be delivered from its power, exclaiming, " O wretched man that I am ! who shall deliver me from the body of this death ?"—this repentance, not admitted under the law of works, is the first-fruit of the Redeemer's atoning work, who is exalted at the right **hand of** God **to** give *repentance* and the remission of sins.

Three things are included **in** that repentance **which is** unto salvation, and which was preached **by** Wesley and the pioneer **preachers of** Canadian Methodism: 1. A *holy sorrow* **for** sin, as dishonourable **to God and** defiling **to the** soul—as ungrateful, hateful, **and destructive.** 2. Confession **of** sin—a confession which **is simply** the language of the inward sorrow of the heart—the giving vent to that sorrow, **in** acknowledgments free without compulsion, **ingenuous** without reserve, cordial without **hypocrisy.** 3. **A turning** from sin—from **all sin, from every sin**—turning to God. **Godly sorrow flows from God, and leads to Him.** Repentance **unto life, is** repentance *towards* God. The repentant heart **turns to** God, **as** the needle to **the** pole. **The** prodigal not only lamented and renounced **his** harlot indulgences, but returned to his insulted father. Such repentance teaches the bitterness **of sin,** shows the nature of pardon, prepares and melts **the heart,** like wax, **to** receive **the** seal **of pardon.**

Such is the repentance **taught by** Wesley,* and his fellow-labourers **and spiritual sons** in **the** United States and **in Canada.** Such a *repentance* is closely and inseparably connected **with** *faith;* a faith, **not a mere** intellectual assent **to**

* **See** Wesley's Sermon **on** *The Way to the Kingdom.*

the doctrine of redemption and all the truths of
the Gospel, but a *trust* in the Redeemer. Repentance is the sorrowful consciousness of guilt, and
a throbbing desire for forgiveness; faith is the
trust of the soul in the sacrificial death of the
Son of God for pardon and eternal life—it is the
resting of the soul upon Christ alone for salvation.
Without *faith*, repentance would be but the
anguish of irreparable sin and folly—the gloomy
foreshadowing of future punishment; without
repentance, faith is the mere assent of the understanding—the heartless and perhaps reluctant
submission of the judgment to facts and doctrines
which cannot be successfully contradicted or reasonably doubted. Repentance gives heart and
hands to faith; faith places that heart upon Jesus
Christ, and clasps those hands around His cross.
Faith is the vital artery of the soul; it unites
the soul to Christ; it receives life from Him;
it quickens the soul from death unto life. "He
that believeth on the Son of God, though he were
dead, yet shall he live." He "is passed from
death unto life."

Hence pardon, adoption, and regeneration immediately follow upon repentance and faith. By
pardon, we are delivered from the punishment
and guilt of sin through the merits of Jesus
Christ; by *adoption*, we are taken into the family
of God, are dignified by His name, and made

partakers of all the privileges of His children; by *regeneration*, we are restored to the moral image of God—we are stamped with the seal of His likeness—we are renewed in righteousness and true holiness. New faculties are not given; but the qualities, the character, the tendency of our intellectual and moral powers are changed and improved—embracing the understanding, the will, the conscience, the affections, the passions, and appetites; and prompting us still, by an ever-increasing hungering and thirsting after righteousness, until the God of peace sanctifies us wholly, preserving our whole spirit, soul and body unto the coming of our Lord Jesus Christ. Often repentance, faith, pardon, regeneration, and adoption are carried in the soul simultaneously, and sometimes nearly instantaneously. Such is a meagre summary of the Scriptural and experimental doctrines which the pioneer preachers of Canadian Methodism proclaimed in public, and taught from house to house, among the new and scattered settlers of the Canadian wilderness; and "the hand of the Lord was with them, and a great number believed and turned unto the Lord."

But it was not merely in the pure and experimental doctrines taught that the *supernatural character* of Canadian Methodism was demonstrated in the early stages of its development; it was also in the recognition and dependence upon

6

the presence and power of God the Holy Ghost
in every ministration and service, public or private. Was ignorance or the darkness of the
understanding dispelled? It was "God who
caused the light to shine out of darkness," and
" shined in the heart to give the light of the knowledge of the glory of God in the face of Jesus
Christ." Was there a stirring of spiritual life,
the quickening sensation of *repentance*? "You
hath He quickened who were dead in trespasses
and sins." Was there faith? It was the "operation" and "gift of God." Was there the act
of pardon? God was present; for "it is God
that justifieth." Did the believing sinner know
that he was pardoned and accepted in the Beloved? The Holy Spirit bare witness with his
spirit that he was a child of God. Was he renewed in the spirit of his mind? Here was a
new creation—making something out of nothing
—the peculiar work of God. Was the believer
preserved steadfast in Christ Jesus? It was because he was "kept by the power of God, through
faith unto salvation."

Thus is the *supernatural character* of Canadian
Methodism evinced in its every doctrine and
service. In this glorious work God was the Alpha
and Omega, the all in all. Though some of its
apostles might plant and others water, it was

God, in every case, that gave the increase.* The
ministration of these devoted men was manifestly

* "Wherever," says Robert Hall, "the apostles had
any distinguished success in the ministry of the Gospel,
they certainly remind us of its being effected by *Divine
agency*. If they preached with success at Antioch, where
it appears that their ministry was attended with great
benefit, it is announced in these words : '*And the hand
of the Lord was with them.*' When Paul had preached
the Gospel to the heathen, after having been commis-
sioned with Barnabas to the work of the Lord to which
they were sent, they represented to the Church '*how God
had opened a way to the Gentiles*,' and the Jewish Christians were compelled, we are told, to magnify the grace
of God in communicating the blessing to them, and
they did so in these words : '*Then hath God also to the
Gentiles granted repentance unto life.*' If Lydia was
converted to the faith of Christ, we are told it was
because '*the Lord had opened her heart to attend to the
things that were spoken.*' Sincere preachers of the
Gospel, then, as they have been successful in the work,
even from the very beginning, from the first communication of Divine truth, have uniformly represented it as
the *work of God*, as the work of His Spirit, independent
of the instrumentality which He employed in the ministry of the Word.

"Human suasion can operate only on principles which
already exist. When Demosthenes, by his powerful elo-
quence, excited the Athenians to combat, he only called
into action, by a skilful grouping of motives, and an
appropriate exercise of his genius, principles already
existing, but which had lain dormant. He created
nothing new ; he transformed them not into new crea-

the "ministration of the Spirit;" and in deep
humiliation, but assured confidence, their constant
language was, "Not that we are sufficient of ourselves to think anything as of ourselves; *but*

tures ; but only roused and stimulated those principles
which had animated the bosoms of nations in resisting
tyranny in every age. But when the apostles went forth
to preach faith in Christ, they enforced and demanded,
if I may say so, a state of things of which there had
been no instance : they proposed to make a change in
the mind and heart of man to which there was no
natural tendency ; they required a creature 'dead in
trespasses and sins' to awake to Christ ; they proposed
to convert him into a devoted servant, a subject most
loyal, most affectionate, and ardent ; and how was it
possible that mere human art or force could effect such
changes as these ?

"It is worthy of observation, that those who have
had the greatest success in preaching the Gospel in
heathen nations, as well as in Christian lands, have ever
been the most deeply convinced of this important truth ;
a truth they enforced in every stage of the progress of
the Gospel, and which, instead of producing discouragement, only awakened greater ardour : their strength
appeared only to lie in an implicit confidence in Him
whose energy is all-sufficient, and who has so fully declared His willingness to exert it. Thus Brainard and
Schwartz and Eliot [and Wesley and the first Methodist
preachers in Canada], and those in every age who have
had the greatest success in turning men to righteousness,
have been the first to declare that they were nothing.
They, of all men, most ardently implored, and most
entirely depended upon, the agency we are contemplat-

our sufficiency is of God." They were well read in the Scriptures, and experienced in the deep things of God. In every congregation and in every house they could say, " That which was from the beginning, which we have heard, which we have seen with our eyes and our hands have handled, of the *Word of Life,* declare we unto you, that ye also may have fellowship with us; and truly our fellowship is with the Father and with His Son, Jesus Christ."

Such was the divine, the internal, the experimental, the practical religion exemplified and taught by the early preachers of Canadian Methodism, and maintained by their successors. Yet, by those who were strangers to its power, it was scoffed at and ridiculed, and often persecuted. Mr. Wesley himself says—" This repentance, this faith; this peace, joy, love; this change from glory to glory, is what the wisdom of this world has voted to be madness—mere enthusiasm, utter dis-

ing; and their success appears to have been more in their earnest solicitude in seeking this blessing, *this Divine agency,* than to any other cause whatever.

" Those who do not believe there is any agency of the Spirit of God, are so conscious that nothing else can produce the desired effect, that they do not venture into the field ; but while they despair of the conversion of men, deal out scorn upon such as are engaged in the work."— Sermon on *The Success of Missions depends upon the Spirit.* Works, Vol. III., pp. 402—404.

traction. But thou, oh man of God, regard them not; be thou moved by none of those things. Thou knowest in whom thou hast believed. See that no man take thy crown. Whereunto thou hast already attained, hold fast, and follow, till thou attain all the great and precious promises."

Among those who maintained this ceaseless warfare against Methodism, as "madness, mere enthusiasm, and utter distraction," many of the clergy and some of the laity of the Church of England, both in England and Canada, occupied a conspicuous place,—aided indeed by some clergy and laymen of other religious persuasions, but much mitigated of late years; yet in no formularies of any Church are more fully recognized and especially stated the distinctive doctrines taught by the Methodist preachers of Canada than in the Articles, Liturgy, and Homilies of the Church of England.

* Sermon on *The Way to the Kingdom.* In another place, in reply to the accusation, " You drive people out of their senses ; you make them mad," Mr. Wesley says : " And first, I grant it is my earnest desire to drive all the world into what you probably call madness (I mean inward religion); to make them just as mad as Paul when he was so accounted by Festus." " I grant, secondly, it is my endeavour to drive all I can into what you may term another species of madness, and which I term *repentance* or *conviction.*"—*Further Appeal to Men of Reason and Religion.* Works, Vol. V., pp. 92, 93, Am. Ed.

In regard to *repentance*, in the *General Con-fession* we acknowledge that "we are miserable offenders," and that "there is no health in us "—indicating a heartfelt sense of guilt, of depravity, of helplessness. In the *Communion Service* we declare that "the remembrance of our sins is grievous unto us, and the burden of them is in-tolerable ;" and in the *Office for the Sick* we pray, "Make us *know* and *feel* that there is no other name than that of Jesus whereby we must be saved." Passages, almost without number, to the same effect could be selected from the *Liturgy* as well as from the *Homilies*, which are declared in the 35th Article of the Church of England to contain wholesome and godly doctrine, such as should be read in the churches. In the Homily on *Fasting* we have the following words :

"When men feel in themselves the heavy burden of sin, see damnation to be the reward of it, and behold with the eyes of the mind the horror of hell, they tremble, they quake, and are in-wardly touched with sorrowfulness of heart, and cannot but accuse themselves, and open their grief unto Almighty God, and call upon Him for mercy. This being done seriously, their mind is so occupied, partly with sorrow and business, partly with earnest desire to be delivered from this danger of hell and damnation, that all desire of meat and drink is laid apart, and loathing of

all worldly things and pleasures cometh in place.
So that nothing thus liketh them more than to
weep, to lament, to mourn, and in both words
and behaviour of body to show themselves weary
of life."

And this deep heartfelt repentance is everywhere represented as the *work of the Holy Spirit ;*
producing faith in our Lord Jesus Christ. Thus,
in the *Collect for Ash-Wednesday* we pray :

" Almighty God, who dost forgive the sins of
them that are *penitent, create and make in us
new and contrite hearts ;* that we, *worthily lamenting our sins, and acknowledging our wretchedness,*
may obtain of Thee perfect remission and forgiveness, through Jesus Christ our Lord." " He
pardoneth and absolveth all them that *truly repent*
and *unfeignedly believe* His holy gospel." And
in the office for the *Visitation of the Sick,* the
minister prays for the sick person as follows :
"Give him [or her] *unfeigned repentance and
steadfast faith,* that his [or her] sins may be
blotted out." And in the *Homily on the Passion,*
we have these expressive words : " When we *feel*
the heavy burden of our sins pressing our souls
with the fear of death, hell, and damnation, we
must steadfastly behold Christ crucified with the
eyes of our heart."

It will be seen by these passages from the
Homilies and *Liturgy* of the Church of England

(which might be indefinitely multiplied), that repentance and faith are not only the result of Divine influences, but *precede justification* or *pardon.*

But it is the doctrine of *justification by faith* and *the witness* of *it by the Holy Spirit* which has been the special object of opposition from various quarters, and especially certain clergy and members of the Church of England, who ought to have known better than to ridicule as "fanaticism" and "enthusiasm" the solemn verities of their own Church. But in this as well as in other doctrines the early Canadian preachers of Methodism were true to the principle and spirit of the Protestant Reformation—to those principles, and to that spirit which commenced the career of Britain's greatness, and which have formed so vital an element in the formation of Canadian liberty and character. On no subject did the fathers and founders of the Protestant Reformation, and the greatest men who have succeeded them, more uniformly agree than on the supernatural character of the work of God in the soul of man, by which he experiences the pardon of sin, adoption into the Divine family, the witness of the Holy Spirit to his sonship with God, and his sanctification from the defilements of sin. Out of a multitude, we will adduce a few authorities.

In the *Second Homily on the Passion*, we have these words :

" The only instrument of salvation required on our part is faith; that is, a sure trust and confidence that God both hath and will forgive our sins, that He hath accepted us again into His favour for the merits of Christ's death and passion."

Again, in the first part of the *Homily on the Sacraments:* "Have a sure and constant faith not only that the death of Christ is available for all the world, but that it hath made a full and sufficient sacrifice *for thee*, a perfect cleansing of *thy* sins, so thou mayest say with the apostle, ' He loved *thee*, and gave himself for thee.' For this is to make Christ thine own, and to apply His merits to thyself."*

But on the internal work of the Holy Spirit renewing our hearts and witnessing our sonship with God, we have testimony equally explicit and very abundant.

The *Homily on Rogation Week* says: " If after contrition we feel our consciences at peace with God, through the remission of our sins, *it is God*

---

* The Roman Catholic Council of Trent says, in the 12th Canon : " If any man shall say that justifying faith is nothing else than confidence in the Divine mercy, remitting sins for Christ's sake, and this confidence in that alone by which we are justified, let him be accursed."

who worketh that great miracle in us;" and then prays that "as this knowledge and feeling is not in ourselves, and that as by ourselves it is not possible to come by it, the Lord would give us grace to *know* these things, and *feel* them in our hearts."

Again, in the *Homily on the Resurrection* are these words: "He died to destroy the rule of the devil in us; and He rose again to send down His Holy Spirit to 'rule in our hearts.' We have the Holy Spirit in our hearts as a seal and pledge of our everlasting inheritance."

The *Homily on Certain Places of Scripture* says: "Good men feel inwardly the Holy Ghost influencing their hearts with the fear and love of God, and they are miserable wretches who have no feeling of God in them at all."

The judicious Hooker says: "The Spirit which God giveth is to assure us that we are the sons of God, and to enable us to call Him our Father."

Calvin says: "Our mind, of itself, independently of the preceding testimony of the Spirit, could not produce this persuasion that we are the sons of God."

Witsius on the Creed testifies: "There is a certain instinct immediately assuring God's beloved people of their adoption."

Bishop Hooper says: "Blessed is that man in

whose heart God's Spirit beareth record that he is the son of God."

And says Bishop Brownrig : "It is one great office of the Holy Spirit to ratify and seal to us the forgiveness of sins."

Out of a score, we will limit ourselves to four other witnesses.

Archbishop Usher says : " From adoption flows all Christian joy : for the spirit of adoption is, first, a witness ; second, a seal; third, the pledge and earnest of our inheritance, setting a holy, security upon the soul, whereby it rejoiceth, even in affliction, in the hope of glory."

Bishop Pearson on the Creed, recognized and used in all the Theological Colleges of the Episcopal Church, of the Methodist Church, and of some other Protestant Churches, Bishop Pearson says :—

" Fifthly—It is the office of the Holy Ghost to assure us of the adoption of sons, to create within us a sense of the paternal love of God towards us, and to give us an earnest of our everlasting inheritance : Rom. v. 5 ; viii. 14; Gal. iv. 6 ; Rom. viii. 15, 16. As, therefore, we are born again by the Spirit, and receive from Him our regeneration, so we are also assured by the same Spirit of our adoption."

The famous Dr. Isaac Barrow is very explicit, as well as edifying on this subject He says :

"It is also a notable part of the Holy Spirit's office to comfort and sustain us in all our religious practice; so particularly in our doubts, difficulties, distresses and afflictions; to beget joy, peace, and satisfaction in us, in all our performances, and in all our sufferings; whence the title of Comforter belongeth unto Him. It is also another part of the Spirit's work to assure us of God's gracious love and favour, and that we are His children;—confirming in us the hopes of our everlasting inheritance."

There is another office of the Holy Spirit's work which has not been noticed—that of *sanctification* —which is well expressed in the following words of the Homily on Whit-Sunday, part first:

"It is the office of the Holy Ghost to sanctify; which the more it is hid from the understanding" (that is, the more particular manner of His working), "the more it ought to move all men to wonder at the secret and mighty workings of God's Holy Spirit which is within us. For it is the Holy Spirit that doth *quicken* the minds of men, *stirring up godly motives* in their hearts. Neither doth He think it sufficient inwardly to evoke the new birth of man, unless He do also dwell and abide in him. 'Know ye not,' saith St. Paul, 'that ye are the temple of God, and that the Spirit of God dwelleth in you? Know ye not that your bodies are the temples of the

Holy Ghost, which is in you?' Again he saith, 'Ye are not in the flesh, but in the Spirit.' For why? 'The Spirit of God dwelleth in you.' To this agreeth St. John, 'The anointing which ye have received' (he meaneth the Holy Ghost) 'abideth in you,' 1 John ii. 27. And St. Peter saith the same: 'The Spirit of glory and of God resteth upon you.' O what comfort is this to the heart of a true Christian, to think that the Holy Ghost dwelleth in him! 'If God be with us,' as the Apostle saith, 'who can be against us?' He giveth patience and joyfulness of heart, in temptation and affliction, and is therefore worthily called 'the Comforter,' John xiv. 16. He doth instruct the hearts of the simple in the knowledge of God and His Word; therefore He is justly termed 'the Spirit of Truth,' xvi. 13. And where the Holy Ghost doth instruct and teach, there is no delay in learning." *

* It may be proper to subjoin Mr. Wesley's own definition of the Witness of the Spirit, especially as it is in entire harmony with the doctrine of the Protestant Reformers above quoted, as well as with the Holy Scriptures. Mr. Wesley says:

"By the testimony of the Spirit I mean an inward impression on the soul, whereby the Spirit of God immediately and directly witnesses to my spirit that I am a child of God; that Jesus Christ hath loved me, and given Himself for me; that all my sins are blotted out, and I, even I, am reconciled to God." "Meantime,

In all these extracts from the authoritative
expositions of the original principles of Protestantism and of the true doctrines of the Church
of England, there is not a word of "sacramental
salvation," either by baptism or the Lord's Supper,

let it be observed, I do not mean hereby that the Spirit
of God testifies this by any outward voice, although He
may do this sometimes. Neither do I suppose that He
always applies to the heart (though He often may) one or
more texts of Scripture. But He so works upon the soul
by His immediate influence, and by a strange though
inexplicable operation, that the stormy wind and troubled
waves subside, and there is a sweet calm ; the head
resting as in the arms of Jesus, and the sinner being
clearly satisfied that 'God is reconciled,' that all his
' iniquities are forgiven, and his sins covered.' "

" That the testimony of the Spirit of God must, in
the very nature of things, be antecedent to the testimony
of our own spirit, may appear from this consideration :
We must be holy in heart and life before we can be
conscious that we are so. But we must love God before
we can be holy at all, this being the root of all holiness.
Now, we cannot love God till we know He first loved
us : 'We love Him because He first loved us,' and
we cannot know His love to us till His Spirit witnesses
it to our spirit. Till then we cannot believe it ; we cannot
say, ' The life which I now live, I live by faith in the Son
of God, who loved me and gave Himself for me.'

" Then, only then we feel
Our interest in His blood,
And cry with joy unspeakable,
Thou art my Lord, my God."

much less by millinery costumes, genuflexions, and external ceremonies. The founders of Protestantism were too wise to substitute the outward for the inward in religion; they were too enlightened and too well taught by the Holy Spirit to sink the greatness of God down to the littleness of dramatic gesticulations, and the mighty energy of faith in the crucified Saviour, which is the power of God unto salvation, to the mutterings of semi-papal penances and the merits of human self-denials. Nothing of the kind was thought of, much less practised, in the days when the resurrection power of Scriptural truth raised England from its previous mental and spiritual debasement, and the Word of God became the infallible medium, and the Spirit of God the supreme agent of communication between God and man, and the atonement of our Lord Jesus Christ the only foundation of reconciliation and acceptance with God. Wesley was the true reviver and witness of the primary and fundamental principles of the Protestant Reformation; and his successors in Canada, as well as throughout America, have proved noble, and often martyr, witnesses and preachers of the same doctrines—constituting as they do the *supernatural character* of the system of truth which they have taught with a success not equalled since the days of the apostles.

It is a source of pleasure and of gratitude to believe and state that among the leading denominations of Protestants at the present day, the different classes of Presbyterians, Baptists, Congregationalists and Methodists recognize and preach the same doctrines of vital and experimental religion ; and that a large and increasing number of the clergy of the Church of England proclaim the same faith as it is in Jesus ; but it is lamentable to be obliged to confess that there is still a clerical *residuum* in that Church who, though superciliously pretentious, appear to be ignorant of, or at least to deny, the vital articles and liturgical offices of their own Church, though ostentatiously pretending to be the exclusive successors of the apostles! They frequently make their way into Methodist families and seek to disparage their ministry and subvert their faith in the doctrines of their fathers.

The above extracts from the Articles, Liturgy Homilies, and great divines of the Church of England, will be the best answer on the part of Methodist families to these ritualistic interlopers ; and for their further refutation, and instruction, if they be susceptible of it, we quote the following words of Bishop Jeremy Taylor, from a discourse entitled " *Via Intelligentiæ,* showing how the scholars of the University shall become most learned and most useful: "

" There is in every righteous man a new **vital** principle. The Spirit of Grace is the spirit of wisdom, and teaches us by secret inspirations, by proper arguments, by actual persuasions, by per- sonal applications, by effects and energies ; and as the soul of man is the cause of all his vital opera- tions, so is the Spirit of God the life of that life, and cause of all spiritual actions and productions." " Unless the soul have a new life put into it— unless there be a vital principle within—unless the Spirit of life be the informer of the spirit of man, the Word of God will be as dead in the operation as the body in its powers and possibili- ties. God's Spirit does not destroy reason, but heightens it. God opens the heart and creates a new one; and without this creation, this new principle of life, we may hear the Word of God, but we can never understand it; we hear the sound, but are never the better."

Having thus treated of the *supernatural char- acter* of Methodism, the subject of the next Essay will be the *Phenomena and Philosophy of Methodist Revivals.*

ESSAY IV.

PHENOMENA AND PHILOSOPHY OF EARLY METHODIST REVIVALS OF RELIGION.

IN my last Essay, on the Supernatural Character of Canadian Methodism, I stood with the reader face to face with that work of God in the soul of man in which he is born into the kingdom of God, and grows up to the stature of the fulness of Christ; I traced that work step by step, from its tears of penitence to its joys of pardon, adoption, regeneration and sanctification, as illustrated in the lives and labours of the early Methodist preachers, as also in the doctrines and ministrations of the early Protestant Reformers. I now propose to consider the peculiar circumstances of that work; or, in other words, the Phenomena and Philosophy of Early Methodist Revivals of Religion in Canada.

The term *revival* simply signifies restoring; recovery from apparent death or drowning, to life; return to activity from a state of languor; recovery from a state of neglect and depression, as the revival of literature or learning; quickening, or re-animating with hopes or joys; awakening men to their spiritual interests, and rousing them to more attention and action in regard to religion.* It is in this last sense that I employ the term *revival* in these Essays.

The term *phenomenon* is defined by Mr. Wesley as "an uncommon circumstance." In nature it is an appearance the cause of which is not immediately obvious, as the phenomena of the heavenly bodies, of terrestrial productions and substances, of heat or colour, etc., etc. But the phenomena in the realm of mind, and in the kingdom of God, in the soul of man, are not less remarkable, though invisible to the bodily eye, than those of the material universe; and though the "Kingdom of God cometh not with observation," its phenomena, whether established in the

* Mr. Wesley, in a letter to a friend, dated February 12th, 1779, says : " The remark of Luther, ' that a revival of religion seldom continues above thirty years,' has been verified many times in several countries. But it will not always hold. The present revival in England has already continued fifty years. And, blessed be God, it is at least as likely to continue as it was twenty or thirty years ago. Indeed, it is far more likely ; as it not only spreads wider, but sinks deeper, than ever ; more and more persons being able to testify that the blood of Christ cleanses from all sin. We have, therefore, reason to hope that this revival of religion will continue, and continually increase till the time when all Israel shall be saved, and the fulness of the Gentiles shall come."—*Works, Am. Edit.*, Vol. VII., p. 180.

heart of a single individual, or of a multitude, are open to examination; and the reasons, or *philosophy*, of the work which gives them birth, may be reverently and profitably studied.

We shall first speak of the phenomena, and then of the philosophy of the revivals of religion among the early Methodists of Canada.

The new birth of every soul into the kingdom of God is not only a phenomenon, but a miracle, and is so recognized by the Church of England herself; for in the Homily on Rogation Week she says: "If, after contrition, we feel our conscience at peace with God, through the remission of our sins, it is God who worketh that *great miracle* in us." In a revival of religion, such a miracle is multiplied by scores, sometimes by hundreds and thousands, as on the day of Pentecost. All these displays of Divine power are attended with phenomena arising from the varied constitution of the human mind, and the "divers manners" in which God manifests Himself unto those whom He calls, pardons, and saves.

The first phenomenon which has arrested my attention in contemplating this wonderful work, is the *special* call and adaptation of the instruments of its commencement and promotion. From the morning of the Protestant Reformation, the candidate for the holy ministry was questioned before his ordination, "Do you trust that *you are in-*

wardly moved by the **Holy Ghost to** *take* **upon you** *this office* **and** *ministration* **to serve God,** for the promotion of His glory and the edification of His people?" But the first instruments of the Canadian work felt that they were not only "moved by the Holy Ghost to take upon them this office and ministry" in the Church of God, but they felt a Divine call to give themselves especially to the work in Canada, as did Paul and Barnabas to preach to the Gentiles, though to reach Canada they would have to travel some hundreds of miles through a wilderness, and then prosecute it through a still more remote wilderness, depending wholly upon the new settlers for their subsistence. Since the days of the apostles, I know not that the history of the Church has presented a phenomenon more remarkable for self-denial and devotion than that of the first Methodist preachers voluntarily consecrating themselves to the work of God in Canada, as detailed in the second of these Essays. They braved perils by water and perils in the wilderness, labouring night and day, and often working with their own hands to minister to their necessities.

If they were sometimes assailed for want of classical learning, and chiefly by men who could not read a classical author themselves without the aid of a lexicon, they showed themselves mighty in the Scriptures,—their clerical and other assailants retiring in confusion.*

* Not only the preachers, but **many of the** converts, from their own experience, **were** able to silence, if not confound, the skeptical assailants of practical and experimental religion—reminding **one of the** remarks and statements **contained in the** *Homily of the Church of England* (first part) *for Whitsunday*, **in the** following words :

"Who will not marvel at that which is written in the Acts of the Apostles, to hear their bold confession before the Council at Jerusalem ; and to consider that they went away with joy and gladness, rejoicing that they **were** counted worthy to suffer rebukes and **checks for the** name and faith **of** Christ Jesus ? **This was the mighty** work of the Holy **Ghost, who, because He** giveth patience and joyfulness of **heart in temptation and affliction, hath** therefore worthily obtained **this name in the Holy Scrip-** tures, **to be** called **the** Comforter. **Who will not also** marvel to read **the** learned **heavenly sermons of** Peter and the other disciples, considering **that they were** never brought up in a school **of** learning, **but** called from their nets to supply rooms of **apostles ?** This was likewise **the mighty** work **of the Holy** Ghost, who, because He **doth instruct the hearts of the simple** in the **true** know- ledge of **God and His holy** word, **is** most justly **termed,** by His name **and title, to be** the Spirit of Truth. **Euse-** bius, in **his Ecclesiastical** History, telleth a **strange story** of a certain learned **and** subtile philosopher, **who, being** an extreme adversary to Christ **and** His doctrine, **could** by no kind of learning be **converted to** the faith, **but was able to** withstand all **the** arguments that **could be** brought **against him** with little or **no labour. At length**

The phenomenon attending these revivals of
religion among the people were chiefly twofold—
the *suddenness* of conversions and the *extraordinary circumstances* connected with many of them
Of the reality of conversion,* and the inward

there started up a poor simple man, of small wit and less
knowledge, one that was reputed among the learned as
an idiot ; and he, in God's name, would take in hand to
dispute with this proud philosopher. The bishops and
other learned men standing by were marvellously
abashed at the matter, thinking that by his doings they
should be all confounded and put to open shame. He
notwithstanding goeth on, and beginning in the name of
Jesus, brought the philosopher to such a point in the
end, contrary to all men's expectations, that he would
not choose but acknowledge the power of God in his
words, and to give place to the truth. Was not this a
miraculous work, that one silly soul, of no learning,
should do that which many bishops of great knowledge
and understanding were never able to bring to pass ?
So true is the saying of Bede : ' Where the Holy Ghost
doth instruct and teach, there is no delay at all in
learning.' "

* Some opposers of conversion have argued that it was
only for heathens and Jews, but not for those in a Christian land who profess to believe the doctrines of Christianity. Dr. Paley will not be accused or suspected of
enthusiasm even by skeptics ; yet he speaks as follows
on this subject :

" Now, of the persons in our congregations to whom
we not only may, but must, preach the doctrine of
conversion, plainly and directly, are those who, with the
name indeed of Christians, have hitherto passed their

assurance of adoption, I have spoken sufficiently in the essay on the "Supernatural Character of lives without any internal religion whatever."—"At this day we have not Jews and Gentiles to preach to; but these persons are really in as unconverted a state as any Jew or Gentile could be in our Saviour's time. They are no more Christians, as to any actual benefit of Christianity to their souls, than the most hardened Jew or profligate Gentile was in the age of the Gospel. As to any difference in the two cases, the difference is all against them. These must be converted before they can be saved. The course of their thoughts must be changed; the very principles upon which they act must be changed. Considerations which never, or hardly ever, entered into their minds, must deeply and perpetually engage them. Views and motives which did not influence them at all either as checks from doing evil, or as inducements to do good, must become views and motives which they regularly consult, and by which they are guided; that is to say, there must be a revolution in principle; the visible conduct will follow the change; *but there must be a revolution within.* A change so entire, so deep, so important, as this, I do allow to be *conversion;* and no one who is in the situation above described can be saved without undergoing it; and he must necessarily both be sensible of it at the time, and remember it all his life afterward. It is too momentous an event ever to be forgotten. A man might as easily forget his escape from a shipwreck. Whether it was sudden, or whether it was gradual, if it was effected (and the fruits will prove that), it was a true conversion; and every such person may justly both believe and say of himself that he was converted at a particular assignable time."—*Sermon on Conversion,* Works, Vol. V., pp. 72-75.

Canadian Methodism," and have adduced ample authorities.

I now speak of the phenomenon of *sudden* conversions, so common in all Methodist revivals of religion, but more especially in the early period of Methodism, both in England, the United States, and in Canada. No one from Wesley to the present day has ever insisted upon the necessity of sudden conversion; but he and his followers have recognized it as the work of God when followed by the fruits of a true conversion. " Mr. Wesley and the Methodists," says Mr. Watson, " never taught that all true conversions are instantaneous, though they believed many of them to be so; but how can any one prove that all sudden conversions are fictitious and imaginary ? To influence the will, and move the affections to serious and spiritual objects, the truths of religion must be presented to the mind, for nothing beside has ever been known to produce those effects. But to some persons these truths may come in the slow process of elementary instruction, and serious advice from childhood; to others they may be presented, in all their great features, at once; or they may be suddenly revived in their minds; and to such they will have the additional interest which arises from novelty, their habits of life having taken them out of the way of regular instruction, and their religious education having either been neglected, or its impressions obliterated by the long practice of vice. In such cases, what reason can even a philosopher give, why the display of the stirring and solemn truths of the Gospel, unfolded by a living preacher with earnestness, perspicuity, and pathos, should not produce strong and sudden effects, and why the impressions thus made should not be deep and lasting?

"A true philosophy teaches that minds are differently constituted; that some men are slow to judge and to feel, and that what they hear rarely produces any immediate effect. The impression is made by subsequent reflection; for, like the ruminating animals, they do not feed for immediate digestion, but reserve that to a second process. In others the intellectual powers are more active and the affections more yielding; and there exists no reason why this peculiarity of mental disposition should not influence religious experience, though a superhuman agent must necessarily be supposed carrying on His designs, and exerting His influence with, and by, our constitutional qualities. It would be as manifestly absurd to deny that true conversion may follow a sudden impression upon yielding minds, as to affirm that it must be confined to slow and hesitating intellects, or that a decisive course of action of any kind cannot follow when motives to it are urged

upon a susceptible spirit, and the force of them
is immediately admitted. Determinations of the
will, and perseverance in effort, are essential to
rational and proper conduct of any kind. But
with whatever variety the Creator has formed the
human spirit, it is not to be supposed that it
has, in any case, a constitution which renders
decisive choice, and perseverance, impracticable.
These effects do not always result from slow
and reluctant operations of mind; they are not
inconsistent with susceptibility. The cautious
need energy ; the ardent, watchfulness and support; but everything rich in sentiment, firm in
choice, and constant in action, may exist in each
class of character. To suppose the contrary
would be a reflection on our Maker, who uses
variety as the means of exhibiting His wisdom,
but never sacrifices it to His own great and
beneficent purposes, and the moral capabilities of
His creatures.

" From these sudden yieldings of the mind to
impressions of a religious kind, what then can be
reasonably concluded ? Why, that conversion is
not a natural process, though carried on through
and by our natural powers. We are better instructed, I hope, in the Scriptures and the doctrine
of all true Churches—that suddenness and slow-
ness are mere circumstances, quite unconnected
with the essence of conversion. We believe the

testimony of Scripture, that the Spirit is not only given to the disciples of Christ, after they assume that character, but in order to their becoming His disciples; that, according to the words of our Lord, He is sent 'to convince the world of sin,' to the end that they may believe in Christ; and that whenever the Gospel is fully proclaimed by the ministers of Christ, it is 'the power of God unto salvation to every one that believeth,' and is made so by the accompanying influence of the Holy Ghost. If this doctrine be allowed, it will be difficult to prove Mr. Wesley a fanatic for his belief in the reality of sudden conversions. Who shall prescribe a mode to Divine operations? Who, if he believes such an influence accompanying the truth, shall presume to say, that when inspired truth is proposed, the attention of the careless shall be roused by a gradual and slow process only? or that no influence on the mind is genuine and divine, if it operate not in the prescribed manner? that the Holy Spirit shall not avail Himself of the variety which exists in the mental constitutions of men, to effect His purposes of mercy by different methods? and that the operations of grace shall not present, as well as those of nature, that beauteous variety which so much illustrates the glory of Him 'who worketh all in all?'

"And who shall say that even the peculiarities
of men's natures shall not, in many instances,
be even set aside in the course of a divine and
secret operation touching the springs of action,
and opening the sources of feeling; giving intensity of action to the one, and a flow to the
other, which shall more eminently mark His
finger in a work which His own glory, and the
humility proper to man, require should be known
and acknowledged as the work of God alone?
Assuredly there is nothing in the reason of the
case to fix the manner of producing such effects
to one rule, and nothing in Scripture. Instances
of sudden conversion occur in the New Testament in sufficient number to warrant us to
conclude that this may be often the mode adopted
by Divine wisdom, and especially in a slumbering
age, to arouse attention to long-despised and
neglected truths. The conversions of the day of
Pentecost were sudden, and, for anything that
appears to the contrary, they were real; for the
persons so influenced were thought worthy to
be 'added to the Church.' Nor was it by the
miracles of tongues that the effect was produced.
If miracles could have converted them, they had
witnessed greater than even that glorious day
exhibited. The dead had been raised in their
sight; the earth had quaked beneath their feet;
the sun had hid himself and made untimely

night; the graves had given up their dead; and Christ Himself had risen from the tomb sealed and watched. It was not by the impression of the miracles of tongues alone, but by that super-venient gracious influence which operated with the demonstrative sermon of Peter, after the miracle had excited the attention of his hearers, that they were 'pricked in their hearts,' and cried ' Men and brethren, what shall we do ? '

" The only true rule of judging of professed conversion is its fruits. The mode may vary from circumstances of which we are not the judges ; nor can we be until we know more both of the mystic powers of the mind, and of that intercourse which Almighty God, in His goodness, condescends to hold with it." *

But the more remarkable phenomena of the revivals of religion are not merely the suddenness of conversions, but the extraordinary circum-stances connected with them—physical agitations and prostrations. The words of the Church of England *Homily on Fasting* may here be repeated:

" When men feel in themselves the heavy burden of sin, see damnation to be the reward of it, and behold with the eye of their mind the horror of hell, *they tremble, they quake,* and are inwardly *touched with sorrowfulness of heart, and cannot but accuse themselves, and open their grief*

* Richard Watson's Works, Vol. V., pp. 414-418.

unto Almighty God and call upon Him for mercy.
This being done seriously, their mind is so
occupied, partly with sorrow and heaviness, partly
with an earnest desire to be delivered from this
danger of hell and damnation, *that all desire of
meat and drink is laid apart, and loathing of
all worldly things and pleasure cometh in place:
so that nothing liketh them more than to weep,
to lament, to mourn, and by both words and
behaviour of body to show themselves weary of life.*"

Mr. Wesley, after quoting these words, com-
ments upon them thus to the objector:

"Now, what if your wife, or daughter, or acquaintance, after hearing one of these field
preachers, should come and tell you that they
saw damnation before them, and beheld with
the eye of their mind this horror of hell? What
if they should 'tremble and quake,' and be so
taken up 'partly with sorrow and heaviness,
partly with an earnest desire to be delivered from
this hell and damnation, as to weep, to lament,
to mourn, and by both words and behaviour to
show themselves weary of life;' would you
scruple to say that they are stark mad; that
these fellows have driven them out of their
senses? These are the words of our own Church.
You may read them, if you are so inclined, in the
first part of the 'Homily on Fasting.' And, consequently, what you have peremptorily deter-

mined to be mere lunacy and distraction, is that 'repentance unto life,' which, in the judgment both of the Church and of St. Paul, is 'never to be repented of.' I grant that extraordinary circumstances have attended this conviction in some instances. While the Word of God was preached, some persons have dropped down as dead; some have been, as it were, in strong convulsions; some roared aloud, though not with an articulate voice; and others spoke the anguish of their souls."*

*Wesley's *Further Appeal to Men of Reason and Religion.* Works, Vol. V., p. 93. Am. Ed. Mr. Wesley adds : "This, I suppose, you believe to be perfect madness. But it is easily accounted for, either on principles of reason or Scripture.

"First, on principles of reason. For how easy is it to suppose that a strong, lively, and sudden apprehension of the heinousness of sin, the wrath of God, and the bitter pains of eternal death, should affect the body as well as the soul, during the present laws of vital union —should interrupt or disturb the ordinary circulations, and put nature out of its course ! Yes, we may question whether, while this union subsists, it is possible for the mind to be affected in so violent a degree without some one or other of those bodily symptoms following.

"It is likewise easy to account for these things on principles of Scripture. For when we take a view of them in this light, we are to add, to the consideration of natural causes, the agency of those spirits who still excel in strength, and, as far as they have leave from God, will not fail to torment whom they cannot destroy ; to tear those that are coming to Christ. It is also

These physical phenomena were not uncommon in the early years of Methodism in Canada, and especially in those great rural assemblages known as "camp-meetings," and they have occurred from time to time to this day. Examples of them are needless; they have been supposed by some to have originated in Canada, and to be a characteristic of Canadian Methodism; but this is a mistake.

remarkable, that there is plain Scripture precedent of every symptom which has lately appeared; so that we cannot allow the conviction attended with these to be madness, without giving up both reason and Scripture." "All these and whatever else conversion effects may sometimes accompany this conviction, are easily known from the common distemper of madness, were it only for this one circumstance—that whenever the person convinced tastes the pardoning love of God, they all vanish away in a moment."—*Ib.*, p. 94.

It should be borne in mind, however, that Mr. Wesley never confounded these phenomena with noise or clamour in public worship; the latter he unhesitatingly condemned. "Perhaps," he says, in one of his discourses, "some may be afraid, lest refraining from these warm expressions, or even gently checking them, should check the fervour of our devotion. It is possible it may check or even prevent some kind of fervour which has passed for devotion. Possibly it may prevent loud shouting, horrid, unnatural screaming, repeating the same words twenty or thirty times, jumping two or three feet high, and throwing the arms or legs about, both of men and women, shocking not only to religion, but to common

These meetings in America originated with the Presbyterians in the Western States; and the most remarkable instances of these phenomena occurred among them, at these vast forest gatherings. "Violent opposers were sometimes seized by a mysterious power which agitated them from head to foot; men with imprecations upon their lips were suddenly smitten down. Drunkards, attempting to drown the effect by liquors, could not hold the bottle to their lips; their convulsed arms would drop it, or shiver it against the surrounding trees. Horsemen charging upon these camp-meetings to disperse them, were seized by the strange affection at the very boundaries of the

decency; but it will never check, much less prevent, true Scriptural devotion."—*Sermon on "Knowing Christ after the Flesh."*

Dr Adam Clarke equally condemned such clamours and confusion. In his Commentary on 1 Cor. xiv. 33, he says: "Let not the persons who act in the congregation in this disorderly manner, say that they are under the influence of God; for He is not the author of confusion: but two, or three, or more praying or teaching at the same place, and at the same time, is confusion; and God is not the author of such work: and let men be aware how they attribute such disorder to the God of order and peace. The Apostle calls such conduct *akatastasasia,*—tumult, sedition; and such they are in the sight of God, and in the sight of all good men. How often is the work of God marred and discredited by the folly of men!"

worshipping circles, and were the more violently shaken the more they endeavoured to resist the inexplicable power. As many as five hundred persons are said to have been thus affected in a single congregation. The nervous affection spread from one denomination to another, and prevailed as an epidemic through much of the valley of the Mississippi.

"Prior to the introduction of camp-meetings, infidelity prevailed generally in the new States of the West, the effect, to a great extent, of the writings of Thomas Paine, and of his great personal influence in America during the then recent revolutionary struggle. Many wise as well as devout men, who witnessed the results of these meetings, believed that they were a providential provision for the counteraction of the deism and corruption which seemed to threaten with utter demoralization that vast country—the seat of future and gigantic States—and that the astonishing physical phenomena which attended them were a necessary means of arresting the popular attention. The 'great revival' which followed, and which swept over the whole valley of the Mississippi, unquestionably broke down the prevalent deism, and opened the way for the most rapid religious development recorded in the history of any modern people."*

* Stevens' History of Methodism, Vol. II., pp. 425, 426; and Dr. Bangs' Life and Times, pp. 149, 150.

Perhaps one illustration of similar work in Canada may be given, from an account of the "first camp-meeting in Canada, which took place in 1803, in Adolphustown, where the first Methodist class in the province was organized in 1790, by its first Methodist preacher, William Losee, and its first Methodist chapel erected in 1792. Camp-meetings had been extensively held in the Western States for about five years. They originated among the Presbyterians. They seemed justified by the necessities of the frontier, where there were few chapels, and where, after the harvests, the settlers could travel considerable distances from home, and avail themselves of a week of camp-life for religious instruction and social intercourse." The first camp-meeting in Canada appeared to Dr. Bangs a salient fact in the history of Canadian Methodism. He therefore made particular notes of it.

"Its announcement beforehand excited great interest far and near. Whole families prepared for a pilgrimage to the ground. Processions of waggons and foot passengers wended their way to the place of assemblage. With two of his fellow-evangelists, Dr. Bangs had to take his course from a remote appointment, through a range of forest thirty miles in extent. They hastened forward, conversing on religious themes, praying and singing, and eager with expectation

for the moral battle-scene about to open. They
arrived, in time to commence the meeting, on
Friday, the 27th of September, though only about
two hundred and fifty people had yet reached
the ground. The exercises commenced with singing, prayer, and a short sermon on the text,
' Brethren, pray.' Several exhortations followed ;
and after an intermission of about twenty minutes
another sermon was delivered on 'Christ, our
Wisdom, Righteousness, Sanctification, and Redemption.' Some lively exhortations followed,
and the Spirit of the Lord seemed to move
among the people. After an interruption of an
hour and a-half, a prayer-meeting was held,
and towards its close the power of God descended
on the assembly, and songs of victory and praise
resounded through the forest. During this day
six persons passed from death unto life.

"At five o'clock Saturday morning a prayer-
meeting was held, and at ten o'clock a sermon
was preached on the words, 'My people are
destroyed for lack of knowledge.' At this time
the congregation had increased to perhaps twenty-
five hundred, and the people of God were seated
together on logs near the stand, while a crowd
were standing in a semicircle around them.
During the sermon I felt an unusual sense of the
Divine presence, and thought I could see a cloud
of the Divine glory resting upon the congregation.

At the close of the sermon I sprang to my feet, and immediately descended from the stand among the hearers. The rest of the preachers all spontaneously followed me, and we went among the people exhorting the impenitent and comforting the distressed; for while Christians were 'filled with joy unspeakable and full of glory,' many a sinner was weeping and praying in the surrounding crowd. These we collected together in little groups, and we exhorted God's people to join in prayer for them. O, what a scene of prayer and tears was this! I suppose that not less than a dozen little praying circles were thus formed in the course of a few minutes. It was truly affecting to see parents weeping over their children, neighbours exhorting their unconverted neighbours to repent, while all, old and young, were awe-struck. This meeting resulted in some forty conversions.

" On Sabbath morning, as the natural sun arose in splendour, darting his rays through the forest, we presented ourselves before its Maker, and poured out our songs of thanksgiving to the Lord of the universe. We felt that our early sacrifice was accepted, for the 'Sun of Righteousness' shone upon our souls, and made all within us rejoice.

" After breakfast, a host being now on the ground, we held a love-feast. The interest and excitement were so great, and the crowd so large, that while some assembled around the stand, a preacher mounted a waggon at a distance and addressed a separate congregation. The impression of the Word was universal; the power of the Spirit was manifest throughout the encampment, and almost every tent was a scene of prayer.

"At noon the Lord's Supper was administered to multitudes, while other multitudes looked on with astonishment and tears. After the sacrament, a young woman, of fashionable and high position in society, was smitten down, and with sobs entreated the prayers of the people. Her sister forced her away. A preacher went forth without the camp, and led them both back, followed by quite a procession of their friends; a circle was formed about them, and we sang and prayed. The unawakened sister was soon upon her knees praying in agony, and was first converted; the other quickly after received the peace of God, and they wept and rejoiced together."*

* Stevens' Life and Times of Dr. Bangs, pp. 150-154.
Dr. Bangs gives an account of a remarkable conversion, but in the more quiet and ordinary way :

"In Oxford, Major Ingersoll, to whom I was first introduced, was a Universalist ; and told me, on my first visit, that he was an unbeliever in the doctrine of depravity ; that he never had himself a depraved heart. 'This assertion,' said I, 'is a sure sign that you

As to the philosophy of these revivals of religion, and the extraordinary circumstances connected with some of them, little need be added to the reasonings of Messrs. Wesley and Watson in the quotations from their writings made in the former part of this paper. I will therefore only subjoin a few remarks.

never knew your heart.' On my second visit, I found him sitting in his chair, with his head inclined on his hands. He looked up to me and said, 'O, what a depraved heart I have!' 'Ay!' said I, 'have you discovered that fact at last?' 'Yes, indeed,' he replied; 'what shall I do to be saved?' 'Surrender up to God, by faith in Christ, and He will give you a new heart and renew a right spirit within you.' He did so, and found the promise verified. He, his wife, who was a very sensible and amiable woman, his two daughters, together with the husband of one of them, were soon converted and joined the Church; and the good work quickly spread through the neighbourhood, sweeping all before it. In this way the revival prevailed in both these places, so that large and flourishing societies were established, and no less than six preachers were raised up. The reformation extended through many settlements, particularly Oxford, where large numbers were 'turned from darkness to light.'"—*Ib.*, pp. 84, 85.

More than thirty years later, Dr. Bangs, while travelling through the State of New York, wrote a private letter, now before me :

"On my way in the canal boat, a young preacher introduced himself to me, and asked if I remembered one Hitchcock, who lived in the township of Oxford,

1. These extraordinary physical phenomena of religious revivals or excitements first occurred long before the time of Wesley himself. They occurred in the mediæval ages in the Roman Church, on the Continent, and in Scotland.*

in Upper Canada, about thirty-four years ago ? I replied, Yes, very well.' ' I am,' said he, ' his son.'

" His father and mother were converted under my ministry on the first circuit I ever travelled, and were soon married together, and here was their son, a minister ! This circumstance brought a thousand pleasant recollections to my mind, and made me thank God and take courage. The grandfather of this youth was a Universalist, a Major Ingersoll, to whom I had a letter of introduction in a new place where I went to preach. Himself, wife, and two of his daughters were soon converted and joined our Church ; and now here is one of the third generation in the itinerant field ! I thought I should pray and preach with greater fervour than ever.'' —*Ib.*, p. 85, in a note.

* In " Historical Collections relating to Remarkable Periods of the Success of the Gospel, and Eminent Instruments employed in Promoting It," compiled by the Rev. Dr. Gillies, one of the ministers of Glasgow, published in 1754, accounts are given of the rapid conquests of the Gospel in less than forty years after the Reformation in Germany, France, Switzerland, Holland, Denmark, and the Low Countries, with Britain and Ireland ; in which, says Dr. Gillies, these things are observable :

" 1. How the truth of the Gospel then came ' not in word only, but in power, in the Holy Ghost, and in

President Edwards has recorded many of them in
his accounts of the great awakening in New
England; and they were known in New Jersey
before Whitfield's arrival there.

much assurance ;' assurance of faith and understanding
of the truth, and with that seal of the greatest enlarge-
ment of comfort ; so as receiving the word in much
affliction was with joy in the Holy Ghost. 2. That in
this blessed Reformed religion, the Church did receive
the Spirit, and an innumerable company in these last
ages were sealed thereby, which is the undoubted seal
and attestation from the Lord of His own truth and
doctrine, so expressly promised to the Church under
the New Testament. 3. That after this blessed day once
began to dawn, and the Lord did so visibly rend the
heavens, and caused the mountains to flow at His presence, with so solemn a downpouring of the Spirit following the Gospel, as there could be no standing before
it, but cities and nations were subjected to so marvellous
a power, to the embracing of the truth. 4. That this
great work of God was not for a short time, but for
many years. Wherever the truth came, it did most
discernibly accompany the same, not only to affect and
convince, by some transient flash upon the spirits of
men, but to that solid and effectual change as visibly
transformed them into that blessed image of Christ, by
the spirit of holiness, so as it was given, both to believe
and suffer for His name."

"I must here instance a solemn and extraordinary
outpouring of the Spirit, about the year 1625, and afterwards, in the west of Scotland. This, by the profane
rabble, was called the Stewarton sickness ; for in that
parish first, but afterward through much of that country,

2. Though arising, directly or indirectly, from religious causes, these phenomena are themselves physical affections; they have not always been followed by a religious life; they are no criterion of a genuine conversion, the proof of which must be sought in its fruits; and the most devout men have not been most under their influence.

particularly at Irvine, under the ministry of Mr. Dickson, it was remarkable ; where it can be said (which divers ministers and Christians yet alive can witness) that, for a considerable time, few Sabbaths did pass away without some evidently converted, or some convincing proofs of the power of God accompanying His Word ; yea, that many were so taken by the heart, that, through terror, the Spirit in such measure convincing them of sin, in hearing of the Word they have been made to fall over, and were carried out of the church ; who afterward proved the most solid and lively Christians."—" The famous Stewarton sickness was begun about the year 1630, and spread from house to house for many miles in the strath where Stewarton water flows, on both sides of it. Serious, practical religion flourished mightily in the west of Scotland about this time.

" I must mention that solemn communion of the Kirk of Shott's, June 20, 1630, at which there was so convincing an appearance of God, and downpouring of the Spirit, even in an extraordinary way, that did follow the ordinances, especially that sermon on the Monday, June 21, with a strange unusual motion on the hearers, who in a great multitude were then convinced of divers ranks, that it was known, which I can speak on sure ground, *near five hundred had at that time a dis-*

3. They have not been identified with any diseased affections; nor have they been followed by any morbid physical effects, or even exhaustion, though they have been known to continue some days without motion, food or drink.

cernible change wrought on them, of whom most proved lively Christians afterwards."

Sir Henry Moncrief Welwood, Bart., in his Life of John Erskine, D.D., states, among many others, the following facts :

"In the following winter (1741-2), very remarkable impressions were observed in the congregation of Camberslong, under the ministry of Mr. McCulloch, the pastor of that parish—a man of genuine piety and considerable capacity, but is said to have had nothing particularly striking either in the manner or substance of his preaching. His hearers, in considerable numbers, were on different occasions *so violently agitated while he preached on the Christian doctrine of regeneration, as to fall down, in the midst of the multitude, under visible paroxysms of bodily agony."—"* The same visible agitations among the people were continued during the whole course of the winter, and his labours and solicitudes were never relaxed The effect of his labours became every day more visible and extensive.

"Similar effects began to appear at Kilsyth, in the barony parish of Glasgow, and in some other adjacent parishes."—"From this time the multitudes who assembled were more numerous than they had ever been, or perhaps than any congregations which had ever assembled in Scotland; the religious impressions made on the people were apparently much greater and more general; and the visible convulsive agitations, which accom-

4. Though the power of the work of grace either in a revival of religion, or in individual conversion, does not consist in these phenomena ; yet their presence is not a proof that a deep and extraordinary work and revival of religion is not being wrought in the hearts of men by the Spirit of God, and that it is not a season of refreshing from the presence of the Lord. Conversion is an individual work, operating upon each heart separately, as much as if there were no other heart in the universe, and evinces the particular providence of God as well as the work of the Holy Spirit. And there is joy before the angels over one sinner that repenteth.

I cannot.better conclude this paper than in the words of the Rev. Dr. F. W. Farrar's " Life and Work of St. Paul," Vol. I., Chapter x., pp. 198, 199 :

" In the course of human lives there have been other spiritual crises analogous to this in their startling suddenness and absolute finality. To many, the resurrection from the death of sin is

panied them exceeded anything of the kind which had yet been obsérved. Whatever opinion we may form of the source of those extraordinary effects, it is, at least, a most remarkable fact that in this period they were neither confined to any one district of country, nor were they exclusively connected with the ministry of any individuals."—*Sir Henry Moncrief* ₁*Welwood's Life oJ John Erskine, D.D.*

a slow and life-long process ; but others pass with one thrill of conviction, with one spasm of energy, from death to life, from the power of Satan unto God. Such moments crowd eternity into an hour, and stretch an hour into eternity.

> ' At such hours
> Of inspiration from the living God,
> Thought is not.'

"When God's awful warnings burn before the soul in letters of flame, it can read them indeed, and know their meaning to the very uttermost ; but it does not know, and does not care, whether it was Perez or Upharsin that was written on the wall. The utterances of the Eternal Sybil are inscribed on records scattered and multitudinous as are the forest leaves. As the anatomist may dissect every joint and lay bare every nerve of the organism, yet be infinitely distant from any discovery of the principle of life, so the critic and grammarian may decipher the dim syllables and wrangle about the disputed discrepancies; but it is not theirs to interpret. If we would in truth understand such experiences, the records of them must be read by a light that never was on land or sea.

"Saul rose another man : he had fallen in death, he rose in life; he had fallen in the midst of things temporal, he rose in awful consciousness of things eternal; he had fallen a proud, intolerant, persecuting Jew ; he rose a humble, brokenhearted, penitent Christian. In that moment a new element had been added to his being. Henceforth—to use his own deep and dominant expression—he was 'in Christ.' God had found him, Jesus had spoken to him, and in one flash had changed him from a raging Pharisee into a true disciple—from the murderer of the saints into the Apostle of the Gentiles. It was a new birth —a new creation." *

* Farrar's Life and Work of St. Paul, Vol. I., Chap. x., pp. 198, 199. (Conversion of St. Paul.)

ESSAY V.

METHODISM **THE** PIONEER **OF** CIVIL AND RELIGIOUS LIBERTY IN UPPER CANADA; COMMENCEMENT OF THE CLERGY RESERVES CONTROVERSY.

F Methodism was **the** first **ministry of re-** ligious instruction and spiritual freedom **to** the first Canadian settlers; if, under **its** minis- trations, men were freed from the slavery **of vice in** every form, and made virtuous, moral, **religious** citizens—were turned from **darkness unto light,** and made partakers of the glorious **liberty of** the sons **of** God; so **also** was Methodism the pre- cursor, the pioneer, the first **and most** effective promoter of civil and religious liberty for the **entire** country. The early Methodist preachers did not interfere with politics; **I can** find no in- stance of **it in the** whole of their history; **but** they taught doctrines which lay at the foundation of a country's freedom, and without which **no** country has ever been free. They preached **the** Gospel of Christ in its purity, fulness, **and power;** and a late writer **has well** observed, "Christ's Gospel did not promise political freedom, **yet it**

9

gave it : more surely than conqueror, reformer,
patriot, that Gospel will bring about true liberty
at last. This, not by theories, nor by schemes of
constitutions, but by the revelations of truths."
(F. W. Robertson.)

There is a fourfold truth which lies at the
foundation of all other truths of the Bible, and
which involves the first elements of civil freedom.

First, God is a Spirit, the Creator and Preserver
of all mankind ; and the counterpart of that truth,
each human being is the child of God by creation
" The rich and the poor meet together ; the Lord
is the *Maker* of them *all*." " We are also His off-
spring." " God, that made the world, and all
things therein, seeing that He is Lord of heaven
and earth, dwelleth not in temples made with
hands,. . and hath made of *one blood* all nations of
men, for to dwell on all the face of the earth."
In the sunlight of these inspired words (words
not found in the philosophy or any writings of
the Greeks or Romans) on the grand truth of
creation, we have the glorious doctrines of the
universal fatherhood of God, and the universal
brotherhood of man, in the presence of which all
earthly distinctions of title, of rank, of attain-
ments, of age, of nations, disappear, and the universal equality of mankind—the foe of despotism
and tyranny—stands forth as the basis and pledge
of universal freedom.

In connection **with** this twofold truth **of crea-**
tion, take the twofold truth of redemption. Jesus
Christ has tasted death for *every man ;* and **by**
, His teaching and **resurrection,** has revealed **and**
demonstrated man's immortality, **and hath** given
" the manifestation **of the Spirit to every** man **to**
profit **withal "**—proofs and teachings suited to
all understandings—sealed **by the** blood **and con-**
firmed by the resurrection of **our** common Lord
and Saviour.

The universality of man's redemption commen-
surate with that **of** his creation, imparts by **the**
riches of Divine grace to every human being **the**
right of access **to** all the nobility and **privileges**
of "heirs of God **and** joint-heirs **with Christ."**

Before these fundamental **and sublime truths**
of revelation—God our **Creator, and all we His**
children ; Christ our **Redeemer, and all we His**
redeemed, and redeemed **for immortality to an**
equality with the angels —how **are all mankind,**
and every man, enfranchised **with the rights of**
an equal freedom **and** dignified with **the grandeur**
of more than angelic glory !

It is unhappily **the case that these great**
truths have been mutilated, separated from each
other, placed one against the other, perverted **and**
abused by the mental narrowness, **cupidity, and**
ambition of men, as **have** been other **truths** of
Revelation, **and many of the** greatest bounties of

Providence, to the oppression and enslavement of their fellow-men; but the perversion and abuse of truths or blessings does not change their nature or lessen their value. Wherever these truths have been proclaimed in their reality and fulness, and the Book which teaches them has been an open book to all interested in them, there have communities and peoples risen, or are rising, to the manhood of true civil freedom; while all other communities and peoples who are untaught,[1] or perverted, and the book which teaches them is a prohibited book, are bound by the claims of despotism, or scarred by the manacles of tyranny.

It is also true that wherever the universality of the atonement has been denied, and its saving benefits shrivelled to a small portion of mankind—the unconditionally elect from all eternity, and the rest, the great majority, of the human race, left unconditionally and eternally reprobate—there the principles of universal freedom, or even of toleration, have neither been practised nor understood, as witness the grinding and persecuting government of Calvin in Geneva and of the Puritans in Massachusetts Bay, against all reprobates. The doctrine of the Papacy which exalts one man and his delegates above all other men, assuming to possess the keys of the kingdom of heaven, to lock and unlock at pleasure, and the doctrine that the eternal blessings of the atonement are limited to the few elected from all eternity, to the exclusion of all others of the human race, are equally. incompatible with the principles of equal rights and freedom among any people. But the Methodist preachers preached throughout the land that "God is no respecter of persons," and that "Jesus Christ is the Saviour of all men, especially of them that believe ;" and they made the wilderness resound, from one extremity of Canada to the other, with the doctrine and song—

> "Lord, I believe were sinners more
> Than sands upon the ocean shore,
> Thou hast for all a ransom paid,
> For all a full atonement made."

With this doctrine the whole country (with a few individual exceptions) became leavened at an early period, whether connected with Methodism in Church fellowship or not, and espoused the cause of equal rights and privileges before the law by all classes of citizens, whenever opportunity offered. The doctrine of universal equality before the law was the natural result of the doctrine of universal equality before God in both creation and redemption ; and with the Bible in their hands, recommending its circulation and reading among the people, early Methodist preachers desired and prayed that all classes might enjoy the rights and privileges which they claimed and exercised for themselves. It was thus that the principles of equal religious rights and liberty became grounded in the public mind of the country far beyond the nominal limits of the religious denomination that first taught them, and long before the question itself became a subject of newspaper discussion.

In this the early Methodist preachers in Canada were the true followers of the Divine Founder of our holy Christianity and of His first apostles—being themselves of the common people, and sympathizing with them in all their wants and privations. The late Rev. Dr. Spring, of New York, has justly observed : " It is remarked of the Divine Founder of the Christian faith, that the ' common people heard Him gladly.' He was himself one of the common people. He was raised from an obscure family in Israel, and was from the humbler walks of life. All His sympathies were with the common people. He knew the heart of the suffering and oppressed, and was touched with the feeling of their infirmities. Of the same character were His apostles, and the principal teachers of His religion. And of the same character do we find all their doctrines and precepts. 'To the poor the Gospel is preached.' ' In Christ Jesus there is neither Greek nor Jew, barbarian nor Scythian, bond nor free.' 'The cultivated heathen,' says Tholuck, ' were offended at Christianity precisely for this reason, that the higher classes could no longer have precedence of the common people.' " *

* *Obligations of the World to the Bible.* Lecture IV., pp. 113, 114.

" It is worthy of remark, that the Bible recognizes and maintains the only principle on which it is possible for a nation ever to enjoy the blessings of civil liberty. That principle is, that *all that is valuable in the institutions of civil liberty, rests on the character which the people sustain as citizens.* The fear of God is the foundation of political freedom.

'He is the freeman whom the truth makes free,
And all are slaves beside.'

Bad men cannot be good citizens. It is impossible that a nation of infidels or idolaters should be a nation of freemen. It is when a people forget God, that tyrants forge their chains. The principles of liberty and the principles of the Bible are most exactly coincident. A vitiated state of morals, a corrupted public conscience, is incompatible with freedom. Nothing short of the strong influence of that system of truth which God has revealed from heaven is competent so to guide, moderate and preserve the balance between the conflicting interests and passions of men, as to prepare them for the blessings of free government. Holland was free, as long as she was virtuous. She was a flourishing republic ; she produced great and enlightened statesmen, until she became corrupt, and infidelity spoiled her of her glory. France would have become free on the accession of her citizen king, but for the radical deficiency of her moral virtue. When the distinguished Perrier,

It was thus that **the early** Methodist preachers
—almost **the only** ministers of religion **in** the
country—**sprung from and** sympathizing with **the**
common people, traversed every county and new
settled township of the land, **holding forth the
Bible** as the only infallible rule of faith and prac-

who succeeded **La** Fayette in the office of Prime Minister
to Louis Philippe, was on **his** death-bed, he exclaimed
with great emphasis and fervour, *La France doit avoir
une religion,* 'France **must have a** religion.' Liberty
cannot **exist without** morality, nor morality without the
religion **of the Bible.** It is a nation's love of law, its
love of **wise and benevolent institutions,** its attachment
to the **public weal,** its peaceful and benevolent spirit, **its**
love of virtue, and these alone, can **make it free.** Take
these away, **and there must be** tyrants **in their place.**
I hold no axiom more true or more important **than this,**
that man must be governed by **truth or by despotic power.**
As soon as a nation becomes corrupt, her liberties degen-
erate into faction ; and then nothing short of the strong
arm of despotism will restrain the passions of men, and
control their selfishness, their love of gold, their thirst for
domination, and their brutal licentiousness. The Bible
alone is the source of that high-toned moral principle
which is necessary to all classes, in all their intercourse,
for the exercise of their rights and the enjoyment **of** all
their privileges. **Without** it rulers become tyrants, and
the people are **fitted only for servitude, or** anarchy.
Without it there is no such thing as an intelligent, lofty,
honourable, **and** disinterested **character.** Nothing else
is capable of combining a nation into one great brotherhood—annihilating **its** divisions—quenching its hate—

tice—the Magna Charta of a people's rights and
liberties—teaching from day to day, and from
house to -house, those first truths of faith, of
morality, of order and of freedom, and thus per-
meating the entire population, from parents to
children, from neighbours to neighbours, with
principles which have developed into the noblest

destroying its spirit of party—bringing all parts with all
their jarring interests into one great whole. Nothing
will rightly control its suffrages ; send up salutary influence into its Senate Chamber ; diffuse its power through
all ranks of office : direct learning and laws ; act on
commerce and the arts. and spread that hallowed influence through every department of society that shall
render its liberties perpetual. Statesmen may be slow
to learn from the Bible ; but they will nowhere find
their interests so watchfully protected and their liberties
defended with such ability and so many counsels of wisdom. The designs of the ambitious and intriguing, the
artifices of demagogues, the usurpations of power, the
corrupting influences of high places, and the punishment
of political delusion, all find the prototype and antidote
in the principles, prophecies, biography and history of
the Bible. * * * We shall be a free people, only as
we remain a Christian people. If a low and degraded
infidelity should ever succeed in its already begun enterprise of sending up from the whole face of this land
her poisonous exhalations, and the youth of our country
become regardless of the God of their fathers ; men in
other lands, who have been watching for our downfall,
will in a few short years enrol us on the catalogue of
enslaved nations."—*Ib.*, 120-123.

elements of Canadian character **and** institutions.

Montesquieu, **one of the** most profound and candid French **essayists of the** last century, has remarked : " Christianity is a stranger **to** despotic power." De Tocqueville, a French statesman and elegant writer **of** the present century, after travelling in England and America, says : " The religion which declares that all men are equal in the sight of God, **will not refuse to** acknowledge that all citizens are equal in the eye **of** the law."— "Religion is the companion of liberty in **all its** battles and all its conflicts ; the cradle of its infancy and the divine source of its claims."

But the influence of Methodism **as** the pioneer of civil and religious liberty in Canada arose not only from its teaching the fundamental truths of religion—especially the doctrine **of** universal redemption **and its** collateral truths, **but in its** earnest appeals, **in all** its ministrations, to the Holy Scriptures **as the only source of** authority in matters of religion ; on every man's undeniable and inviolable right of private judgment in all matters of religious faith and duty, irrespective **of** the civil governmental authority, whether **of Pope** or **King** or **President ; and consequently on the** great principle that religion being **a** spiritual system of inspired truth, must be promoted only by **moral and** spiritual influences, and not by the coercion of civil government or legal statute, by pains and penalties, which do not reach the heart, or conscience, or understanding.

It was not the practice of the Methodist preachers to deliver formal theses on these subjects, but they constituted the warp and woof of all their teachings, as the writer well recollects in listening to their ministrations in the days of his boyhood and youth—they thus being not the heralds of salvation to an otherwise religiously destitute people, but the harbinger-voices in the wilderness for the coming struggles of religious right against religious proscriptions, of equal political freedom against class political exclusion —the day-star of the sunlight of civil and religious liberty which was, in a few short years, to shine with impartial and unclouded splendour upon the entire population of Upper Canada.

But the dawn of that day of equal religious and civil liberty was accompanied with clouds and storms which agitated all classes of society, and which developed into an entire change of the relations of different Christian persuasions and in the whole system of government in Upper Canada. These great religious, social, and constitutional changes were involved in what has been known as the " Clergy Reserve Controversy " —which will be the subject of my next essay.

In the meantime, I think it proper to devote

the rest of this essay to the preliminaries of that great contest.

It was assumed and avowed by the leading clergy of the Church of England, that that Church was the Established Church not only of England and Ireland, but of the empire, and that the clergy of that Church were alone duly authorized to preach the Gospel, and administer the sacraments and ordinances of religion. This doctrine, or rather pretension, excluded all ministers and members of all Christian persuasions but Episcopalians from even the pale of the Christian Church. In maintenance of such pretension, not only was the one-seventh of the public lands of the province claimed for the support of the clergy of the Church of England, but earnest applications were made to the Propagation Society and Parliament in England for large additional support. It was with this view that the venerable Archdeacon of York—the late Right Reverend Dr. Strachan, then and long afterwards, until his decease at the age of ninety years, as the first Bishop of Toronto, the acknowledged head of the Church of England in Upper Canada—prepared and delivered a sermon, the 3rd day of July, 1825, on the death of the Bishop of Quebec (Dr. Mountain)—the diocese of Quebec then embracing all Upper as well as Lower Canada. In this discourse, of remarkable ability, the history of the

Church of England, from the beginning, was traced, and the obstacles and difficulties which it encountered, with an earnest appeal to the British Parliament and Propagation Society in England for grants to support and extend the Church of England in Upper Canada. The sermon was evidently intended more for England than for Canada; it was not printed until the spring of 1826, on the eve of its author's departure for England, in order to procure large additional supplies and a University Charter for the Church of England, endowed out of the public lands of Upper Canada. A copy of this plausible and able discourse fell into the hands of a member of the Methodist Church, and he brought it to a social and religious meeting of its principal members, who assembled once a month for social and devotional purposes, on the meeting of their two preachers after their three weeks' tour of eleven townships, west, north, and east of the town, preaching each two Sabbaths out of four in the town. At one of these social meetings, the discourse of the Archdeacon of York was read, containing attacks on different religious denominations, but chiefly on the Methodists. It thrilled the whole company, who with one voice insisted that the unjust attack and misrepresentations of the Archdeacon should be answered; and when the question was proposed as to who should write the answer, the common voice pointed to a young preacher, who had just finished the twenty-third year of his age, but not the first year of his probation in the Methodist ministry—the youngest, though now the oldest minister of the Methodist Church. He objected on the ground of his youth, inexperience, etc.; but finding his remonstrances unavailing, he proposed that the Superintendent of the Circuit (the late Rev. James Richardson, D.D.) and himself should each write something during their next tour round the Circuit; and out of what they should both write, something might be compiled that would meet the case. This was assented to; and at the next monthly meeting, inquiry was made as to what had been done in answer to the sermon of the Archdeacon of York, when it was found that the Superintendent of the Circuit had written nothing. The junior preacher replied that he had endeavoured to obey the wishes of his brethren. He was pressed to read what he had written, which he did with great reluctance. The effect of the paper (which occupied only twenty-seven octavo pages) seemed to be electrical; and the publication of it was instantly demanded. The author remonstrated, when one of the brethren present seized him by the arms from behind, and another wrested the manuscript from his hands, and said he would take it to the printer. Seeing that he could not recover the manuscript, he said if **it would** be returned to him he would **not** destroy **it,** but revise and re-write it, and give it back to his brethren to do what **they pleased** with it. This was agreed to, **and the** paper, which was written in April, 1826, **was** published, under the title **of " A** Review **of a Sermon** preached by the Hon. and Rev. John Strachan, D.D., at York, U. C., 3rd of July, 1825, on the death of the late Bishop **of** Quebec. By a Methodist Preacher."

This " Review " produced a sensation and alarm scarcely less than that of a Fenian **inva**sion ; **it was the** first publication put forth **by** the Methodists **in** Upper Canada in their **own** defence, and **in** which the exclusive claims **of the** Church of England to an **ordained ministry, and** to the status and endowments **of** *the* Established Church, were called in question, and the claims **of** other denominations **to** equal rights and privileges with the Church of England were defended and maintained; **it** was the sole topic of conversation, and the subject of universal excitement in **town and** country. In the course of a fortnight, **four** answers appeared in the public papers to the " Review"—three of them written by clergymen, and one by **a** layman **of** the Church of England ; by all **of** whom the unknown author of the " Review " was treated in the most contemptuous **and** bitter **terms.** By one he was called an "ignoramus;" by another, "a proud boaster of his learning;" by a third, no Methodist preacher, but "a crafty politician;" by a fourth, "a rebel and a traitor." One of them retired after the first shot; the other three continued the contest for a year or more, during which time the public mind became much excited. Public meetings were held, at which resolutions and petitions to the Legislature were adopted. A Central Committee was formed in the town of York, of which the late Rev. William Ryerson was the animating spirit, and the late Jesse Ketchum, Esq., was a most active member. This Committee sent out drafts of resolutions and petitions into various parts of the country.

Thus the "Clergy Reserve Controversy" was fairly inaugurated; the House of Assembly, in compliance with the petitions presented, appointed a Select Committee to examine into the allegations involved. The proceedings of the House of Assembly, the testimony of upwards of fifty witnesses examined, and the report and address of the House of Assembly to the King, will be adduced in my next essay. In the remaining pages of the present paper I will give some extracts from the sermon which caused the controversy, together with a few passages of the discussion which followed its publication. The whole discussion, on both sides, was afterwards published in a book.

I may state at the outset that upwards of fifty years have passed away since these papers were written. On the reperusal of them, after the lapse of so long a time, the impression upon my own mind is, that Dr. Strachan was honest in his statements and views ; but he was so wrapt up in the doctrine of Episcopal Succession and a Church Establishment, that he was incapable of doing justice to those who differed from him, or of giving a fair account of the different religious persuasions in the country. He was more moderate and liberal in his views and feelings in his later years, and became the personal friend of his old antagonist, " The Reviewer," who, he said, had "fought fair."

In the course of his sermon, referring to the obstacles which retarded the progress of the Church of England in Canada, Dr. Strachan said:

" Even when churches are erected, the persons who give regular attendance are so few as greatly to discourage the minister, and his influence is frequently broken or injured by numbers of uneducated itinerant preachers, who, leaving their usual employment, betake themselves to preaching the Gospel, out of idleness, or a zeal without knowledge, by which they are induced to teach what they do not know, and which from their pride they disdain to learn."

To this " The Reviewer " replied:

10

" With respect to the small numbers who give
regular attendance to the ministrations of the
Church of England, I am of the Doctor's opinion.
For I believe those instances are not very rare,
which compel the venerable clergyman to say,
with Dean Swift, ' My dearly beloved Roger, the
Scripture moveth us in sundry places,' etc. And
as a remedy for this doleful complaint, we may
say with the. eloquent Chalmers, ' to fill the
church well, we must fill the pulpit well.'

" As to the Doctor's remarks on the qualifications, motives, and conduct of the Methodist
.itinerant preachers, they are ungenerous, unfounded, and false. The Methodist preachers
do not value themselves upon the wealth, virtues,
and grandeur of their ancestry ; nor do they consider their former occupation an argument against
their present employment or usefulness. They
have learned that the ' venerable ' Apostles were
once fishermen ; that a Milner could once throw
the shuttle ; and that a Newton was not ashamed
to watch his mother's flock. By these examples,
and a hundred more, they feel themselves sufficiently shielded from the envious shafts of a
bigoted ecclesiastic. They are likewise charged
with ' preaching the Gospel out of idleness.' Does
the Doctor claim the attribute of omniscience ?
Does he know what is in man ? How does he
know they preach ' the Gospel out of idleness ? '

Let the Doctor remember that ' with what judgment he judges, he shall be judged.' (Matt.
vii. 2.)

" What does the Doctor call ' idleness ? ' Not
the reading of one or two dry discourses on Sabbath ; not the preaching to one congregation at
an annual income of two or three hundred
pounds. No ; this is hard labour, this is indefatigable industry. Two or four hundred pounds
per annum is no inducement, no motive for
preaching the Gospel. Those who labour in this
apostolic manner, and for this small pittance,
cannot be otherwise than the 'venerable successors' of Apostles. Who are they, then, that
' preach the Gospel out of idleness ? ' Those in-
dolent, covetous men who travel from two to three
hundred miles and preach from twenty-five to
forty times every month. Those who, in addition to this, visit from house to house, and teach
old and young 'repentance towards God, and
faith in our Lord Jesus Christ.' (Acts xx. 24.)
Those who continue this labour year after year,
and are elevated with the enormous salary of £25
or £50 per annum; these are the men who
' preach the Gospel out of idleness.' O bigotry,
thou parent of persecution ! O envy, thou
fountain of slander ! O covetousness, thou god
of injustice ! Would to Heaven ye were banished
from the earth !

"The Methodist preachers are said to be 'uneducated,' and to preach the Gospel without any
'preparation.' To a collegiate education they do
not make pretensions. But it should not be forgotten, that there are other ways and places of
education besides the Doctor's academy at ——;
and if this objection may be brought against the
Methodist preachers in Canada, it cannot be
brought against those who composed their Articles
and Discipline, and who formed their Constitution. The founders of Methodism were not inferior to the most illustrious of their age, both in
the republic of letters, and in scientific knowledge
in general. But the Methodist preachers are not
destitute of learning; nor do they undervalue it.
They consider it indispensably necessary to an
able minister of the Gospel. They go farther.
They say, 'to human learning, we must add
Divine grace;' 'that man is not properly qualified,'
say they, 'who can only translate some of the
classics, read a chapter or two in the Greek Gos-
pels, rehearse the Lord's Prayer and Ten Com-
mandments in Latin, possibly write a Latin sermon; if he be destitute of that wisdom which
comes down from heaven, "he cannot discern the
things of the Spirit of God."' (1 Cor. ii. 14.)
'Old things must pass away, and all things must
become new.' (2 Cor. v. 17.) St. Paul's learning,
though extensive, did not qualify him for the

ministry. His sins must be washed away, and he be filled with the Holy Ghost. (Acts ix. 17.) The Son of God was revealed in his heart before he was qualified to preach Him among the heathen. (Gal. i. 16.) 'Learning and piety,' says an able divine, 'accompanied with a consciousness of the Divine call, constitute the accomplished and able minister of Jesus Christ.'" [Then follows an account of the various tests and examinations, religious, literary, and theological, through which each candidate for the Methodist ministry had to pass before his admission to the ministry, and a vindication of the qualifications of Methodist ministers for their work.]

Several pages of Dr. Strachan's sermon were devoted to the wretched state of morals and the want of improvements in Canada, and the very serious impediments in procuring support for the clergy either from England or from the Provincial Legislature; in consequence of which the Lord Bishop of Quebec applied to the Society for the Propagation of the Gospel in Foreign Parts to increase the number of their missions in Canada. " His lordship's request being favourably received," says the Doctor, "the next difficulty was to procure clergymen. For when the Society had assented to the Bishop's prayer, in as far as they were able, clergymen of enlightened piety could not be found willing to leave England for Canada;

gentlemen of education and zeal refused to forsake their homes, and the endearing associations of early years, to come to so distant and inhospitable a colony."

On this "The Reviewer" remarks : "If 'gentlemen of enlightened piety and zeal would not sacrifice their homes and the endearing associations of their early years ' to preach the Word of Life to the destitute and uncultivated inhabitants of this colony, who would ? Would those of less piety and zeal do it ? If this be the character of the 'gentlemen of *enlightened piety and zeal*,' what notions are we left to entertain of the great mass of the English clergy ? Can these be the true followers of Him who declared with the most solemn asseverations, 'if any man love father or mother, wife or children, houses or lands, more than me or my Gospel, he cannot be my disciple ?' (Luke xiv. 26.) Can these be the followers of Him ' who counted all things but dross for the excellency of the knowledge of Christ Jesus ?' (Phil. iii. 8.) Of Him who was 'willing not only to be bound at Jerusalem, but to die for the Lord Jesus ?' (Acts xx. 13.) Can these gentlemen of ' *enlightened piety* and **zeal** ' be the ' venerable successors of Him who went from country to country strewing His way with the wrecks of Satan's kingdom ?' We would fain exculpate the enlightened and pious clergymen of England from the indelible reproach that the Doctor has cast upon them; but we fear the task would be too tedious at present."

At this time nearly ten thousand pounds sterling were expended by the British Parliament and the Propagation Society for the support of the Church of England in Canada; yet the Archdeacon of York demanded far larger supplies to save the Church of England from being swallowed up by "sectaries," and the country from becoming republican. He exclaimed, "What can fifty-three clergymen do, scattered over a country of greater extent than Great Britain? Is it to be wondered at that, under such circumstances, the religious benefits of the ecclesiastical establishment of England are little known or felt, and that sectaries of all descriptions are increasing on every side? And when it is considered that the religious teachers of the other denominations, a very respectable portion of the ministers of the Church of Scotland excepted, come almost universally from the republican States of America, where they gather their knowledge and form their sentiments, it is quite evident that if the Imperial Government does not immediately step forward with efficient help, the mass of the population will be nurtured and instructed in hostility to our parent Church, nor will it be long till they imbibe opinions anything but favourable to the political institutions of England."

The following are some passages **of** "**The Reviewer's**" reply **to Dr.** Strachan's despairing exclamations **and** philippics against the teachers **of** other religious denominations :

"We **are** sorry **to** see the Doctor reduced **to such a** dilemma **of** agitation and distress ; but **we** fear his recovery will not **be** immediate. He **asks, in** the language **of** despair, "What can fifty-three clergymen do, scattered **over a** country **of greater** extent than Great Britain ?' For the Doctor's reflection and encouragement I would **ask, What did twelve** apostles **do** in the midst **of an** obstinate, barbarous and persecuting world ? **What did a Waldus do in the** valleys of Piedmont ? **What did a Wycliffe do in** England ? **What did a Luther do in Germany ; nay, in** the **Christian world ?** What did a Wesley **and** his contemporaries **do in** Europe ? **What** have the **Methodists done in America ?** The most of these **were not** endowed with miraculous gifts. **Why did** *they* **not cry out in the** tone of discouragement, 'What can **one man do in** the face of an **anti-christian world ?'** Why did they not apply **to some Legislature for** pecuniary aid ? **Simply because** they **had** learned that 'the **race** is not **to the swift, nor the battle to the strong.'** (Eccl. **ix. 11.)** Because **they felt the force of** that saying, '**Cursed is the** man that trusteth in man, **whose** heart departeth **from** the living God' (Jer.

xvii. 5); because they knew that the victories of the Cross did not owe their extension to legislative influence and support; because they believed the weapons of their warfare were not carnal, but mighty through God to the pulling down of strongholds (2 Cor. x. 4); because they had the sword of the Spirit, which divideth asunder the joints and marrow, and is a discerner'of the thoughts and intents of the heart (Eph. vi. 17; Heb. iv. 12); because they were convinced 'that the manner of propagating the Gospel in the first days of its glory, must be the most judicious manner of propagating it now.' And 'according to their faith it was done unto them.' (Matt. ix. 29.) Let the 'venerable successors of the Apostles' in Canada go forward in the spirit of Him whose residence was among the habitations of distress and the tabernacles of the poor; let them in reality be the followers of Him who 'declared the whole counsel of God, in season and out of season, from house to house, reproving, rebuking, exhorting with all long-suffering and doctrine' (Acts xx. 27; 2 Tim. iv. 2), and they will soon exclaim, not in the language of apology, but in the song of triumph, 'What *have* fifty-three clergymen done in the British colony of Canada!' Would to God they might so do, and that every house might become a house of prayer, and every heart a temple of the Holy Ghost!

"One particular reason which the Doctor assigns for imploring the aid of the Imperial Parliament is, that republican principles will be instilled in the minds of the people by the 'religious teachers of other denominations, who,' he says, 'come *almost universally* from the republican States of America.'"

"The Reviewer" replied to this:

"To put the Doctor at rest on this point, and to remove this cause of complaint, I remark that the 'religious teachers of other denominations' do not talk or think quite so much about politics as does the Doctor. They have something else to do. They leave others to attend to temporal affairs, that they may 'give themselves to prayer, and to the ministry of the Word.' (Acts vi. 4.)

"But the assertion is not true. They are not republicans; neither are they infected with republican principles; nor have they come 'almost universally from the republican States of America.'

"Seven-eighths of the teachers among dissenters are British-born subjects. And out of the whole body of Methodist itinerant preachers, who seem to be the principal butt of the Doctor's hatred, there are only eight who have not been *born and educated in the British dominions.* And of those eight, all except two (of whom the late Rev. Dr. Green was one, have become naturalized

British subjects, according to the statute of the Province.

"The hue-and-cry that 'dissenters are disaffected to the Imperial Government,' has stunned the ears of almost all Europe for more than two centuries. It was first raised to make dissenters contribute to the support of the Establishment, to increase the revenues of the clergy, and to give more unlimited sway to ecclesiastical domination, such as enforcing the Act of Uniformity, etc.; and doubtless it is for the same purpose that it has been transported to America, and now continues its hideous shrieks through the dreary wastes of Canada.

"Have the 'dissenters' in this country ever shown a disposition in any way hostile to the true interests of the colony? Have they not been quiet in time of peace and bold in time of war? Answer, ye parents who mourn the loss of patriotic sons, who yielded up the ghost on the field of battle! Speak, ye fatherless children, the dying groans of whose dissenting fathers proclaimed that they could die in defence of the British Constitution, and yet be unconnected with a religious Establishment! Bear testimony, ye disconsolate widows, whose dissenting husbands' loyalty has doomed you to perpetual melancholy! Lift up your voices, ye unfortunate invalids, whose lacerated limbs speak more than volumes, that they are slanderers and liars who say that the religious any more than the political dissenters in Canada are not true to the 'political institutions of England.'"

I have given these extracts that the Methodist readers of the present generation may know how their forefathers were assailed, and through what reproaches and trials they passed, and what was the first attempt to defend their rights and vindicate their character.

But "The Reviewer" was not allowed to escape unscathed; his Church opponents seem to have exhausted upon him the vocabulary of the English language, aided by the Latin, in terms of contempt and denunciation, and seemed not to allow him a place in the pale of Christendom, much less of British loyalty. He was for a time greatly depressed, finding himself against his intentions, and wishes, and remonstrances, and in the first year of his ministry, involved in a controversy embracing the profoundest questions of ecclesiastical polity and civil government, besides the character and rights of his fathers and brethren. Finding that his only alternative now was to flee or fight, he chose the latter; devoted a day to fasting and prayer, recovered his calmness and confidence, and went at his antagonist in good earnest.

I will subjoin two or three passages of his

rejoinders upon the attacks made upon him, and the mode of argument employed to refute him.

It was said that the Review was the "prodigious effort of a party." "The Reviewer" replied, "On this I observe, that only two preachers, besides the Reviewer, knew that anything of the kind was in contemplation till the Review appeared in print; and the Reviewer wrote it in less than eight days, during which time he rode nearly a hundred miles, and preached seven sermons."

"The Reviewer" was charged with not having defined his principles; to which he rejoined, "I do not build my faith upon that of my fathers or grandfathers, but upon Jesus Christ and the authority and practice of His Apostles. My principles are contained in the Articles and Homilies of the Church of England; in James i. 27, is my definition of the Christian religion; and I will substitude the 19th Article of the Church of England in place of a 'religious Establishment.'"

"The Reviewer" having been charged with being an alien, and having "black intentions upon the Government," replied, "This is the old watchword. To this I reply, that however many and great objections I may have to a religious Establishment in Canada, I have no objections to the civil government. I am a British-born subject; and by my paternal loyalty and personal feeling, I am unwaveringly attached to the British Constitution. Hence the Church of England man may learn that his antagonist, whom he considers to be an enemy of 'God and man,' is by birth, education, and attachment a truly British subject."

The several advocates of a Church Establishment in Canada differed in their premises, though they agreed in their conclusions. "The Reviewer" took advantage of this diversity, and reduced it to a syllogistic form, which caused much amusement at the time, and produced considerable popular effect. He said:

"That a religious establishment is essential to a Christian nation, is also denied by Dr. Paley, who says, 'a religious establishment is no part of Christianity, but a means of diffusing it.' So say Gisborne, Whitgift, Pretyman, and Stillingfleet. But the testimony of my opponents carries its own confutation, if we consider it in the light of a matter of fact.

"Dr. Strachan declares that a Christian nation 'without an establishment is a *contradiction.*' The Brockville clergyman denies it. The Kingston gentleman forbids the freedom of man's unstable will in religious matters. His learned predecessor announces that 'every man among us maintains his privilege to unshackled freedom of judgment in matters of religion.' Two contrary propositions cannot be true at the same time. Such are the harmonious sentiments of these Church members, who, our Doctor assures us, 'are never divided by a variety of opinions.'

"However, that their arguments may appear in their true light, and have their full force on the reader's mind, I will reduce them to the simple syllogistic form.

"I. (1) 'A Christian nation without a religious establishment is a contradiction.' .

"(2) 'The establishment is a circumstance purely adventitious, and is by no means necessary to the existence of the Church.'

"(3) *Therefore*—England ought to pay £1,108,-000 per annum to support a religious establishment.

"II. (1) 'The Church of Christ must not be built on mankind's unstable will.'

"(2) 'Every man among us maintains his privilege to unshackled freedom of judgment in matters religious.'

"(3) *Therefore*—The King and Parliament ought to make laws to prevent us from changing our religious opinions.

"III. (1) 'The King is declared to be the Head of the Church in no sense at variance with the spiritual supremacy which belongs to Christ alone.'

"(2) 'The King or Queen may forbid the exercise of the sacred commission derived from Christ.'

" (3) *Therefore*—The **King** or Queen ought to be the Head of the Church, seeing that He or She had and yet has not a right to interfere in spiritual matters.

"**Are** these the guardians of the flock of Christ in this colony ?

" *Infelix ô semper, oves, pecus !* "

The controversy thus inaugurated continued upwards of a year, and developed into public meetings, petitions to the Legislature, the appointment by the House of Assembly of a Select Committee who examined fifty-two witnesses, and reported to the House, which adopted the Report and an Address to the Kng. These proceedings will be duly noticed in the next essay.

ESSAY VI.

THE CLERGY RESERVE CONTROVERSY ; OR, THE CON-
QUEST FOR EQUAL RIGHTS AND PRIVILEGES AMONG
ALL RELIGIOUS DENOMINATIONS IN UPPER CANADA.

IN my last paper, after having shown that
Methodism was the pioneer of civil and
religious liberty in Upper Canada, I stated the
circumstances which preceded the Clergy Reserve
controversy, caused by the attacks of the Archdeacon of York upon the several religious persuasions not connected with the Church of
England (called "Dissenters"), especially the
ministers of Methodism. In reply to that discourse, *The Reviewer* did not confine himself to
the defence of the Methodist ministers, but
included the ministers of other religious denominations, by several of whose ministers he was
recognized as their champion—they furnishing
him with all the books in their possession on the
questions of dispute, together with information
in regard to the birth and education of their
ministers. Among the Baptist ministers were

11

the late Rev. George Barclay, of Pickering, and the Rev. Alex. Stewart, of the town of York—the first agent of the local Bible Society—a man of general intelligence and great energy. Among the Presbyterians was a congregation at Brockville, under the pastorate of the Rev. Wm. Smart, of which the late Sheriff Sherwood, of Brockville, was a principal member. There was also another Presbyterian congregation in Kingston, called the American, of which the late Dr. Edward Armstrong and Marshall S. Bidwell were active members.

An Act had passed the Legislature some years before authorizing Lutheran-*Calvinist* ministers to solemnize matrimony; and the ministers of the Church of Scotland and some Baptist ministers qualified under this Act. This privilege conferred distinction and profit upon those who possessed it; but they showed little interest in obtaining for Methodist ministers the same right which they enjoyed themselves. The Methodist ministers were not only denied the right of solemnizing matrimony, but the Methodist people were without a law to enable them to hold a foot of land on which to erect a place of worship or in which to bury their dead. The writer of these papers had to get a Presbyterian clergyman to perform his marriage service—travelling twenty miles for that purpose; and his elder brother,

the late Rev. John Ryerson, had to employ a
Church of England clergyman to perform the
same service at his marriage. All the Presbyterian clergymen opposed the exclusive pretensions of the Church of England to be *the*
Established Church of Canada; but the few
clergymen of the Church of Scotland who had
been excepted in Dr. Strachan's attack upon the
ministers of other denominations, did not advocate
equal rights and privileges for all religious
denominations, but advocated equal status of the
Church of Scotland with the Church of England
as the Church establishment of Canada, and an
equal right to participate in Clergy Reserve
appropriations for " the support of a Protestant
clergy." * Many Presbyterian laymen, as well as
Baptists, united with the Methodists at public
meetings, and in adopting and signing petitions

---

* In the first of six letters addressed by the venerable
Archdeacon of York to the Hon. Wm. Morris, in the
autumn of 1837, Dr. Strachan says :

" For a time you made common cause with other denominations against the Established Church ; but since your
connection with the National Church of Scotland has been
indirectly acknowledged by the General Assembly, you have
deemed it prudent to drop your former associates. You
have made use of them as long as they could be turned
to your advantage, and now you cast them off as a tattered
garment, and bring forward with equal violence and per-
tinacity a claim to an equality with the Church of England,

in favour of equal rights and privileges for all
denominations of Christians in Upper Canada, for
the application of the proceeds of the Clergy
Reserves to purposes of education and internal
improvements, and against the establishment and
endowment, at public expense, of a university
under the sole control of the Church of England.
But the burden of that great struggle, together
with the reproaches, abuse, and in some instances

without any regard to the provisions of the 31 Geo. III.,
chap. 31, or to the smallness of your numbers." (p. 6.)

To this charge Mr. Morris replies, January 1838, as
follows :

"In the whole proceeding from that day (1823) to the
present time, it does not appear that the members of the
Church of Scotland 'made common cause with other denominations against (what you call) The Church,' but what
would more properly be styled the unreasonable pretensions
of yourself and a few other of her members. Whatever
you may think of my conduct regarding the various shapes
in which the questions came up during the period between
the years 1823 and 1832, the clergy and members of the
Scottish Church cannot be justly said to have made common
cause with other denominations against the Reserves, for
that cause was that they should be sold and the proceeds
applied to 'education and general improvement;' and when
the address to the King to that effect passed, on the 20th
March, 1828, the members of the Assembly of that body,
including your humble servant, voted against it.

"But you say, further, for what object I cannot tell,
that after using the other sects for our own purposes, we
'cast them off like a tattered garment.' Where is the

persecutions, had to be borne by the Methodists, who—laymen and ministers—were a unit in the contest for equal rights and privileges in behalf of all religious denominations.

It may be remarked, that the investigation was not based on the sermon of the Archdeacon of York, **July, 1825,** referred to in my last paper, but on an official letter and chart addressed by him to the Right Hon. R. J. Wilmot Horton, Under-Secretary of State for the Colonies, for the information of Lord Goderich, Principal Secretary of State for the Colonies. The letter and chart were intended to procure additional grants for the support of the Church of England in Canada,

proof? In what instance did the ministers and members of the Scots Church act in the way you represent? If my communication to Her Majesty's Government may be regarded as speaking the voice of the parties accused, the very reverse is the fact. Surely you could not have noticed my letter to Lord Glenelg, of the 26th June last (1837), when you made this assertion; for so far from 'casting off' the denominations you speak of, I proposed that one-third part of the Clergy Reserves should be given to them! And if it is an object to secure the affection and good-will of all classes, the sooner this is done the better. And, notwithstanding that my letter proposing such a distribution of the Reserves has been some months before the public, I have not heard any objection on the part of the Scot Church to the plan I proposed." (*Reply of William Morris, Member of the Legislative Council of Upper Canada, to Six Letters addressed to him by John Strachan, D.D., Archdeacon of York, pp. 15, 16.*)

and a charter and endowment for a university.
The letter is dated "19 Bury Street, St. James's,
May 16th, 1827;" and the principal passages
of it are as follows :

" Sir,—I take the liberty of enclosing, for the information of Lord Goderich, an Ecclesiastical Chart of Upper
Canada, which I believe to be correct for the present
year, 1827, and from which it appears that the Church
of England has made considerable progress, and is
rapidly increasing.

" The people are coming forward in all directions,
offering to assist in building churches, and soliciting
with the greatest anxiety the establishment of a settled
minister. Indeed, the prospect of obtaining a respectable
clergyman unites neighbourhoods together ; and when
one is sent of a mild, conciliatory disposition, he is sure,
in any settlement in which he may be placed, to form
the respectable part of the inhabitants into an increasing
congregation.   There are in the province 150 townships,
containing from 40 to 500 families, in each of which a
clergyman may be most usefully employed ; and double
this number will be required in less than twelve years.

" When contrasted with other denominations, the
Church or England need not be ashamed of the progress
she has made. Till 1818, there was only one clergyman
in Upper Canada, a member of the Church of Scotland.
This gentleman [Rev. Mr. Bethune] brought up his
two sons in the Church of England, of which they are
now parish priests. After his death his congregation
was split into three divisions, which, with another
collected at Kingston in 1822, count four congregations
in all which are in communion with the Kirk of Scotland.
Two are at present vacant, and of the two Scotch

clergymen **now** in the province, **one has applied for** holy **orders in the** Church of England.

"The teachers of **the** different denominations, with the exception of two **ministers of the** Church **of** Scotland, **four** Congregational **ministers** [or rather Presbyterian ministers not **connected with the** Church **of** Scotland], **and a** respectable **English missionary** who presides over a Wesleyan **Methodist meeting in** Kingston, **are** for **the most part from** the **United** States, where they **gather** their knowledge **and form** their **sentiments. Indeed, the** Methodist teachers are subject to the orders of the United States of America [not **so, for there was a Conference in** Upper **Canada** since 1824, controlling **and** appointing **all the preachers]; and it is** manifest that **the Colonial Government neither has nor** can have any **other control over them, or prevent them** from gradually rendering **a large portion of the** popu-lation, by their **influence and instructions, hostile to our** institutions, **civil and religious, than by increasing the** number of **the Established clergy.**

"Two **assertions** have **been made** respecting **the** Church of England **in** Upper **Canada, which, if correct,** ought certainly to have **considerable** influence. First, that the clergymen **have no** congregations. Now, I affirm **from** personal knowledge, **that in** fifty-eight places where regular or occasional service is performed, **numer-**ous and respectable congregations assemble.*

* In his sermon on the death of **the first Bishop of Quebec,** quoted in my last paper, and **printed the year** before **this** letter to Mr. Wilmot Horton **was written, the Archdeacon** of York said, "What can fifty-three clergymen **do, scattered** **over** a country larger **than** Great Britain? **Is it to be** wondered at that, **under such** circumstances, **the religious**

" The second is, that in the House of Assembly,
consisting of forty-four members, only two belong to
the Church of England. Now, the fact is that eighteen
out of forty-four profess to belong to the Church of
England, of the truth of which I pledge myself, and can,
if necessary, furnish the names ; the remaining twenty-
six are of various denominations, but not more than
three or four are Scotch Presbyterians.

"The Church of England in Canada was supported for
many years out of the very limited and fluctuating
revenue of the venerable Society for Promoting the
Gospel in Foreign Parts, which did its utmost to increase
the number of the clergy ; but its means were so
inadequate to the demand, that it was at length obliged
to solicit the aid of Government to continue and extend
its efforts ;—accordingly a small sum in aid of its funds
has been for some years voted by the Imperial Parliament, of which Upper Canada receives a portion. How
inefficient this aid is to supply the increasing necessities
of the colony, has been sufficiently shown ; for the tendency of the population is towards the Church of England,
and nothing but the want of moderate support prevents
her from spreading over the whole Province."

The Archdeacon then proceeds to give reasons
why the Clergy Reserves had not been more productive, and concludes his letter in the following
words :

" Two or three hundred clergymen living in Upper
Canada, in the midst of their congregations, and re-

benefits of the ecclesiastical Establishment of England are
little known or felt, and that sectaries of all descriptions
are increasing on every side ? "

ceiving the greater portion of their income from funds deposited in this country [England], must attach still more intimately the population of the colony to the Parent State. Their influence would gradually spread; they would infuse into the inhabitants a tone of feeling entirely English, and acquiring by degrees the direction of education, which the clergy of England have always possessed, the very first feelings, sentiments, and opinions of the youth must become British."

In the Ecclesiastical Chart of Upper Canada accompanying this letter, the names and places of the clergy of different denominations are professedly given. The number of the clergy of the Church of England is set down as thirty-nine, although only thirty-one names are given; the number of Presbyterian ministers not connected with the Kirk of Scotland is stated to be six —all born and educated in Scotland or England except one, the Rev. R. McDowell, long a resident or pastor in Bay Quinte, Midland District. The number in communion with the Kirk of Scotland is stated to be two, with two vacancies. In a note to the Chart the Archdeacon adds:

"As the Methodists have no settled clergymen, it has been found difficult to ascertain the number of itinerants employed; but it is presumed to be considerable—perhaps from twenty to thirty in the whole province. One from England, settled in Kingston, appears to be a very superior person. The other denominations have very few teachers, and those seemingly very ignorant. **One of the two remaining** clergymen in communion with the Church of Scotland has applied to be admitted **into** the Established Church."

Such were **the** statements **on** which petitions to the House of Assembly were founded, and on which the investigations were instituted.

The petitions were the same **in** form, adopted in different parts of the Province. The first name attached to the first petition presented to the House of Assembly, March, 1828, was that of Bulkley Waters—a Methodist farmer in the Midland District. The petition runs as follows:

' " The Petition of **Christians** of Different Denominations in Upper Canada.

" To the Commons of **Upper Canada, in** Provincial Par. liament assembled.

" We, His Majesty's faithful and loyal subjects, **Christians** of all denominations in Upper Canada, beg **leave to draw** the attention of your honourable House to the alarming misrepresentations and advice contained in a letter and ecclesiastical chart which were addressed to the Under-Secretary of State for the Colonies, for the information of Lord Goderich, on the 16th of May last, by the honourable and venerable Dr. Strachan, Archdeacon of York, and a number of the Legislative and Executive Councils of this Province, and printed by order of the House of Commons of Great Britain.

" In this communication His Majesty is informed that the ministers of the different churches in this Province, unconnected with the Protestant Episcopal Church, 'are for the most part from the United States, where they gather their knowledge and form their sentiments.' The Methodist preachers are particularly stigmatized with the charge of mixing up sedition with the word of God ; and 'the other denominations' are represented as having few teachers, and those seemingly very ignorant.

"Could it be true that the Methodist preachers were rendering, by their influence and instructions, a large portion of the population hostile to our institutions, both civil and religious, the evil would be most alarming ; and if the charge be credited in any degree by our gracious Sovereign, we feel with deep regret how low we must sink in his estimation, and how hopeless is our expectation of enjoying his royal confidence. Your petitioners know no difference between those who preach disaffection, and those who habitually hear it. We notice with much anxiety in the same document a disposition expressed and recommended to pursue a policy which shall augment the numbers of the clergymen of the Protestant Episcopal Church from 300 to 2,000 ; and by the addition of wealth, to be shared by no other denomination of Christians, gradually to acquire to themselves exclusively the superintendence of the education of our children in the public schools. The end of such a system must be ecclesiastical dominion. It is asserted with much confidence by this sworn adviser of the representative of His Majesty, that 'the tendency of the population is towards the Church of England,' and that 'nothing but the want of moderate support prevents her from spreading over the whole Province.'

" We have ascertained that a Royal Charter has been granted for the establishment of an university amongst us ; the principle of which, we have good reason to fear, will be found inconsistent with the unimpaired preservation and maintenance of our civil and religious rights and privileges.

" We humbly pray that your honourable House would inquire into the principle upon which an university is to be established among us ; so that no power to hold lands or other property be granted to, nor any addition to the number of members composing the House of Assembly made from, or out of, any ecclesiastical or literary body corporate, at whose hands danger could or might be apprehended to the Constitution, or to our religious liberties; and also, that your honourable House would inquire into the truth of the above recited cruel charges and statements against the ministers and the people, and further to take such steps upon the premises, and to preserve us and our children from ecclesiastical domination, as to your wisdom shall seem fit.

"And your petitioners, as in duty bound, will ever pray."

To this petition, and others referred to the Committee on the same subject, are attached the names of 5,697 persons.

The names of the Committee of Investigation, appointed by the Legislature, were:—M. S. Bidwell (Chairman); Messrs. Perry, Matthews, H. C. Thompson (of Frontenac), and Hamilton (after whom the city of Hamilton is named).

The following are the names of the persons examined by the Committee : *

> Elder William Case.
> Rev. Wm. Ryerson.
> Rev. Egerton Ryerson.
> John A. Wilkinson, Esq., M.P.
> Donald McDonald, Esq., M.P.
> John J. Lefferty, Esq., M.P.

* Of the fifty-two witnesses examined, as also the other members of Parliament who took part in the proceedings in 1828, all have passed away except two—namely, Francis L. Walsh, for many years Registrar of the county of Norfolk, now in the 91st year of his age, and Egerton Ryerson, now in his 78th year.

Rev. Alex. Stewart.
Duncan McCall, Esq., **M.P.**
Reuben White, Esq., M.P.
Zaccheus Burnham, Esq., **M.P.**
Rev. James Richardson.
Jas. Wilson, **Esq.**, M.P.
Wm. Morris, **Esq.**, M P.
Robt. Randal, **Esq.**, M.P.
Paul Peterson, Esq., M.P.
Thomas Horner, Esq., M.P.
Wm. Scollick, Esq., M.P.
Ed. McBride, Esq., M.P.
B. **C.** Beardsley, **Esq.**, **M.P.**
Rev. Geo. Barclay.
Jas. Jordan, Esq., **M.P.**
Thomas Coleman, Esq., **M.P.**
P. VanKoughnet, Esq., **M.P.**
Mr. Ebenezer **Perry.**
Francis **L.** Walsh, Esq., **M.P.**
Chas. Fothergill, Esq., M.P.
Dr. Dunlop, Warden Canada **Co.**
Wm. Thompson, Esq., M.P.
Francis Baby, Esq., M.P.
Alex. McDonell, Esq., **M.P.**
Rev. **Jas.** Harris.
Dr. Morrison.
D. Cameron, **Esq.**, **M.P.**
Rich. Beasly, Esq., M.P.
Capt. Mathews, M.P.
John Clarke, Esq., **M.P.**
Jas. Lyons, Esq., **M.P.**
Archibald McLean, Esq., M.P.
Jno. Wilson, Esq., Speaker House of **Assembly.**
Rev. Angus McDonell.

J. B. Robinson, Esq., Attorney General.

Hon. Wm. Dickson.

Hon. Thos. Clarke.

Hon. Jas. Baby.

John Rolph, Esq., M.P.

David Jones, Esq., M.P. [York.

Hon. and Ven. Dr. Strachan, Archdeacon of

Peter Jones (an Indian), a missionary among the Indians.

John Jones (his brother), Indian S. Teacher.

John Fenton, Clerk of Episcopal Church.

Wm. Andrews, Sexton, do.

The questions put by the Committee were printed, and written answers were handed in by the witnesses. The questions were fourteen in number, as follows :

" 1st. Do you think that the teachers or ministers of the different Christian denominations in this Province, unconnected with the Church of England, are for the most part from the United States, and that they there gather their knowledge and form their sentiments ? "

The answers to this question are almost universally in the negative. In the few instances in which no opinion is expressed, the witnesses state that they had not the necessary information to enable them to form an opinion on the subject.

" 2nd. Do you think that the influence and instruction of the Methodist preachers in this Province are rendering, or have a tendency to render a large portion of the population of this Province hostile to our institutions, both civil and religious ? "

The answers to this question furnished a noble testimony to the loyalty of the early Methodist preachers, and to the beneficial influence of their labours. The Rev. William Ryerson, after giving his testimony, adds, that "during the late war with the United States, the Methodists were as active and zealous in defence of the Province as any other part of the population. Several of their clergymen voluntarily served in the flank companies, and were in several engagements, and two of them were wounded.*

"3rd. Do you think that the people of this Province would become more attached to our institutions, civil and religious, by increasing in this Province the number of missionaries of the Church of England?"

The answers to this question are wonderfully strong in the negative, with few modifications and exceptions.

* It is passing strange, that there should have been such a persevering effort to fasten upon the Methodist ministers the charge of *disloyalty*, when, as has been shown in the first and second of these Essays, the first Methodist preachers in Canada were officers of the British army, the first members of the Methodist Church in Canada came to Canada on account of their loyalty, and the first Methodist missionary preachers had been Loyalists during the American Revolution; so that Methodism had been established and spread in Canada under the influence and prestige of Loyalty that could be claimed by no other Church. No charge could be

"4th. Is the tendency of the population of this Province towards the Church of England? Is it spreading over the Province? Is it not as well supported by its members, and have they not, in proportion to their numbers, equal means of supporting it, as the members of any other Church in the Province?"

The answers to this threefold question are very strong, with few exceptions, against the statements and pretensions of the representative-advocate of the Church of England.*

brought against the apostles of Methodism upon the ground of morals and religious doctrines; but they preached practical Christianity against immorality of every kind; they preached and professed inward experimental Christianity in contradistinction to mere outward formalism and sinful amusements. Hence they were subject to the reproach of their Divine Master, who was charged with not being a friend to Cæsar; and of his apostles, who were charged with turning the world upside down.

* Perhaps it may be fitting for me to give extracts from the answers to this question of the four Methodist ministers examined:

The Rev. James Richardson (afterwards Bishop Richardson) said:

" I believe, from what knowledge I have, that but a small portion of the people of this country are members of the Church of England, compared with some other denominations; and though it has increased in the number of its churches and ministers, yet I believe it does not increase in the number of members, in proportion to the increase of the population of the Province.

"5th. Do you think that the people of this Province wish that any one or more churches or denominations of Christians should be established by law in this Province with exclusive or peculiar rights, privileges, or endowments?"

The answers to this question were virtually unanimous in the negative.

"6th. Do you think that the people generally wish the proceeds of the Clergy Reserves should be given to the clergymen of the Church of England?"

The answers were decidedly in the negative.

To my certain knowledge, many of her members have withdrawn themselves from her communion, and joined themselves to the Methodists. This may arise from several causes, principally from the want of a Christian discipline being exercised, and a dislike to certain practices of some of her ministers."

Elder William Case—" I believe but a small portion of the population (comparatively speaking) is attached to the Church of England. The progress of her establishment is very slow, compared with that of some other denominations. This may arise from various causes, as 1st—From a dislike in the people to her ceremonies and forms of worship. 2nd—From the matter and manner of preaching. 3rd—From a want of proper exercise of discipline among her members and professors, and, in some instances, from (as the people consider it) the unchristian-like conduct of her clergymen. The ministers of the different religious denominations are supported entirely by the voluntary contributions of their congregations ; and the congregations of the Church of England being composed of a fair proportion

12

" 7th. To what purpose do you think the people would generally prefer to see the proceeds of the Clergy Reserves applied?"

The answers generally favoured the application of the proceeds of the Clergy Reserves to general education and internal improvements; a few favoured the moderate endowment of pastors and the building of churches of different denominations.

" 8th. Of which of the various denominations of Christians in this Province do you think the clergymen or teachers interfere most in political matters?"

. The answers to this question are various, and some of them amusing. Some of the witnesses

of the opulent class of the people, are as able to support their ministers, according to their numbers, as those of other denominations. Understands that the clergymen of the Church of England receive severally an annual salary from England of £200 sterling: they derive besides a considerable income from marrying."

Rev. William Ryerson "concurs in the foregoing answer; and adds, that two years ago the number of persons in regular communion in the Methodist Church in this place [the town of York, now Toronto] (about the 8th of October, 1825), was 50; in 1826, in September, numbers 99; at present (1828) about 150; the present number of hearers vary from 400 to 600, and the increase has been about the same as in the commencement."

The Rev. E. Ryerson (a) "concurs in the foregoing

(a) He was appointed to preach in the town of York (now Toronto) from September, 1825, to September, 1827—

declined expressing any opinion, declaring themselves incompetent to do so; most thought the
Episcopal clergy interfered most in politics, and
several thought that Dr. Strachan alone interfered
in politics, as he was both a Legislative and
Executive Councillor; some thought the clergy of
the different denominations did not interfere at
all in politics; others thought that they interfered too much, and that the Presbyterian, Methodist, and Baptist ministers interfered quite as
much as Episcopalian ministers.

answers; and adds, that Dr. Strachan admits in his
sermon (26th page) preached on the death of the late
Lord Bishop of Quebec, delivered the 3rd of July, 1825,
that the benefits of the Church of England are little felt
or known, and that sectaries of all descriptions are
increasing on every side. Dr. Strachan has also stated,
in a pamphlet published in London (England), under his
own name, that if the proceeds of the Clergy Reserves
were not exclusively given to the clergy of the Church of
England, that Church would be annihilated."

the first year in connection with the Yonge Street Circuit
—the late Rev. James Richardson being Superintendent;
the second year in connection with the Credit Indian
Mission, where he was the first Indian missionary—the Rev.
William Ryerson being the Superintendent of the town of
York, in connection with the Yonge Street Circuit. In
1827, E. Ryerson was appointed to the Cobourg Circuit,
which, at that time, extended from five miles east of
Bowmanville to the Trent, including the towns of Port
Hope, Cobourg, Colborne, and Brighton, and all the town-
ships south of Rice Lake, including also the township of
Seymour.

"9th. What proportion, in your opinion, do the members of the Church of England in this Province bear
to the whole population?"

The answers to this question were diversified.
Some of the witnesses could express no opinion;
but the witnesses generally said "a very small
proportion," others said "very trifling," others
said from one to ten, or one to twenty or twenty-
five. The Attorney-General, J. B. Robinson (afterwards Sir John Robinson), said,—"I do not know,
nor do I think anybody else does."

"10th. What denominations in this Province do you
think the most numerous?"

The witnesses were almost unanimous in stating
the Methodists as the most numerous; some
of them said, "The Methodists, beyond question."

"11th. Do you think that there are several, and what,
denominations of Christians in this Province more numerous than the Church of England?'

In answer to this question, nearly all the
witnesses said, "Methodists, Presbyterians, and
Catholics;" some placed Baptists before Catholics.
The Honourable John Wilson, Speaker of the
House of Assembly, in his answer to the question,
placed the religious denominations in the following order:

"I think they might, in regard to numbers,
be arranged thus:

"1st. Methodists.

" 2nd. Presbyterians (including Scotch Kirk, Seceders, Independents, Congregationalists, etc.).

" 3rd. Catholics.

" 4th. Baptists.

" 5th. Church of England."

" 12th. Has the Church of England laboured under greater difficulties in this Province than any other Church?"

All the witnesses agreed that the Church of England had enjoyed greater pecuniary advantages than any other Church. The Rev. William Case said:

" The Church of England has certainly greater pecuniary advantages than any other religious denomination in this Province ; and I know of no other hindrances to her prosperity than those alluded to in my answer to question the fourth. [See the answer on page 177.] The ministers of the Church of England have always freely enjoyed certain privileges which the ministers of several other denominations have been deprived of, to the great grief of the people under their charge, and for the exercising of which several respectable ministers belonging to different churches have been arrested and imprisoned (one put in a dungeon), tried without the privilege of counsel, and sentenced to banishment from the Province for fourteen years. The Methodists have always considered marriage a religious rite, and thought themselves entitled to perform this, as a religious service, under the 31st George the Third, chapter 31st ; but two of their ministers (Mr. Ryan and Mr. Sawyer) were arrested, tried, and banished ! Another (Mr. Smith) was acquitted, as also Mr. Pope, a British missionary.

Witness has understood that there were one or two Baptists, and one of the Presbyterian ministers, convicted for the same. The denial of their clergymen to solemnize matrimony, in behalf of their people, has always been considered by the Methodists as a grievance, though they are looking forward to the period when a more just and liberal policy will correct the evil. They cannot, for want of a law for that purpose, hold lands for sites of churches, etc., in succession."

The best apology for the Church of England, in answer to this question, is contained in the evidence of the Attorney-General, J. B. Robinson (since Sir J. B. Robinson), which is as follows:

"It has had encouragement and assistance which other Churches in this Province have not had; but at the same time it labours under difficulties beyond some other Churches, which operate against its extending. The clergy of the Church of England, as well as the clergy of the Church of Scotland and the Roman Catholic Church, cannot obtain ordination without a long and expensive previous course of study. The nature of that Church Establishment is such, that its ministers are stationary, and, to answer the purpose of their mission, must be able to maintain themselves competently, though moderately, by the profession to which they have devoted themselves; and to subsist from the casual contributions of their flocks, is not consistent with the nature of the Church of England.

"The preachers of some other sects, and perhaps more especially of the Methodists, seldom pass through the same expensive preparation for their ministry; they derive from their flocks, and from other sources, perhaps, a support not much greater probably than is considered sufficient for subsistence in any station of life, and the consequence is, that the preachers of these sects are more easily multiplied. For instance, I imagine no clergyman of the Church of England is appointed to a mission unless £150 or £200 can be secured to him." *

"13th. Do you think that the Ecclesiastical Chart now shown to you exhibits a fair and correct view of the different denominations of Christians in this Province? Can you point out any inaccuracies in the Chart within your own knowledge?"

The various witnesses agreed that the Ecclesiastical Chart was not a fair representation of the state and character of the different denominations of Upper Canada, and pointed out errors in it in the localities of their residences and knowledge.

The Hon. Attorney-General, J. B. Robinson, gave the most favourable answer in behalf of his old master and patron. He said:

" I have never made the necessary inquiries to enable me to answer this question, further than that I perceived a few inaccuracies in the Chart, so far as it regards the Church of England ; some churches are erroneously stated to be built, under the impression, no doubt, that they had been built ; but either the subscription list had not been completed, or some other cause of which the

* It is worthy of note that the question did not relate to the number of the clergy of the Church of England and other religious persuasions, but the number of members, the success and usefulness of the clergy, and the comparative advantages enjoyed by the Church of England and other denominations.

compiler of the Chart, was doubtless not aware, has caused the execution of the design to be abandoned or delayed. I notice also some omissions in the Chart as it regards the Church of England. I could not pretend, from any information I possess, to construct one more accurate upon the whole."

The Rev. Egerton Ryerson gave in a minute and exhaustive answer, founded chiefly on the different statements which had been made by the Archdeacon of York. But his answer is too long for insertion in this summary of evidence before the Select Committee.

` " 14th. Are the teachers of the various denominations of Christians not specified in the Letter and Chart before you, few and seemingly ignorant?"

The answers to this question were nearly all in the negative; some of the witnesses spoke of the denominations not mentioned in the Letter or Chart as more numerous than the Church of England, and referred to many of their teachers as men of education and talents.

Then there were three questions put, not numbered, relating to the Methodists. The first question was put to and answered by the Rev. William Case, as follows:

"Are the Methodist preachers in this Province accountable to the Conference of the United States?"

To which Mr. Case answered:

" The Methodist preachers who came into this Province were from the Methodist Conference in the State of New York, about the year 1790. They continued to be accountable to that Conference for their moral deportment, and their characters were carefully examined, till August, 1824 ; since which time the affairs of the Methodist Church in Canada have been transacted by the Canadian Conference.

"At no time did the Methodist Conference in the United States exercise or claim any control of a spiritual nature over the Methodists in Canada. Their services were purely of a spiritual nature. To supply the wants of a destitute country, they laboured freely and for many years at considerable sacrifice of property, and even of health and life ; and some of their ministers, by excessive toil in a new country, expended both.

"The Colonial Government, I conceive, has the same control over the Methodists in this country, that the British Government has over others of its subjects both in Europe and America." *

The Rev. William Ryerson was asked, " What income or salary do your preachers receive ? " He answered (1828):

"Our *unmarried* travelling preachers are allowed

---

* It has been shown in the first and second of these Essays, that the first two Methodist preachers in Canada were officers of the British army ; that the first members of the Methodist Church were the first refugee Loyalists from the United States ; that the first regular Methodist preachers from the State of New York came to Canada as volunteers, having been Loyalists during the American Revolution, and that those who volunteered and were appointed to Canada for twenty years were ordained

£25 per annum, besides their travelling expenses, which average each year from £2 to £3, and consist principally of ferriage, horse-shoeing, etc., as the preachers are generally entertained gratuitously at the houses of our members. Our *married* preachers are allowed £50 per annum, besides the table allowance of their families ; these generally amount to £15 or £25 in the country where the preacher has a wife and two or three children ; and in town to something more, on account of the additional expense of house rent. All the preachers, and also our bishops, are allowed the same. No other expenses or contingencies are provided for or allowed."

Another question put to Mr. Ryerson was, " Can you give the Committee a brief account of the history and progress of your Church in this Province?" in answer to which Mr. Ryerson gave a brief sketch of the rise and progress of the Methodist Church in Canada, which has been anticipated in previous numbers of these Essays.

Thomas D. Morrison, M.D., a member of the Methodist Church, was Secretary of the Com-

and appointed by Bishop Asbury, himself an Englishman, who lived in concealment during a great part of the Revolutionary War, refusing to take the oath of allegiance to the United States until after the acknowledgment of their independence by Great Britain. The Rev. William Ryerson, in his answer to the second question, states that some of the Methodist preachers volunteered into the militia flank companies during the war of the United States against Great Britain in 1812-1815, fought in several battles, and two of them were wounded.

mittee **which** prepared and presented **to** the
Legislative Assembly the petitions **on which** the
investigation was founded. In his **evidence, in**
answer to the first question **of the** Committee, he
said :

" By documents **in** my possession, **on which** an Ecclesiastical Chart **of** Upper Canada has been formed,
the principal **part of the** ministers **of** the Christian
denominations unconnected with the Church of England
are natives of Europe and the Colonies, and have there
alone gathered their knowledge and formed their sentiments. Nine alone **of the** whole are lately from **the**
United States, **and they are now** under circumstances
to be naturalized, **by** the **Act** lately passed by **the**
Legislature of this Province. **Such** others **as may be**
natives of the United States **have been in the Province a**
number of years, probably **since their** youth, **and are**
naturalized ; and they have consequently gathered their
knowledge and formed their sentiments in **his** Majesty's
dominions."

The Committee say **to Dr. Morrison, "You**
speak, in answer to some **former** question, of an
Ecclesiastical Chart; **how was** that formed ?" Dr.
Morrison **answers :**

" At a public meeting **in York** (now Toronto), **a**
Committee **was appointed,** called **the** Central Committee
of Upper Canada, **and** directed **to** correspond with **the**
other parts of the Province, to suggest the appointment
of Committees, and to request that they would carefully
collect and transmit to the Central Committee at York,
accurate information respecting the number of persons
belonging to the religious denominations in their neigh-

bourhood. In consequence · of these, communications were received from various parts of the Province, containing correct and full information on this subject, obtained from personal knowledge or inquiry, and authenticated by the signatures of respectable inhabitants. This information was pretty general with respect to the Methodists and Baptists, and with regard to others, the Committee, in addition to the information obtained in this way, collected from all other sources the most accurate information that could be got. The Chart was formed from the materials thus obtained, and it presents, in my opinion, a very fair and complete view of the number of ministers and number of ˙ different religious denominations in this Province. I have a copy ˙of this Chart, which I leave with the Committee."

In this comprehensive Chart we have, in each district of Upper Canada, the names of the clergymen of the several denominations; where born; where educated; how long in Canada, and if naturalized; number of regular communicants; of churches or chapels; of places of regular worship; of places of various worship; of regular hearers.

The much labour and time devoted by Dr. Morrison in collecting materials for and compiling this Chart, were gratuitous. He had been chief clerk in the Surveyor General's Office, and without charge or the slightest deficiency in faithfulness and efficiency, was dismissed—for the simple reason that he had become a Methodist. He then devoted himself to the medical profession, for which he had studied in early life. He was once elected member of the House of Assembly for the town of York, defeating the Attorney-General ; he was also once elected Mayor of the city. He was the writer's physician during life, died in great peace, strong in faith, giving glory to God.

The following correspondence took place between the Chairman of the Committee and the Archdeacon of Toronto :

"House of Assembly Committee Room,
"15th February, 1828.

"SIR,—The Committee of the House of Assembly to whom have been referred the petitions of Bulkley Waters and others, and a number of similar petitions from others, have directed me to transmit to you a copy of said petition.

"The Committee have also directed me to say that they will be most happy to receive from you any information, in any form that you may think proper, and that you may consider likely to assist them in their inquiries.

"I am, Sir, your most obedient, humble servant,
(Signed) "M. S. BIDWELL.
"Honourable and Venerable The Archdeacon of York."

The Archdeacon's reply was as follows:

"York, 19th February, 1828.

"SIR,—I thank the Committee for having transmitted to me last evening a copy of a petition referred to their consideration, in which the petitioners are made to convey imputations upon myself.

"I do not feel it necessary to avail myself of the Committee's offer to receive explanations in respect to statements which were not voluntarily given ; but when called upon for information by the King's Government, and in defence of the Church of England, against attacks that had been made upon her, I deemed it my duty to furnish them, with a sincere conviction of their accuracy.

"As the duty committed to me in England would not otherwise have required any such communication on my part, I made it at the time chiefly from memory.

"For my opinions I am responsible to no one. I had no desire to conceal them, and they were therefore publicly and openly expressed. No consideration could have prevailed upon me to deny or misstate them; but in applying them, every candid mind will feel that the general expressions used admit the existence of exception.

"I desire it only to be borne in mind, that they were given from memory, and in reply to an attack for which I could not have been prepared. Being thus given for a public purpose, they were also given that there could be no danger of any part escaping detection, if it turned out not to be perfectly correct.

"Though I have no wish to communicate with the Committee further on this subject, I beg it may be understood that, with the leave of His Excellency the Lieutenant-Governor and the Legislative Council, I am ready, if the Committee desire it, to attend them upon the usual summons, for the purpose of answering, and giving any information that may be required.

"I am, Sir, your most obedient, humble servant,

(Signed) "JOHN STRACHAN.

"To Marshall S. Bidwell, Esq., M.P., Chairman."

The Archdeacon ultimately appeared before the Committee, delivered to them a copy of the Royal Charter of King's College, and answered various questions. He adhered to the views and general accuracy of the statements of his Letter and Chart laid before the Imperial Government, by which they had been printed by order of the House of Commons, and thus became known in Canada.

The answer of the Archdeacon to several questions throws light upon the early history of the Church of England in Upper Canada.

Question.—" How many clergymen were there of the Church of England when you took orders in 1803?" *Answer.*—" I believe five—Mr. Addison, Dr. Stewart, Mr. Langhorn, Mr. (now Dr.) Stuart, and Mr. Rudd."

Question.—" What are the emoluments of the clergymen of the Church of England in this Province?" *Answer.*—" Till 1815, the salary of a missionary was £150 sterling per annum, paid chiefly by the Society for the Propagation of the Gospel in Foreign Parts, established in London. Since 1815 it has been, to a Missionary in Priest's orders, £200 ; to a Deacon, £100 sterling, paid from the charitable funds of the same society."

Question.—" This, then, is exclusive of perquisites for marriages and other services?" *Answer.*—" There is no other service than marrying for which any fee is charged or received, except for baptism—one shilling generally for registration."

Question.—" Are not the members of the Church of England in this Province, in proportion to their numbers, as well able to bear the expense of supporting the preaching of the gospel, etc., as those of other denominations?" *Answer.*—" They probably are ; but they have never been called upon. The funds of the Society in England have furnished the means hitherto."

Question. — " Does that include the building of churches?" *Answer.*—" The people frequently subscribe toward that object ; but in that they have likewise, in most places, been assisted by aid from England, collected by subscription."

Question.—" Do you know the number of the members of the Church of England in this Province?" *Answer.* —" I only know in those cases which have been communicated to me, from which it appears that from one-half to two-thirds of all the people in those places are favourable to our Church—and I believe it is so throughout the Province, except the Eastern District."

Question.—" By the expression 'favourable to our Church,' do you mean members of the Church?"᾿ *Answer.*—" I would not say members ; but I mean preferring our service, when opportunities offer, to all others."

Question.—" Have you any other corrections to your Chart, or any further remarks upon the subject under consideration of the Committee, which you wish to offer?" *Answer.*—" I would desire to state to the Committee, in drawing up my letter to Mr. Horton, and the accompanying Chart, I was called upon suddenly to do it, to repel an attack of the Kirk of Scotland, and I had not an opportunity to correct the proofsheets ; some trifling inaccuracies (but no ways affecting the argument), in consequence of this, have unavoidably crept in, but, for the information of the Committee, I will leave with them a Chart which I have compiled from authentic sources."

This completed the Committee's investigation. The Committee embodied the results of their investigation in a report to the House of Assembly, and the draft of an address by the House of Assembly to the King, both of which were adopted by the House of Assembly by a majority of more than two to one.*

Not to protract this Essay to an undue length, I will give these important documents in my next paper, together with the names of the yeas and nays in the votes of the House respecting them, together with the subsequent phases and results of the Clergy Reserve controversy.

* In the first paragraph of his letter of 1827, to the Colonial Secretary, accompanying his Ecclesiastical Chart of Upper Canada, Archdeacon Strachan says :—

"From this religious picture of Upper Canada, it evidently appears that the Church has made considerable progress, and is rapidly extending. In 1791 there was only one English clergyman in the Province, settled at Kingston ; two more arrived in 1793, and for many years the number continued six. In 1818, they amounted to twelve ; in 1824, to twenty-two ; and from recent ordinations they are now (in 1827) about thirty."

In an appendix (No. 1) to this letter is a long extract from the address of the British of Quebec and the Clergy of Upper Canada in 1823. In this address the imagination is drawn upon for most of the statements, and the appeal to starve the clergy of other denominations, as essential to build up the Church of England, was as original as it was contemptible, and a self-confessed refutation of the statements which preceded, and a practical acknowledgment that the Church of England could not exist upon equal terms with other denominations. The statements are as follows :—

"The population, now greatly increased, and embracing in its bosom many denominations of Christians, still

13

retains its prominent feature of being attached to the Church of England ; the members of which, together with the Dutch and Lutherans, who join them in communion, comprise by far the most numerous description of Christians in Upper Canada."

" The very little progress made by the other denominations compared with that of the Church of England, and the very recent establishment of their scanty congregations, has generally created in the minds of the people a veneration for it as the established form of worship—a light in which it has always been presented to the inhabitants of the Province from their earliest years ; for the venerable Society for the Propagation of the Gospel in Foreign Parts, ever attentive to the spiritual wants of the colonies, sent missionaries to the principal stations of the Province on its first settlement, multiplying them as the population increased, till it pleased his Majesty to form Lower and Upper Canada into the diocese of Quebec, and to appoint a Bishop to cherish, extend, and govern the infant Church."

" Nearly forty applications for clergymen have been made to the Bishop and Government from various parts of the Province, at most of which churches are built or in progress ; and twice that number of applications may be expected before the former can be supplied ; for, owing to the want of means, one-fourth of the clergy necessary for the population cannot be supported."

" When new missions are established in any quarter, not only do those persons join who are not yet particularly attached to any denomination, but even Presbyterians and Congregationalists attend public worship with their families, so that on many occasions the whole neighbourhood becomes united with the Church ; and not only are their dead buried according to their rites, but

likewise the bodies of their friends and relatives are
frequently collected from private places for interment,
and again consigned to the grave in the public burial-
ground with the solemn offices of the Church. More-
over, their children are educated in the bosom of the
Church, and the greater number at length confirmed by
the Bishop, and thus a congregation is formed in a few
years strongly attached to our venerable Establishment.
Even in those remote parts of the country where the
Methodist itinerants are the most active, so soon as the
population is sufficiently compact to admit and require
the ministrations of a regular clergyman, he finds his
congregation increasing by the gradual accession of
their more respectable adherents.

"The Church is increasing so rapidly as to afford
great encouragement to respectable families to bring up
their children to the sacred profession; accordingly
more than thirty students are preparing for the Church,
and many more than can possibly be provided for are
presenting themselves to the Lord Bishop as candidates
for Holy Orders.

"There is every reason to believe that the greater
proportion of all denominations of Protestants may be
expected to conform, so as at length to include the great
mass of this population, a result which appears highly
probable from the following facts:—1st. The Lutheran
clergymen have generally conformed, and brought their
congregations with them. 2nd. Several Presbyterian
or Congregational clergymen—for both names are used
promiscuously in the country—have solicited the Lord
Bishop to be admitted as candidates for Holy Orders,
and the only Presbyterian clergyman in communion with
the Kirk of Scotland, who lived in the Province before
1818, educated two of his sons for the Church of Eng-

land (but none for his own Church, though he had three
other sons), one of whom was in orders many years
before the death of his father, and the other has just
been admitted. 3rd. No objection is made by parents
against teaching their children the Church Catechism
and the service of the Church from the Book of
Common Prayer ; on the contrary, all denominations
are desirous of obtaining both, for their own and their
families' edification. 4th. The whole neighbourhood
bring their children to the resident clergymen to be
baptized, and submit in great numbers, both old and,
young, to the rite of confirmation, send their youth to
the Sunday-schools, and allow them, after their tasks
are heard, to walk in procession to the church. In fine,
there manifestly appears the fairest prospect that the
Church of England, from the favourable disposition that
now exists towards it, will be able to collect within its
bosom the bulk of the inhabitants of the Province,
should no prospect of supporting their clergy be held out
to the various Protestant denominations.

"With the exception of the Methodists, who have
been deserted by their brethren in England, and left for
instruction to itinerants from the United States (unless
one respectable congregation in Kingston, who have an
excellent missionary from England), there appears no
prominent denomination of Protestants in the Province
but the Established Church capable of exciting public
attention ; for the Congregationalists or Independent
Presbyterians, who are next in number to the Methodists, have only six small congregations." [Representa-
tion of the Bishop of Quebec, and the Clergy of the
Church of England in Upper Canada in 1823, to counteract in England the claims of the clergy of the Church
of Scotland in Canada (said to be seven in number);

claiming a share of the Reserves, as one of the National Churches, and supporting this claim under the supposed ambiguity of the Act, " A Protestant Clergy."]

Remarks.—It is not easy to condense in the same space a greater number of fictions and misrepresentations than are contained in the above extracts of the representation to England in 1823 by the Bishop of Quebec and the Episcopal Clergy of Upper Canada, and all for the purpose of obtaining money and endowments for their Church, from the Propagation Society and the British Government. But these statements will be found abundantly refuted by the evidence given before a Select Committee of the House of Assembly of Upper Canada, in 1828, quoted in the subsequent part of this Essay.

In less than two years after making these representations, the then Bishop of Quebec (Dr. Mountain) died, and his funeral sermon was delivered by the Archdeacon of York, July 3rd, 1825, referred to in my last essay. It is not surprising that in the presence of such representations, Dr. Strachan should have deprecated the agitation of the Clergy Reserve question in Canada, where all the facts and pretensions could be canvassed, and that he should have complained that his famous Letter to Mr. R. Wilmot Horton, with an Ecclesiastical Chart of Upper Canada, should have found their way from England to the Canadian newspapers. In the first of his six letters addressed to the Hon. W. Morris, dated Toronto, 17th November, 1837, the Archdeacon of York says :—

" Up to this time (1837) the clergy and friends of the Established Church have been content with quietly urging the impropriety of debating the appropriation of the Clergy Reserves in the Colony, where it might pro-

duce much angry feeling, but could never be satisfactorily disposed of, and their readiness to submit to any
measure which her Majesty and Parliament might see fit
to adopt, and which should be final and unequivocal, in
making such appropriations as should appear most consistent with a due regard to religion, to the principles of
the Constitution, and to the permanent welfare and
tranquillity of the Province." (p. 6.)

It is singular that the Archdeacon of York should
have thus expressed himself, when the Clergy Reserve
question had been discussed for ten years in newspapers,
in both Houses of the Legislature, in Church newspapers
and pamphlets as well as others. On the 20th of March,
1828, the Archdeacon delivered his famous speech before
the Legislative Council in vindication of his proceedings
and policy on the question of the Clergy Reserves, or of
the establishment of the Church of England as the
Established Church in Upper Canada—and which
speech was printed at the request of the Legislative
Council, and, of course, at the expense of the Province.
History records that writers in favour of Dr. Strachan's
pretensions and policy, were not remarkable for meek-
ness and quietness in their discussions.

ESSAY VII.

CLERGY RESERVE CONTROVERSY, CONTINUED ; VOICE
OF THE LEGISLATIVE ASSEMBLY OF UPPER CAN-
ADA IN FAVOUR OF EQUAL CIVIL RIGHTS AND
LIBERTY AMONG ALL CLASSES, AND IN VINDI-
CATION OF THE EARLY METHODIST MINISTRY.

IN my last Essay I gave some account of the
preliminary discussions which awakened
public attention to the infringement of the civil
rights and liberties of the great majority of the
people, and the further threatened invasion of
them ; the Petitions which were adopted and presented to the House of Assembly on the subject ;
the appointment by the House of a Select Committee to investigate the complaints contained in
the Petitions ; the examination of fifty-two witnesses by that Committee, and the purport of
their evidence.

I now proceed to give the conclusion and sequel
of the investigation. The Committee presented
a Report to the House detailing their proceedings, and the conclusions at which they had

arrived; they also submitted a draft of an Address or Petition to the King on the subject. Both of these documents were adopted by a large majority of the House of Assembly; they presented (especially the Report) a brief but graphic view of the early religious condition of the country, the labours of the different religious persuasions, and a most complete vindication of the character, privations, labours and successes of the Methodist ministry—stronger and more eulogistic than I have written in preceding Essays. And be it remembered, that this testimony to the character and labours of the early Methodist ministers is not merely the testimony of an individual writer, but that of the elected Representatives of the People of Upper Canada in 1828, during the first thirty years of those labours. Perhaps the reader will be interested in reading the account of the proceedings of the House of Assembly in the words of the official record. They are as follows:

" Proceedings of the House of Assembly on the Report of the Select Committee to which was referred the Petition of Bulkley Waters and others, and other Petitions from Christians of various denominations, on the same subject; and also the Petitions of E. W. Armstrong and others, relating to the University of King's College, lately established at York by Royal Charter."

" *March 17th, 1828.*—Mr. Bidwell, from the Committee to which was referred the Petitions of Bulkley

Waters and others, and the various petitions from the different parts of the Province on the same subject, informed the House that the Committee had agreed to a Report, and an Address to His Majesty founded on the same, which he was ready to submit whenever the House would be pleased to receive the same.

" The Report was ordered to be received and read.

" The Address to His Majesty, as reported, was then read the first time.

" Mr. Bidwell, seconded by Mr. Perry, moves that the House do resolve itself into a Committee of the Whole, to-morrow, on the Report of the Select Committee on the Petition of Bulkley Waters and others, and on the Address to His Majesty, reported by that Committee ; and that it be the first thing on the order of the day for to-morrow, after any third readings ; which was ordered.

" *Tuesday, 18th March, 1828.*—Agreeably to the order of the day, the House went into Committee of the Whole on the Report of the Select Committee to which was referred the petition of Bulkley Waters, and other petitions of the same nature.

" Mr. Hamilton was called to the Chair.

" The House resumed.

" Mr. Hamilton reported the Report of the Select Committee, and the Address to His Majesty founded thereon, both as adopted by the Committee.

" On the question of receiving the Report, the House divided, and the yeas and nays were taken :

"YEAS.—Messrs. Beardsley, Beasley, Bidwell, Cameron, Coleman, Fothergill, Hamilton, Hornor, Lefferty, McBride, McCall, McDonald of Prescott and Russell, McDonell of Glengarry, Matthews, Morris, Perry, Peterson, Randal, Rolph, White, Wilkinson, and Wilson—22.

" NAYS.—Messrs. Attorney General, Burnham, Clark, McLean, Scollick, Thompson of York, Vankoughnett, and Walsh—8.

" The question was carried by a majority of fourteen ; the Report was received and adopted, and the Address read a second time, adopted, and ordered to be engrossed and read a third time on Thursday next.

" *Thursday, March 20th, 1828.*—Agreeably to the order of the day, the Address to His Majesty on the subject of a religious establishment and university was read the third time.

" Mr. Morris, seconded by Mr. McDonell, of Glengarry, moves that the Address do not pass, but that it be recommitted ; which was lost.

" Mr. Morris, seconded by Mr. McDonell, of Glengarry, moves that the words ' and internal improvement,' in the fifth page of the Address, in the fifth line from the top, be expunged : on which the House divided, and the yeas and nays were taken :

" YEAS.—Messrs. Beasley, Bidwell, Cameron, Lefferty, McCall, McDonell of Glengarry, McLean, Morris, Perry, Rolph, Thomson of Frontenac, and Vankoughnett—12.

" NAYS.—Messrs. Baby, Beardsley, Burnham, Coleman, Fothergill, Hamilton, Hornor, J. Jones, McBride, McDonald of Prescott and Russell, Matthews, Peterson, Randal, Scollick, Thompson of York, White, Wilkinson, and Wilson—18.

" The question was decided in the negative by a majority of six, and lost accordingly.

" On the question for passing the Address, the House divided, and the yeas and nays were taken :

" YEAS.—Messrs. Baby, Beardsley, Beasley, Bidwell, Coleman, Fothergill, Hamilton, Hornor, Lefferty, McBride, McCall, McDonald of Prescott and Russell, Matthews, Perry, Peterson, Randal, Rolph, **Thomson** of Frontenac, White, Wilkinson, and Wilson—21.

" NAYS.—Messrs. Burnham, Cameron, J. Jones, Mc-Donell of Glengarry, McLean, **Morris,** Scollick, Thompson of York, and Vankoughnett—9.

" The question was carried in the affirmative by a majority of twelve, and the Address was passed, **and** signed by the Speaker."

Nothing **could** have **been** more deliberate, formal, and dignified than the proceedings of the Select Committee and House of **Assembly** in the presentation and adoption **of the** Report and Address to the King. The elaborate and masterly Report **of** the **Select Committee,** adopted **by the** House **by a majority of** more than two to one—a majority **of 22 to 8—was as follows :**

"To the Honourable the House of Assembly :

" The Select Committee **to** whom **were referred** the petition **of** Bulkley Waters and others, and **various** other petitions of the same tenor, signed **by** nearly 6,000 persons, and also the petition of **E. W.** Armstrong and others, submit the following report :

" The **first** object of **the Committee was to** obtain a correct copy of the **letter and chart referred to in the** petitions. Before proceeding to the examination **of the** statements **contained in the letter and chart, the** Committee directed **the Chairman to transmit to the honourable** and venerable Doctor **Strachan a copy of the petition** referred to them, and **to inform him that the Committee** would **be** happy to receive **from** him **any information** upon the matter submitted to their consideration.

" **The** Committee **have examined all the** members of the

House of Assembly whose testimony they could obtain ; some members of the Honourable the Legislative Council, of long residence, high standing, and large possessions in the Province ; various clergymen of different denominations in York and its vicinity, and a few other individuals.

"From the evidence it will be perceived that the letter and chart were calculated to produce in many respects erroneous impressions respecting the religious state of this Province and the sentiments of its inhabitants. As it seems from Dr. Strachan's evidence that they were drawn up suddenly from memory and without the means of reference to sources of authentic information, it is much to be regretted that these circumstances had not been at least hinted in the letter itself, and the more so when it is considered that as he stated to the Committee he had never known the number of members of the Church of England in this Province. The assertions in the letter, that 'the people are coming forward in all directions offering to assist in building churches, and soliciting with the greatest anxiety the establishment of a settled minister,' and that 'the tendency of the population is towards the Church of England, and nothing but the want of moderate support prevents her from spreading over the whole Province,' are completely contradicted by the evidence.

" Upon this subject the Committee would remark that the Church of England has always had, in this Province, peculiar advantages. It has been the religion of those high in office, and been supported by their influence and countenanced more than any other Church by the favour of the Executive Government. Its clergymen have had the exclusive right of marrying persons of all denominations indiscriminately ; although, by a Provincial statute, the Justices of the Peace, in general quarter sessions, are empowered, if they shall deem it expedient, to authorize Lutheran and Calvinist clergymen and ministers of the Church of Scotland to marry any two persons of whom one has been for six months previously to such marriage a member of the congregation of the clergyman who performs the ceremony. This right the clergymen of the Church of England still exclusively enjoy, notwithstanding that the House of Assembly has for several sessions successively, by a large majority, passed a Bill (which has not been concurred in by the honourable the Legislative Council) to extend this right to the clergymen of Christian denominations in this Province generally : the clergymen of the Church of England have also been liberally supported, and their churches partly or wholly built from the funds of a society in England. The solitary disadvantage mentioned by Dr. Strachan in his evidence before the Committee, of being obliged, for want of a bishop resident in the Colonies, to resort to England for episcopal ordination, has never existed since the Province has had its present form of government ; for during all that time a bishop has resided at Quebec. Still, the number of members of that Church has not increased in the same proportion as that of several other denominations. These facts confirm the opinion so generally expressed by the witnesses, that the tendency of the population is not towards that Church. The contrary opinion entertained by a few of the witnesses may have arisen very naturally from a considerable increase recently in the number of missionaries of that Church, which, however, ought probably to be ascribed to the liberality with which salaries for their support are furnished by the Society for Propagating the Gospel in Foreign Parts, rather than to any

strong wish of the people to have clergymen of that
Church settled among them.

"In reference to the aid furnished by this Society
(from whose funds an annual salary is paid to every
clergyman of the Church of England in this Province,
in priests' orders, £200 sterling, and in deacons' orders,
£100 sterling), and as an argument for further assistance,
it is said in the letter, 'How ineffectual this aid is to
supply the increasing necessities of the Colony has been
sufficiently shown ; for the tendency of the population is
towards the Church of England, and nothing but the
want of moderate support prevents her from spreading
over the whole Province.'

"According to the concurring testimony of the witnesses,
the members of the Church of England in this Province,
in proportion to their number, have at least equal means
of supporting their clergymen with other denominations.
The latter have a large number of clergymen in the Province. Without any aid, therefore, from Great Britain,
the members of the Church of England are able without
difficulty to support as many clergymen of their Church
as the number of their members requires. If, however,
they are not willing to furnish for this purpose the same
means which other sects furnish for a similar purpose,
there can be but little tendency, even among those who
are nominally its members, to the Church of England.
If they are willing, there can be very little necessity for
the aid now received from Great Britain, and much less
for any further assistance, unless to carry on a system of
proselyting to that Church the members of other denominations.

"The insinuations against the Methodist clergymen
the Committee have noticed with peculiar regret. To

the disinterested and indefatigable **exertions of these**
pious men this Province owes much. **At an early period**
of its history, when it was thinly **settled and its inhabi-**
tants were scattered through **the** wilderness and **destitute**
of all other means of religious **instruction, these ministers**
of the Gospel, animated **by** Christian **zeal** and benevolence, at the sacrifice **of health** and interest and comfort,
carried **among the** people **the** blessings **and** consolations
and sanctions **of our** holy religion. Their influence and
instruction, far from having (as is represented in the letter)
a tendency hostile to our institutions, have been con-
ducive, in a degree which cannot easily be estimated, to
the reformation **of** their hearers **from** licentiousness, **and**
the diffusion **of** correct morals, **the** foundation **of all**
sound loyalty **and** **social order.** **There is no reason to**
believe that, as **a body, they have failed to** inculcate, by
precept and **example, as a Christian duty, an attachment**
to **the** Sovereign **and a cheerful and conscientious** obedience to the laws **of the country.** **More than 35 years**
have elapsed since they commenced their labours in the
Colonies. In that time the Province has passed through
a war which put to the proof the loyalty of the people. If
their influence and instructions **have** the tendency men-
tioned, the effects by this time must be manifest ; yet no
one doubts that the Methodists **are as loyal as** any of His
Majesty's **subjects.** **And the very fact** that while their
clergymen **are** **dependent for their support** upon the
voluntary contributions **of their people, the number of**
their members **has increased so as to be now, in the**
opinion of almost all the **witnesses, greater than that of**
the members of any other **denomination** in this Province,
is a complete refutation **of** any suspicion that their influ-
ence and instructions **have** such a tendency ; for it
would be a gross slander on the loyalty of the people to

suppose that they would countenance and listen with complacency to those whose influence was exerted for such base purposes.

"There can be no doubt that, in addition to the Methodists, there are, in the Province, several denominations of Christians who are more numerous than the members of the Church of England. Besides these, there are probably many other persons who are not attached to any particular Church or form of worship. Compared with the whole population, the members of the Church of England must, therefore, constitute an extremely small proportion. It would be unjust and impolitic to exalt this Church, by exclusive and peculiar rights above all others of His Majesty's subjects who are equally loyal, conscientious, and deserving. A country in which there is an Established Church, from which a vast majority of the subjects are dissenters, must be in a lamentable state. The Committee hope that this Province will never present such a spectacle. It is well known that there is in the minds of the people generally a strong and settled aversion to anything like an Established Church ; and although, from the conviction so happily and justly entertained, that His Majesty's Government will never adopt a measure so deeply affecting the interests and feelings of the inhabitants of this Province without the most indulgent consideration of their wishes on the subject, there is less anxiety than would otherwise exist, yet the apprehension that it was the intention of His Majesty's Government to incorporate the Church of England or any other Church with the Government as an appendage of the State, and to invest it with peculiar rights or privileges, civil or pecuniary, from which other sects were excluded, would excite alarm through the country, and the actual execution of such a measure would produce the most general and lasting discontent. There is, besides, no necessity for such an establishment. It cannot be necessary for the security of the Government ; the loyalty of the people is deep and enthusiastic, and it may be doubted how far it would be improved or increased by any State establishment of clergymen. Religious instruction, it is true, will promote and strengthen loyalty and all other virtues ; but no more when communicated by clergymen of the Church of England than by those of other sects, and probably less if they are or appear to be political teachers and servants of the State rather than ministers of the Gospel. It cannot be necessary for the ends of religion ; other denominations, of course, will not be benefited by it, and the Church itself will derive probably but little if any real advantage. The piety and religious prosperity of a Church can gain but little from men who are induced by secular motives to assume the sacred functions of the clerical office. Men may, and in fact do, entertain the most conscientious objections either against the particular doctrines or form of worship of any given Church, or in general against the civil establishment of and ·Church whatever, and its union with the State: if the Church is incorporated with the State, they are compelled by the obligations of conscience to oppose one of the civil institutions of the country, a part of the Government itself. It is in fact their duty to do so ; but by doing so they become objects of jealousy and suspicion, and in addition to their unjust exclusion from privileges to which they are as much entitled as those who are more fortunate though not more conscientious, and perhaps not more correct in their opinions upon this subject, their very conscientiousness comes by degrees to be regarded and treated as a crime. Laws are made to guard against any attempts to injure the establishment. To curtail and counteract their influence

14

they are excluded from the offices and honours of the State and subjected to civil disabilities, and thus, in effect, freedom of conscience is legislated against ; and religion, the rules and sanctions of which are of an infinitely higher nature, is made to rest upon the precepts and penalties of human laws ; at the same time, the harmony and charity which would otherwise prevail between the members of different sects are disturbed, and sectarian pride and intolerance and animosity take their place.

" Upon this subject His Majesty's Government ought to be fairly and distinctly apprised of the sentiments and wishes of the people ; and as the House of Assembly is the constitutional organ to convey to the Throne their sentiments and wishes, the Committee respectfully submit to the House the expediency of addressing His Majesty upon the subject.

"In the course of their enquiries the Committee obtained information, which to their surprise and regret gave them reason to believe that to create in the minds of the Indians recently converted under the Divine blessing to the Christian religion, an influence unfavourable to their present religious teachers, through whose exertions this change has taken place, the name of His Majesty's Government had been used ; and even that intimation had been made of an intention to compel them to come under the Church of England. The great and surprising change which has occurred within a short period of time in the character and condition of large bodies of the Mississagua Indians is well known ; from a state of vice and ignorance, wretchedness and degradation, almost brutal, they have been brought to habits of industry, order, and temperance, a thirst for instruction and knowledge, a profession of the Christian religion, and apparently a cordial and humble belief of its truths and enjoyment of its blessings.

In this change the Methodists have been chiefly instrumental. **They** have manifested the most benevolent **zeal** in accomplishing it ; they have **sent missionaries and** established schools among **them** which are supported by voluntary contributions, **and they are still labouring** among them with the **same disinterested spirit and the** same surprising encouragement **and success.**

" The recent statute of the Imperial Parliament author**izing** the sale of a part of the Clergy Reserves, the Com**mittee** have not seen, and therefore **do** not know whether it directs the application of the proceeds to any particular purpose. They have been informed that according **to this** statute a part of **these reserves are to be sold, and the** proceeds, after **deducting the** expenses **of the sale, are** to be paid into the funds of the **Imperial Government, and** a certain sum **to be** appropriated **to the** improvement of **the** remainder. **Assuming that by a proper application it could be obtained for the benefit of this Province, it is an** interesting question **what use shall be made of it.** The people generally desire **to** see it appropriated **in** a judicious manner to public improvements, and to the support of education upon such principles as will not countenance any distinction on account of religious profession or belief. The House of Assembly, by the Bill authorizing the sale of these **lands, and** the **appropriation of** the proceeds to the **purposes of education, passed during the** last session, have expressed **their opinion against the policy and prac**ticability **of devoting it to the** purposes originally in**tended. With the aid of** the monies arising **from this** source, the Province **can** undertake many **works for** internal improvement, **by which its prosperity would be** greatly promoted, and some of which seem almost indispensable, but which, for **the want of means, cannot, with**out such aid, be attempted. **The anxiety of His Majesty's**

Government to advance our interests, assures us of their assent to all our reasonable wishes on the subject. The Committee are therefore of opinion that an application should be made to have this fund placed at the disposal of the Provincial Legislature, in order that it may be applied to the purposes which have been mentioned. As to the remainder of the Clergy Reserves, the Committee, without an examination of the British statute last alluded to, are unable to say whether the right of directing their sale remains with the Provincial Legislature, or is by that statute confined to the British Parliament. In either case they think that measures should be taken to have them sold, if possible, and the proceeds applied to the same purposes as those which they have recommended for the avails of that part of which the sale is already authorized.

"Upon an examination of the copy of the Charter of the University of King's College, transmitted to the House by His Excellency and referred to them, the Committee find that the following are some of its provisions :

" The Bishop of the Diocese is to be visitor, and as such may disapprove of the by-laws made for the college by the Council, which thereby become void, unless His Majesty in Privy Council afterwards reverses this order ; the Governor, Lieutenant-Governor, or person administering the Government is to be Chancellor ; the President is to be a clergyman in holy orders of the Church of England ; the hon. and venerable Dr. Strachan, Archdeacon of York, is to be the first President ; the corporation is to consist of the Chancellor, President, and Scholars of King's College, and is authorized to take and hold real estate not exceeding the yearly value of £15,000 sterling. The College Council is to consist of the Chancellor, President, and seven other persons, who are to be members of the Church of England, and to sign the 39 Articles of that

Church. The Council, under certain restrictions, are to make by-laws for the college ; one of these restrictions is that no religious test or qualification shall be required of or appointed for any persons admitted or matriculated as scholars in the college, except that those admitted to the degree of Doctor in Divinity shall make the same declarations and subscriptions and take the same oaths as are required of persons admitted to any degree of Divinity in the University of Oxford. From the message of His Excellency it appears that His Majesty has been pleased to grant as an endowment for the University 225,944 acres of the Crown lands, and to appropriate from the revenues of the Crown the sum of £1,000 sterling per annum for 16 years, for the erection of the buildings ; and also that several of the religious societies in England have contributed to the institution by donations of money for the purchase of books and by the foundation of scholarships for missionaries to the Indian tribes.

" From the foregoing abstract of some of the provisions of the Charter, the sectarian character and tendency of the institution will be manifest. Doctor Strachan, by whose representations and exertions, in a great measure, the Charter in its present shape seems to have been procured, in a pamphlet published in London, entitled 'An Appeal to the Friends of Religion and Literature, in behalf of the University of Upper Canada,' distinctly states that it will be essentially a missionary college, 'for the education of missionaries of the Church of England ;' and as an argument to obtain from the members of that Church contributions towards the funds of the college, maintains that the effect of establishing this university will be ultimately to make the greater portion of the population of the Province members of the Church of England. That such must be the natural tendency of putting into the

hands of that Church the only seminary of learning in the
country where a liberal education can be obtained, is
obvious; but the alarm and jealousy which this very
circumstance will produce through the Province, and has
in some measure already produced, and which will prevent parents and guardians from sending their children
to it, will perhaps counteract this tendency, although at
the same time it will, in an equal degree, limit the benefits
which might otherwise be derived from the institution.
A university adapted to the character and circumstances
of the people would be the means of inestimable benefits
to this Province. But to be of real service, the principles
upon which it is established must be in unison with the
general sentiments of the people. It should not be a
school of politics or of sectarian views. It should have
about it no appearance of a spirit of partiality or exclusion. Its portals should be thrown open to all; and upon
none who enter should any influence be exerted to attach
them to a particular creed or church. It should be a
source of intellectual and moral light and animation, from
which the glorious irradiations of literature and science
may descend upon all with equal lustre and power. Such
an institution would be a blessing to the country, its pride
and glory. Most deeply, therefore, is it to be lamented
that the principles of the Charter are calculated to defeat
its usefulness, and to confine to a favoured few all its advantages. That His Majesty's Government could even
have contemplated such a limitation of its beneficence,
that they could have ever intended to found it upon such
terms as must either preclude from its benefits the greater
part of those for whom it was intended, or subject them,
at an age ill qualified to guard against such attacks, to
the silent but powerful influence of a prevailing spirit and
regular system of proselytism, no one will believe. They

could not have been aware of the insurmountable objections to which, from the circumstances of the country, and the sentiments of the people, some of the provisions of the Charter were liable. They acted undoubtedly under the impression, and with the intention, of providing, in the most gracious and liberal manner, an institution much needed and desired by the people. There is therefore every reason to believe that any representations from the House of Assembly upon the matter will be most favourably regarded. Under this impression the Committee strongly recommend this subject to the consideration of the House.

"With this Report, the Committee present to the House the draft of an Address to His Majesty upon the various subjects which have been mentioned, and they respectfully recommend that it be adopted by the House.

"All which is respectfully recommended.

"MARSHALL S. BIDWELL, Chairman.

"Committee Room, 15th March, 1828."

The Address to the King, founded on the Report of the Select Committee, and also adopted by a majority of more than two to one—a majority of 21 to 9—was as follows:

"TO THE KING'S MOST EXCELLENT MAJESTY.

"*Most Gracious Sovereign:*

"We your Majesty's dutiful and loyal subjects, the Commons of Upper Canada, in Provincial Parliament assembled, humbly beg leave to represent to your Majesty, that we have seen, with equal surprise and regret, a letter and ecclesiastical chart, dated 16th May, 1827, and addressed by the Honourable and Venerable Doctor Strachan, Archdeacon of York, a member of your Majesty's Legislative and Executive Councils of this Province, to the

Right Honourable R. J. Wilmot Horton, at that time Under-Secretary of State for the Colonies, for the information of Lord Goderich, then at the head of the Colonial Department ; as they are inaccurate in some important respects, and are calculated to lead your Majesty's Government into serious errors.

"We beg leave to inform your Majesty, that of your Majesty's subjects in this Province only a small proportion are members of the Church of England ; that there is not any peculiar tendency to that Church among the people, and that nothing could cause more alarm and grief in their minds than the apprehension that there was a design, on the part of your Majesty's Government, to establish, as a part of the State, one or more Church or denomination of Christians in this Province, with rights and endowments not granted to your Majesty's subjects in general, of other denominations, who are equally conscientious and deserving, and equally loyal and attached to your Majesty's Royal person and government. In following honestly the dictates of their conscience as regards the great and important subject of religion, the latter have never been conscious that they have violated any law or any obligation of a good subject, or done anything to forfeit your Majesty's favour and protection, or to exclude themselves from a participation in the rights and privileges enjoyed by your Majesty's other subjects.

"We humbly beg leave to assure your Majesty that the insinuations against the Methodist preachers in this Province do much injustice to a body of pious and deserving men, who justly enjoy the confidence, and are the spiritual instructors of a large portion of your Majesty's subjects in this Province. We are convinced that the tendency of their influence and instruction is not hostile to our institutions, but, on the contrary, is eminently favourable to religion and morality ; that their labours are calculated to make their people better men and better subjects, and have already produced, in this Province, the happiest effects.

" While we fully and gratefully appreciate your Majesty's gracious intentions in granting a Royal Charter for the establishment of an University in this Province, we would beg most respectfully to represent, that as the great body of your Majesty's subjects in this Province are not members of the Church of England, they have seen, with grief, that the Charter contains provisions which are calculated to render the institution subservient to the particular interests of that Church, and to exclude from its offices and honours all who do not belong to it. In consequence of these provisions, its benefits will be confined to a favoured few, while others of your Majesty's subjects, far more numerous and equally loyal and deserving of your Majesty's paternal care and favour, will be shut out from a participation in them. Having a tendency to build up one particular Church, to the prejudice of others, it will naturally be an object of jealousy and disgust. Its influence as a seminary of learning will, upon these accounts, be limited and partial. We, therefore, humbly beg that your Majesty will be pleased to listen to the wishes of your Majesty's people in this respect, and to cause the present Charter to be cancelled, and one granted free from the objections to which, emboldened by a conviction of your Majesty's paternal and gracious feelings to your loyal subjects in this Province, as well as by a sense of duty to the people, and a knowledge of their anxiety upon the subject, we have presumed to advert.

" We would also beg leave to state that it is the general desire of your Majesty's subjects in this Province that the monies arising from the sale of any of the lands set apart

in this Province for the support and maintenance of a
Protestant clergy should be entirely appropriated to purposes of education and internal improvement. We would
most humbly represent, that to apply them to the benefit
of one or two Christian denominations, to the exclusion
of others, would be unjust as well as impolitic, and that
it might perhaps be found impracticable to divide them
among all. We have no reason to fear that the cause of
religion would suffer materially from not giving a public
support to its ministers, and from leaving them to be supported by the liberality of their people.

"Many works for the internal improvement of the Province, of great importance to its prosperity and to the ease
and comfort of your Majesty's subjects, are necessarily
neglected for want of money in the Provincial treasury ;
for although the taxes are only of a trifling amount, yet,
from the scarcity of money, and the want of even a toler-
able price for the productions of their farms, they are
paid with great difficulty by many of your Majesty's
people. It is impossible, therefore, to raise by taxation
the means necessary to undertake and carry on those
works. It is also most desirable that a larger sum than
is at present at our disposal should be employed to extend
through the country the advantages of education.

"We therefore humbly pray that the monies arising
from the sale of the lands set apart in this Province for
the support and maintenance of a Protestant clergy may
be placed at the disposal of the Legislature of this Province, for the purposes we have mentioned.

"JOHN WILLSON, Speaker.
"Commons' House of Assembly, 20th March, 1828."

These documents are no less remarkable for
their statesmanlike views than for their spirit of

Christian patriotism. But the twofold controversy on the Charter of King's College and of the Clergy Reserves was rather opened than closed by these proceedings of the Legislative Assembly. The publication of the Charter of King's College and the representations on which it was obtained were largely and warmly discussed. The author of these Essays wrote eight letters (which were widely published in the newspapers, as well as in a pamphlet) on the subject; the Legislative Assembly adopted, during successive Parliaments, resolutions, addresses, and acts against the sectarian provisions and character of King's College Charter; but the proceedings of the Legislative Assembly were long counteracted by the Legislative Council, of which the venerable author of the Charter was a controlling member. It was not until after a contest of more than fifteen years that King's College was converted into a Provincial institution, under the title of Toronto University, when the venerable Archdeacon of York, now become Bishop of Toronto, renounced all connection with the Toronto University, and, with characteristic energy, obtained a Royal Charter and large funds, both in England and Canada for the establishment of Trinity College, Toronto.

The discussion on the Clergy Reserves was still more protracted, if not more vehement, than that on King's College. The Legislative Assembly proceeded in every possible form, and with great unanimity, to extinguish the sectarian monopoly of the Clergy Reserves; the Methodist Conference annually remonstrated against the Clergy Reserve monopoly, as did the annual assemblies of other religious denominations; the intensity of public feeling on the subject was increased by the last act of Sir John Colborne (afterwards Lord Seaton), who, on leaving the Government of Upper Canada in 1835, created *fifty-seven* rectories of the Church of England, and endowed them with glebe lands out of the Clergy Reserves. But all the efforts against the twofold sectarian monopoly of the Clergy Reserves and King's College proved unavailing, while both the Executive and Legislative Councils were in the hands of the monopolists, irresponsible to public opinion, and had the absolute control of a revenue sufficient for the support of the Government, independent of any vote of the House of Assembly, and against its remonstrances.

ESSAY VIII.

CLERGY RESERVE CONTROVERSY CONTINUED : VOICE OF
THE LEGISLATIVE ASSEMBLY OF UPPER CANADA
IN FAVOUR OF EQUAL CIVIL RIGHTS AND LIB-
ERTY AMONG ALL CLASSES, AND IN VINDICATION
OF THE EARLY METHODIST MINISTRY.

WHEN the writer of these Essays was appointed as representative of the Canadian Conferences to the British Conference to
negotiate the first union between the two Conferences in 1833, he carried a Petition to the
King, signed by upwards of 20,000 inhabitants,
against the Clergy Reserve monopoly and the
establishment of a dominant Church in Upper
Canada. This Petition was presented through
Lord Stanley, afterwards the Earl of Derby,
then Colonial Secretary, and then a professed
Liberal, and professedly opposed to the Church
of England possessing any civil advantages in
Canada not enjoyed by other religious denominations.*

* But an earlier Petition to the Crown had been presented, immediately after the publication of Dr. Strachan's
famous Letter and Chart, and a Committee of the House

But a check was given to the progress and
settlement of this question by a design formed
between Messrs. Hume, Roebuck Papineau, and
W. L. Mackenzie, to erect Canada into an in-

of Commons was appointed on the Civil Government of
Canada, which investigated Canadian affairs at the same
time that a Select Committee of the House of Assembly
of Upper Canada was investigating the Letter and Chart
on Petitions from various Christian denominations. Sir
Francis Hincks, in his pamphlet on the Clergy Reserves,
etc., published in London, 1869, says :

"There was much in Dr. Strachan's Letter and Chart that
was deemed offensive to the members of other denominations,
and on its publication was not only taken by the House of
Assembly of Upper Canada, but by the inhabitants, who
entrusted a petition, signed by 8,000 people, to Mr. George
Ryerson, an influential Wesleyan Methodist, who was examined before a Committee of the House of Commons
in 1828. The report of that Committee, of which Mr. Huskisson was Chairman, and Mr. Stanley (now Earl of Derby),
Mr. Labouchere (now Lord Taunton), Sir Franklin Lewis,
Mr. Sturges Bourne, Sir James McIntosh, and others were
members, was, 'That they cannot avoid recommending in
the strongest manner the propriety of securing for the future
any provision which may be deemed necessary for the religious
wants of the community in these Provinces, by other means
than the reservation of one-seventh of the land, according to
the enactment of the Act of 1791.'

"With regard to the doubts which had arisen as to the
meaning of the term 'Protestant clergy,' the Committee
observe, 'The law officers of the Crown have given an opinion
in favour of the rights of the Church of Scotland to such
participation, in which your Committee entirely concur ; but
the question has been raised, whether the clergy of every

dependent republic. The **writer of these papers was in England from November, 1835, to March,**

denomination **of** Christians, except **Roman** Catholics, **may not be included.'** While abstaining from offering any opinion on the legal definition of the term, the Committee declared its opinion **that the** intention **of the** framers of the Act **of** 1791 was **'to** reserve to the **Government** the right to apply **the money, if they saw** fit, to any Protestant clergy.' "(pp. 5, 6.)

Lord Stanley, **in** his **speech, the 2nd** May, 1828, **in** reference to the Report **on** the **Civil** Government of Canada, as reported in the *Mirror of Parliament* (corrected by his own hand), said

"That if **any exclusive privileges be given to the Church of** England, **not only will the measure be** repugnant **to every** principle of sound legislation, **but contrary to the** spirit **and** intentions **of the** Act of **1791, under which the Reserves were** made **for the** Protestant clergy. **I will not enter further into** it at present, except **to** express **my hope that the House will** guard Canada against the evils which **religious dissensions have** already produced **in** this country **and in** Ireland, **where we** have examples to teach us what **to shun. We have seen the** evil consequences **of** this system **at home. God** forbid we should not profit by experience; **and more especially in** legis- **lating for** a **people** bordering **on a** country where religious intolerance **and** religious exclusions are **unknown—a** country to which Parliament looked in **passing the** Act **of 1791,** as all the great men **who argued the question** then expressly **declared.** It is important that **His Majesty's Canadian subjects should** not have occasion **to** look **across the narrow boundary that** separates them from **the United States and see anything there** to envy."

It is singular **that** when **it was proposed to** pass **the Duke of** Newcastle's **Bill in the House of Lords,** in 1853, **to repeal the** Clergy Reserve **Act, Lord Stanley, now** be-

1837, seeking aid and a Royal Charter **for what
is now known as Victoria** University. Almost
every gentleman to whom **he** was introduced,
or whom he met, said, "**You** people in Canada

come the **Earl of Derby and the leader of the** Conser-
vative party, opposed the **Bill, declaring that** the Clergy
Reserves were intended **and set apart for the** Church of
England—the very **reverse of what, as both an** historical
fact and a principle of legislation, **he had** declared twenty-
five years before **in** the House **of Commons.**

Sir George **Murray,** Secretary **of State for the Colonies
under the Duke of Wellington's Government, in a speech
in the House of Commons, July, 1832, on a motion for**
a grant **to the Episcopal North American** Clergy, said :

"This country **is bound to provide religious instruction** for
the people of **our Colonies. At the same time, he (Sir George**
Murray) begged **to say that, so far from** approving **the maintenance** of any **exclusive system in the** Colonies, **he thought**
any such system there **bad and dangerous. He was** of opinion
that the pastors of all **religious** persuasions **in the** Colonies were
equally entitled **to support,** and he deprecated **the establishment of any one Church over** all others."

One can **hardly avoid** the reflection, that had the venerable Archdeacon **of** York, and **the** clergy of the Church
of England **in** Canada, acquiesced forthwith in the deci-
sions of the high Imperial authorities, instead of resisting
them, **and recognized the** constitutional rights **of their
fellow-subjects in Canada, instead of denying and** seeking
to paralyze, if not destroy them, **how different** would have
**been the Canadian history for more than twenty-five
years** from **what it was! how much more harmonious
and rapid the progress of the** country, **and** how much
better **for the Church of England** itself !

are going to set up a republican government for yourselves, and separate from us." I denied it, when I was told, it so appears from letters of Mr. Hume, who is understood to be the agent of the Reformers of Upper Canada, and Mr. Roebuck, agent of the House of Assembly of Lower Canada, and their correspondents in Canada. My answer was, that the people of Upper Canada were not Republicans, were truly loyal to the King and British connection, but desired and insisted upon the impartial administration of the government to all parties, and equal civil rights and privileges among all classes of the people. So deeply mortified did I feel at these unjust and injurious suspicions in regard to the people of Canada, that I sat down and addressed to Messrs. Hume and Roebuck six letters, through the *Times* newspaper, in which I showed, from their own letters and the words of Messrs. Papineau and W. L. Mackenzie, that they were the originators and advisers of the departure from reform to revolution in Canada, the new scheme for throwing off what Mr. Hume called "the baneful domination of the mother country," and for establishing a republic in Canada. These letters were signed "A Canadian," were reprinted and widely circulated in Canada, were collected together under the auspices and at the expense of the British

15

American Association of Merchants in London, and a copy of them sent to each member of both Houses of Parliament.

When these letters were written in London, as also one in reply to a personal attack of Mr. Peter Perry, in the U. C. House of Assembly, in the spring of 1836, the author had no idea of a new election in Upper Canada ; but in May, 1836, Sir F. B. Head dissolved the House of Assembly, and adroitly turned the issue, not on the question of the Clergy Reserves, or of other practical questions, but on the question of connection with the mother country, and of Republicanism *versus* Monarchy, as had been recommended by Messrs. Hume and Roebuck, and advocated by Messrs. Mackenzie and Papineau. This was successful, inasmuch as those Reformers who would not disavow their connection with Messrs. Mackenzie, Hume, and Roebuck lost their elections ; for though not more than half a dozen of them had any sympathy with the sentiments of Messrs. Hume, Roebuck, Papineau and Mackenzie, they did not wish to break the unity of the Reform party by repudiating them, and suffered defeat in consequence at the elections. The successful candidates generally, while they repudiated republican separation from the mother country, promised fidelity to the often-expressed and

well-known wishes of the people in the settlement of the Clergy Reserve question. which,
however, they failed to fulfil, as will presently
be seen.

In the meantime, the Mackenzie, or revolutionary section of the Reformers, resolved to
carry their views into effect by *force of arms,*
and formed secret clubs or societies for that purpose, counselled and guided by a secret Revolutionary Committee in Toronto. An attack was
made upon the city by the rebels, headed by
Mackenzie, on the 4th of December, 1837; but
the citizens volunteered and took arms in its
defence, from the Chief Justice downwards.
The rebels, invading the city from Yonge Street,
were repulsed with considerable loss, and the
rebellion was crushed, the rebels in the west, in
the county of Oxford, headed by Dr. Charles
Duncombe, being dispersed by the militia volunteers under the command of Sir Allan McNab.
There was no rebel rising east of Toronto, and
few, if any, rebels.

In the elections of 1836, the Earl of Durham
says that Sir F. B. Head "succeeded in putting
the question in such a light before the Province
that a great portion of the people really imagined
that they were called upon to decide the question of *separation* by their votes" Had the
constitutional and loyal Reformers *declared* their

opposition to the avowed sentiments and objects of Messrs. Mackenzie, Hume, and Roebuck,
Sir F. B. Head would have had no grounds for
placing such an issue before the country, and
hardly would have done so. The elections would
have taken place on the grounds of responsible
government and equal civil and religious rights
among all Christian denominations. After the
most thorough inquiry, the Earl of Durham, in
his Report, says that "the Assembly of Upper
Canada did not possess the public confidence."
The great body of the Reformers were as loyal
to British connection in 1836 as they are now
in 1880 ; and Sir F. B. Head himself boasted of
the loyalty of the Reformers generally, equally
with the Conservatives, in putting down the
rebellion ; but afterwards, the leaders of the
majority in the new Assembly (which the Earl
of Durham said "did not possess the public
confidence") endeavoured to implicate the loyalty
of the whole Reform party on account of the
rebellion of a small section of them, just as
attempts are now made by certain partizans to
fasten, alternately, annexation sentiments and
designs upon the whole Conservative and Reform parties on account of the annexation
avowals of some individuals of both parties.
The error of the leaders of the Constitutional
Reform party in 1836 was their not at once

disavowing all sympathy and connection with the sentiments and designs of Messrs. Hume, Roebuck, Mackenzie, and Papineau to sever Canada from England with a view to its annexation to the United States. Sir F. Hincks says, in an admirably written pamphlet, published in London in 1869, " The unfortunate rebellion of 1837 had for a time almost annihilated the Reform party, which only began to revive on the appointment of Lord Durham as Governor-General and High Commissioner. On the publication of his Lordship's report it received an immense accession of strength."*

It may be advisable to give in this place a summary view of the legislative proceedings on this subject. I do so by epitomizing an Address

* _Religious Endowments in Canada—The Clergy Reserve and Rectory Questions. A Chapter of Canadian History. By Sir Francis Hincks, K.C., M.G.C.B._ Published in London, by Dalton & Lacy, 28 Cockspur Street, booksellers to the Queen and H. R. H. the Prince of Wales ; pp. 109.

As early as 1832, Lord Goderich, by the command of the King, sent positive instructions to the Lieutenant-Governor of Upper Canada to submit to the Canadian Legislature the settlement of the Clergy Reserve question, by " varying or repealing the provision for support of a Protestant clergy, as it might judge best for the religious and general interests of the country." But the order was evaded ; and the question was still kept open as a subject of agitation.

to the Queen, adopted by the House of Assembly
in 1850, by a majority of 46 to 23, and accompanied by an excellent despatch from the Earl
of Elgin and Kincardine:

1. The reservation of a large portion of the
public domain of the Province, for the support
of a Protestant clergy, by an Act passed in the
reign of King George the Third, has been for
many years a source of intense dissatisfaction
to the great majority of His Majesty's subjects
in Upper Canada.

2. In the early settlement of the Province the
reserve lands were of little value, and as no
sales had then been authorized by the Imperial
Parliament, the question attracted but a slight
share of public attention.

3. The power given by the 41st clause of the
above-mentioned Act (31 George III. chap. 21)
to the Provincial Legislature, to " vary or repeal" the provisions respecting the allotment
and appropriation of lands for the support of
a Protestant clergy, affords sufficient evidence
that, in the opinion of the Imperial Parliament,
the question was one that ought to be settled
with reference to the state of public opinion
in the colony rather than to that of the mother
country.

4. But so soon as the intention of the Government to dispose of the land reserved in Upper

Canada became known, the representatives of the people of that Province took the whole subject into most serious consideration, and, with an unanimity that prevailed on no other question, endeavoured to remove a grievance complained of by the people, save and except by those interested in the maintenance of Church Establishments.

5. In the year 1827, a Bill to authorize the sale of the Clergy Reserves, and the application of the proceeds thereof to the purposes of general education, was passed through the House of Assembly of Upper Canada, the division on the second reading having been 22 to 6; but this Bill was rejected by the Legislative Council.

6. A dissolution having taken place soon afterwards, the tenth Parliament of Upper Canada met in the year 1829, when a Bill for the sale of the Clergy Reserves, and the application of the proceeds to educational purposes, passed through the various stages in the House of Assembly without a division, but was again rejected by the Legislative Council.

7. In the year 1830, during the second session of the tenth Parliament, another Bill, containing similar provisions to the former ones, was passed by the House of Assembly without a division, and was rejected by the Legislative Council.

8. A dissolution having taken place, a new

Parliament met in 1831, when resolutions expressing the same views were adopted by a large majority in the House of Assembly—an amendment proposed by the Solicitor-General (Hagarman) having been rejected on a division by 29 to 7.

9. In the year 1832, during the second session of the eleventh Parliament, an Address to the Crown, praying for the application of the Clergy Reserves to educational purposes, was carried by a large majority in the House of Assembly.

10. After the Address last referred to, a Message was sent down to the House by Lieutenant-Governor Sir John Colborne, in which His Excellency states that he had His Majesty's commands to make a communication to the House of Assembly in reference to the lands set apart for the support and maintenance of a Protestant clergy ; that His Excellency informed the House that the representations made to His Majesty, and to his royal predecessors, of the prejudice sustained by his faithful subjects in the Province, from the appropriating of the Clergy Reserves, had engaged His Majesty's most attentive consideration ; that His Majesty had considered with no less anxiety how the power given to the Provincial Legislature by the Constitutional Act, to vary or repeal this part of its provisions, could be called into exercise

most advantageously for the spiritual and temporal interests of His Majesty's faithful subjects in the Province.

11. After the reception of the above Message, a Bill to re-invest the Clergy Reserves in the Crown, discharged of all trusts whatsoever [that is, to convert them into Crown Lands, pure and simple], was introduced and read a second time on a division of 29 to 7.

12. In the year 1833, during the third session of the eleventh Parliament, a Bill, similar in its provisions with that formerly adopted by the House, was read a second time on a division of 26 to 2.

13. In the year 1834, during the fourth session of the eleventh Parliament, a Bill of similar character was passed through its several stages in the House of Assembly by considerable majorities, though opposed with the whole weight of the Government, but was rejected by the Legislative Council.

13. In the year 1835, during the first session of the twelfth Parliament of Upper Canada, a Bill for the sale of the Clergy Reserves, and the application of the proceeds to educational purposes, was passed by a majority of 40 to 4, but was rejected by the Legislative Council.

15. During the same session, resolutions were sent down to the House of Assembly by the

Legislative Council, in which the opinion was expressed, that as the Legislature of the Province had been unable to concur in any measure respecting the Clergy Reserves, it was expedient to address His Majesty and both Houses of Parliament, requesting that *the Imperial Parliament should legislate on the subject !*

16. This monstrous proposition to abandon the legislative functions which the Imperial Act had conferred upon the Provincial Legislature, to "vary or repeal" the Clergy Reserve provisions, and transfer them to the British Parliament, was promptly rejected by the House of Assembly, which resolved thereupon, by a majority of 24 to 12, that the House had heretofore repeatedly passed Bills providing for the sale of the Clergy Reserves and the appropriation of the moneys arising therefrom to the support of education, which Bills had been rejected without amendment by the Legislative Council. With the same view the House had repeatedly made known, by humble and dutiful addresses to His Majesty, their wishes and opinions—the wishes and opinions of His Majesty's faithful subjects in this Province—on this highly important subject, and the House took that opportunity of declaring that these wishes and opinions, both on the part of the House and of their constituents, remained entirely

unchanged. That during the second session of the then last Parliament, His Excellency the Lieutenant-Governor, by Message, informed the House that he had His Majesty's instructions to invite the House to consider how the powers given to the Provincial Legislature by the Constitutional Act, to "vary and repeal" the provisions which it contains for the allotment and appropriation of the Clergy Reserves, might be most advantageously exercised for the spiritual and temporal interests of his faithful subjects in the Province. That the House, in compliance with His Majesty's wishes thus graciously expressed, and with the strong and well-known desires of His Majesty's faithful subjects in the Province, had passed a Bill during the then present session to provide for the sale of the Clergy Reserves, and to apply the moneys arising from such sales to the support of education. That the Legislative Council had not passed said Bill, had not amended it, and had not passed any other Bill on the subject.

17. In the year 1836, during the second session of the twelfth Parliament, a Bill embodying similar principles to those repeatedly passed by the House of Assembly, was again introduced, and was carried on a division by a majority of 35 to 5. The said Bill was amended by the Legislative Council by expunging all the

enacting clauses, and substituting provisions for investing the Reserves in the Crown for the maintenance of public worship and the support of religion. The House of Assembly adopted, by a majority of 27 to 1, certain amendments to the amended Bill sent down by the Legislative Council affirming the principles of their original Bill.

18. During the same session, a despatch from Lord Glenelg, His Majesty's Principal Secretary of State for the Colonies, to Lieutenant-Governor Sir Francis Head, was communicated to the House of Assembly, in which his Lordship treated the question as one to be settled by the Provincial Legislature, and declined to interfere with the deliberations of the Legislature by offering any suggestions of his own.

19. The twelfth Parliament having been dissolved by Sir Francis Head, a general election was held at a period of great excitement, and the question of the disposal of the Clergy Reserves was lost sight of during the political struggle which ensued. During the first three sessions of this thirteenth and last Parliament of Upper Canada, various efforts were made to settle the question, but without any satisfactory result. At length, in the course of the third session, a Bill which had passed the Legislative Council, providing for the re-investment of the

said Reserves (not in the Crown, but) in the *Imperial Parliament,* was brought down to the House of Assembly, and, by dint of every sort of persuasion and influence on the members, a majority of *one* was obtained for passing it— the vote being 22 to 21. But the Bill was disallowed by the Imperial Government, " there being an insuperable objection to it on point of form." The Governor-General, Lord Sydenham, in announcing the disallowance of this Bill, states " that, in the opinion of Her Majesty's Government, the Provincial Legislature would bring to the decision of the question an extent of accurate information as to the wants and general opinion of society in this country, in which the Imperial Parliament was unavoidably deficient."

20. Another attempt at settlement was made during the last session of this last Parliament of Upper Canada, when a Bill passed both Houses providing for the sale and disposal of the Clergy Reserves, which Bill having been reserved did not receive the Royal assent ; but instead of which, Lord John Russell, then Principal Secretary of State for the Colonies, introduced a Bill into the Imperial Parliament (3 and 4 Vic., chap. lxxviii.), and which passed, providing that the entire Clergy Reserve revenue, from the investments made before the passing

of that Act (1840), should be assigned to the Churches of England and Scotland alone, to the exclusion of all other religious denominations. The provisions of this Bill not only took from the people of Upper Canada the control of the revenue of property which their own labour had rendered valuable, and which their Constitutional Act gave their representatives the right to " vary or repeal," but actually disposed of that revenue by the Imperial Parliament, at variance with and against the views and wishes of the representatives of the people of Upper Canada in nine sessions of four successive Parliaments.

Messrs. William and Egerton Ryerson had been appointed representatives of the Canadian Conference to the British Conference, which met in Newcastle-upon-Tyne in 1840. On their arrival in England, they found Lord John Russell's Bill for the disposal of the Canadian Clergy Revenues to the Churches of England and Scotland before Parliament; and as representing the largest religious denomination in Upper Canada, they requested an interview with Lord John Russell on the subject of his Lordship's Bill before Parliament. In the interview granted, they pointed out to his Lordship the injustice, impolicy, and danger of the Bill, should it become law, and respectfully and earnestly prayed his Lordship to withdraw the Bill; but he was inflexible, when the Messrs. Ryerson prayed to his Lordship to assent to their being heard at the Bar of the House of Commons against the Bill; at which his Lordship became very angry —thinking it presumptuous that two Canadians, however numerous and respectable their constituency, should propose to be heard at the Bar of the British House of Commons against a measure of Her Majesty's Government. But the Messrs. Ryerson knew their country and their position, and afterwards wrote a respectful but earnest letter to his Lordship against his measure, and faithfully warned him of the consequences of it if persevered in; they went so far as to intimate that the measure would prove an opening wedge of separation between Great Britain and the people of Upper Canada; and lest they should be considered as endeavouring to fulfil their own predictions, they did not publish their letter to Lord John Russell, or write a line on the subject for more than ten years—knowing that a wound so deep would, without any action or word on their part, fester and spread so wide in the people of Upper Canada as ultimately to compel the repeal of the Act or sever their connection with Great Britain. The result was as the Messrs. Ryerson

had apprehended; for in 1853 the Act was
repealed by the British Parliament.*

Early in 1852, the Government of which Earl

* Earl Grey had intended to propose its repeal in 1850-51,
and had requested the writer of these papers (who was
then on an Educational tour in Europe) to remain in
England in order to furnish his Lordship with data and
details to enable him to answer objections which might
be made to his Bill in the House of Lords, and wrote to
Lord Elgin, then Governor-General of Canada, requesting
the protracting of Mr. Ryerson's leave of absence for two
or three months. But the Bill had to be deferred until
another session, and Mr. Ryerson returned immediately
to Canada. Sir Francis Hincks, in the pamphlet above
referred to, on page 18, refers to the proceeding on the
part of Earl Grey on the subject. He says :

"On the 11th of January, 1851, Earl Grey addressed a despatch to the Earl of Elgin, announcing that it appeared to
Her Majesty's Government to be impossible for them, consistently with the principles on which they have always held that
the Government of Canada ought to be conducted, to advise
Her Majesty to refuse to comply with the prayer of the address
of the Assembly" [for the repeal of Lord John Russell's Act
of 1840].

"It had been the intention of Earl Grey to have introduced a Bill into Parliament during the session of 1850-51 ;
but in a despatch dated the 27th January, 1851, he made
Lord Elgin acquainted with the circumstances under which
'Her Majesty's Government are compelled to postpone to
another session the introduction of the Bill.' When the Canadian Assembly met in 1851, an address of thanks to Her
Majesty for the promise conveyed in Earl Grey's first despatch,
was proposed and carried. No other action could be taken."
(p. 56.)

Grey was Secretary of State for the Colonies
was superseded by that of the Earl of Derby,
with Sir John Pakington as Secretary of State
for the Colonies, who, in a despatch to Lord
Elgin, dated April 22, 1852, says :

"By a despatch from my predecessor, Earl Grey, of
the 11th July last, you were informed that Her Majesty's
then servants found themselves compelled to postpone to
another session the introduction of a Bill into Parliament
giving the Canadian Legislature authority to alter the
existing arrangements with regard to the Clergy Reserves.

"With reference to that intimation, I have to inform
you that it is not the intention of Her Majesty's present
advisers to propose such a measure to Parliament this
session." Two reasons assigned by Sir John Pakington
for this decision were—first, that a general election had
just taken place in the Province, and "it was yet uncer-
tain what the views of the new Assembly as to the disposal of the Clergy Reserves may be ;" second, that "the
result would probably be the diversion to other purposes"
of the Clergy Reserves than "the support of Divine
worship and religious instruction in the Colony." Sir
John Pakington was soon undeceived as to continued
Canadian sentiment on the subject; for Sir Francis Hincks,
then Inspector-General and Premier of Canada, who hap-
pened to be in London on official business in behalf of
the Canadian Government, enclosed to Sir John Pakington
an "Extract from a Report of a Committee of the Honourable the Executive Council on Matters of State," dated 7th
April, 1852, approved by His Excellency the Governor-
General (the Earl of Elgin) in Council on the same day.
The Executive Council instructed "the Honourable the
Inspector-General to ascertain the views of Her Majesty's

16

Government on the subject of the repeal of the Imperial Act 3 and 4 Vic., chap. 78, in conformity with the addresses to Her Most Gracious Majesty, from both branches of the Canadian Legislature, at its last session, on the subject of the Clergy Reserves."

"The assurances of Her Majesty's late Government that such action would be taken, had prepared the people of Canada to expect that no further delay would take place in meeting their just wishes upon a question of such paramount importance to them ; the Council, therefore, recommend that their colleague, the Inspector-General, be requested by the Provincial Secretary to seek an inter-view with Her Majesty's Ministers, and represent to them the importance of carrying out the pledges of their pre-decessors on the subject of the Clergy Reserves, and thus empower the Colonial Legislature to deal with the ques-tion in accordance with the well-understood wishes of the people of Canada."

Sir Francis Hincks enclosed this minute of the Executive Council of Canada, with a noble letter, dated May 3, 1852, in the course of which he said :

"I have already had an opportunity of urging, during the interview with which you were good enough to honour me, the importance of settling this long-vexed question as speedily as possible. It was my duty to state that the number of those who insist on the present settlement is very small, and I may now add, that one of the leading opposition newspapers in Upper Canada, and in the in-terest of the Church of England, has come out distinctly for a new scheme of distribution. I would press on Her Majesty's Government more formally what I have already urged in conversation with you, that if, as has been alleged, the present Canadian Parliament is favourable to the views of the Church of England, it is surely the best time for that Church to procure a settlement that will be regarded as constitutional.

"I can assure Her Majesty's Government with the utmost sincerity, that there will be no end to the agitation in Canada if the attempt be made to settle the question permanently according to public opinion in England, instead of that of the Province itself; and I may add, that it is well known that many who are opponents of the secularization of the Clergy Reserves are, on constitutional grounds, in favour of a settlement by the Provincial Parliament. I believe that, after the assurance given by the late Government, it will be impossible to protract very long the repeal of the Imperial Act."

In another letter addressed by Sir Francis Hincks to Sir John Pakington, dated May 10, 1842, Sir Francis says:

"I am bound by a sense of duty to express to her confidential advisers that it is with the most serious alarm I have read the concluding portion of your despatch. Most devoutly attached as I am to the maintenance of the subsisting connection between the Mother Country and the British American Colonies, I cannot view without grave apprehension the prospect of collision between Her Majesty's Government and the Parliament of Canada, on a question regarding which such strong feelings prevail among the great mass of the population. Such a difficulty is the more to be regretted because the question of the Clergy Reserves is the only one, so far as I am aware, at all likely to lead to collision. It happens, most unfortunately, that public opinion in England differs widely from that in Canada on questions partaking of a religious character ; and as the people of Canada are convinced that they are better judges than any parties in England can be of what measures will best conduce to the peace and welfare of the Province, Her Majesty's Government will, I trust, perceive the danger, which, I apprehend, is at least deserving of the most grave consideration.

" I cannot have the slightest doubt that the members of Her Majesty's Government are actuated by the most earnest desire to promote the best interests of Canada, and that if they could be brought to believe that I have given a faithful account of the state of public opinion there, they would be disposed to yield their own wishes for the sake of the peace of the Colony.

" I am quite ready to acknowledge the high respec- 'tability of the petitioners against the repeal of the Clergy Reserves Act. The bishops, clergy, and an influential portion of the laity of the Church of England, the clergy and a portion of the Church of Scotland, are doubtless in favour of the present settlement, which, indeed, confers on the Church of Scotland an income wholly beyond its requirements in Canada ; while a majority of the Pres- byterian population receive no share of the endowment, nor desire to participate in it.

" While, however, I admit the respectability of the petitioners, I think I am justified in affirming that they do not represent anything like a majority of the popula- tion of Canada ; indeed, the very fact that they, on all occasions, endeavour to accomplish their wishes by appeal- ing, not to their representatives in Parliament, but to the Imperial Parliament, is conclusive proof that they are themselves conscious that their views are not in accord- ance with public opinion in Canada."

The Derby Ministry had to resign office in December, 1852, and the Duke of Newcastle succeeded **Sir John Pakington** as **Secretary of State for the Colonies** ; and on the 15th January, 1853, the Duke addressed a despatch to the **Earl** of Elgin, announcing **the** decision **of the new Ministry** to propose **the** repeal of the Imperial **Act of** 1840, which was successfully **accomplished.**

Thus was a struggle of more **than twenty-five** years ended, equality before **the law of all** religious denominations **established, and the constitutional** rights of the people of Upper **Canada** secured, to their great joy. But the Bishop of Toronto, whose policy **and measures had caused** so much agitation in **Upper Canada, regarded** this settlement **of the Clergy Reserve** question as an irreparable calamity **to the Church of England** in Canada. **On the 16th of March, 1853,** the Bishop addressed a letter **to the Duke of** Newcastle, **of** which the following **are extracts** :

" Power and violence are to determine the question ; vested rights and the claims of justice are impediments to be swept away. Hence the spoliation sought to be perpetrated by the Legislature of Canada has no parallel in Colonial history. Even in the midst of the American Revolution, the old colonists, during the heart-burnings and ravages of civil war, respected the ecclesiastical endowments made by the Crown against which they were contending." * * *

[The grants made by the Crown were all held by the same tenure—whether to individuals or corporations—

not reservations for certain purposes with power expressly given to Colonial Assemblies to "vary or repeal" them.]

"I feel bitterly, my Lord Duke, on this subject. Till I heard of your Grace's despatch, I had fondly trusted in Mr. Gladstone and his friends, of whom you are one, notwithstanding the present doubtful Administration; and I still argued in my heart, though not without misgivings, that the Church was safe. I have cherished her with my best energies for more than half a century in this distant corner of God's dominions; and after many trials and difficulties I was beholding her with joy, enlarging her tent, lengthening her cords, and strengthening her stakes, but now this joy is turned into grief and sadness, for darkness and tribulation are approaching to arrest her onward progress. Permit me, in conclusion, my Lord Duke, to entreat your forgiveness if in the anguish of my spirit I have been too bold, for it is far from my wish or intention to give personal offence. And of this rest assured, that I would most willingly avert, with the sacrifice of my life, the calamities which the passing of your Bill will bring upon the Church in Canada."

There is a touching pathos in the close of this letter; but the Bishop himself lived to see his apprehended calamities turned into blessings; for the most prosperous and brightest days of the Church of England in Upper Canada have been from 1853 to the present time.

ESSAY IX.

DIVISIONS IN THE WESLEYAN METHODIST CHURCH.

By the late Rev. John Ryerson, written at Brantford, 1864; with notes by E. Ryerson.

THE *Ryan Division—Hallowell Conference, 1824.* In July of the year 1824, the first Canada Conference was held in Hallowell, now Picton. It was during this year that what were called the Ryan difficulties commenced; and because of the importance attached to this matter, I will here give some account of the origin, progress, and first consummation of this unhappy affair, until its termination in the organization of a separate body of Methodists, under the name of the " Canada Wesleyan Methodist Church."

For several years previous to 1824, the question of what was called the election of "Presiding Elders " was much agitated in many parts of the Methodist Episcopal Church. These Elders had always been, as they still are in the United States, appointed by the Bishops. The so-called reform sought for was to take away this power

from the Bishops, and place it in the Annual
Conferences—making the office elective. As
none but the General Conference could effect this
change in the Discipline of the Church, great
exertions were used at the Annual Conferences
to elect delegates to the General Conference who
sympathized with, and would vote for, the "reform."

This was the case in the Genesee Conference,
of which Canada then formed a part. Messrs.
Ryan and Case, the two Presiding Elders in
Canada, were strongly opposed to the electing
of Presiding Elders by each Conference, and were
consequently left out of the delegation, and the
Rev. Isaac B. Smith and the Rev. Wyat Chamberlayne were elected to represent the Canada
section of the Conference. At that time there
was a large majority of the members of the
Genesee Conference in favour of the contemplated reform. Mr. Case bore his defeat with
apparent composure; not so Mr. Ryan, who was
annoyed at the defeat itself, and more so at the
prospective changes in the mode of appointing
Presiding Elders.

In the evening after the adjournment of the
[Genesee] Conference, Mr. Ryan called a meeting
of the preachers from Canada, with the exception
of Mr. Case and such as were known to be
favourable to the proposed reform. In this meet-

ing, held in the open air, Mr. Ryan talked a
great many things, the import of which I could
not quite understand; but among other things,
he said, " A dark cloud hung over the Church;
that this pseudo reform business would split the
Church in pieces from end to end; that the
people, especially in Canada, would never submit to it," etc., etc. By one of the preachers
present it was observed, that " Methodists in Canada did not know or care much about the matter;
and even if some agitation should arise, you,
Elder Ryan and Elder Case, can easily keep all
quiet." To this Mr. Ryan tartly replied that he
knew better than other preachers did the state of
feeling in Canada, and that *we* should get away
from strife before it was meddled with.

Not long after this session of the Conference,
there was a good deal of conversation and cen-
sorious feeling excited in the Church, in the
bounds of Mr. Ryan's district—the Bay of Quinté
District. Late in the autumn of the same year
a Convention was called by Mr. Ryan, to meet
at Hallowell, to take into consideration the state
of the Church. Mr. Ryan did not notify the
delegates to the General Conference to meet him,
nor several of the travelling preachers. At this
Convention, the question of separation from the
Methodist Episcopal Church in the United
States was agitated, and resolutions favourable

to a separation were ultimately adopted by a considerable majority. A Memorial founded on these resolutions was drawn up and signed, to be sent to the American General Conference, asking that body to set off the Methodists in Canada, and constitute them an independent Church. Messrs. Ryan, Case, and David Breakenridge, sen., were appointed a delegation to present and advocate the said Memorial.

With the prayer of this Memorial the General Conference did not altogether comply, but instead set off Canada as an " Annual Conference of the M. E. Church in Canada." The first Conference was appointed to be held the 21st day of the following August, 1824. In reply to the petition of the Canadian memorialists for a separation, the General Conference said that " they thought such a measure at present would be premature ; that sufficient time had not been given to consider the important changes asked for ; that vastly momentous measures should not be hastily adopted. In the meantime they had set apart the Canada part of the Genesee Conference as a separate Conference ; that during the four years that would intervene between that time and the next General Conference, the Canada brethren would manage their own matters as an Annual Conference ; that this would give them full time to deliberate, and better prepare them to conduct their affairs as an independent Connexion, should the taking of such a position be ultimately judged desirable."

This decision of the General Conference by no means pleased Mr. Ryan, who returned to Canada much chafed and disappointed. He complained loudly of the treatment which he and his colleague, Mr. Breakenridge, had received [Mr. Case having declined to go]; he declared that it was the determination of the American Conference never to set off Canada, but to hold the Societies under their control to the last!

But a short time elapsed before there was a great amount of uneasiness created within the bounds of the Bay of Quinté District, which then extended from Port Hope to Ottawa, and the next thing heard of respecting this affair was the assembling of a Convention of Local Preachers of the Bay of Quinté District, for the purpose of taking into consideration the state of the Methodist Societies in Canada.

Mr. Ryan was known to be the mover and promoter of this Convention, during the sittings of which he was on hand in the neighbourhood, though he avoided meeting publicly with the local preachers. The result of these deliberations was the passing of a number of resolutions, the purport of which was, declaring themselves separated from the M. E. Church in the United

States. They also sent out an address to the travelling and local preachers, as also to the members of the Church, calling upon them to unite in forming the Methodist Societies in Canada into a separate and independent Church. Agents were sent out, and meetings were called in most of the principal places within the limits of the Conference, but especially within the bounds of Mr. Ryan's district, who not only headed, but with great activity urged on the movement with all possible haste. Meetings after meetings, principally in the country east of York (now Toronto), made declarations in favour of the local preachers' movements; and everything for the time seemed to indicate that the schism would be a very extensive one.

In the meantime information was communicated to the Bishops of the Church of these doings in Canada; and pressing requests were sent for them to lose no time in visiting this distracted part of their ecclesiastical charge. Accordingly, Bishops George and Hedding, and Dr. Bangs, made arrangements to come to Canada without delay, so as to visit as many Circuits as possible previously to the assembling of our Conference, which was to take place the 26th of August. Bishop George entered the province at its eastern extremity, where he met Elder Case. Bishop Hedding and Dr. Bangs came into the western part of the province. These two deputations (if I may so call them) visited as many Circuits as possible during their very limited time—everywhere preaching and meeting the Societies, and explaining to them the whole matter of the General Conference respecting Canada, and the views and feelings of the bishops and ministers of the General Conference of the M. E. Church respecting that branch of it situated in Canada. These explanations corrected the erroneous impressions the people had received, and proved entirely satisfactory to them. Those who had declared themselves separated from the Church, with the exception of some half a dozen local preachers (who, as Bishop Hedding said, having *tasted* the *pie* of power [as they supposed] did not like to be driven from so sweet a meal), —excepting these few, all retraced their steps, and returned to the fellowship of the Church with more speed and unanimity than they had gone out of it.

This sudden and great revolution of feeling much surprised and disconcerted Mr. Ryan. Bishop George and Elder Case met Mr. Ryan at Mr. Hawley's, near the village of Bath, on the Bay of Quinté Circuit. Mr. Ryan appeared much disconcerted and humbled, for he saw that his plans were being defeated; and in conversation with Bishop George, he said, "I am in your power ; I throw myself upon your generosity ; I leave myself in your hands ; perhaps I have erred and sinned, but I hope my misdoings are not beyond the reach of forgiveness."

Bishop George's deportment towards Mr. Ryan on this occasion was of the most conciliatory character ; he did everything he consistently could to heal Mr. Ryan's wounded feelings, as also did Bishop Hedding and Dr. Bangs at the Conference —endeavouring to reconcile differences between him and other ministers, and to bring back peace to the Church. The Conference, as before stated, was held at Hallowell, now Picton, the 26th day of August, Bishops George and Hedding alternately presiding, accompanied by Dr. Bangs. Numbers of local preachers and laymen from different parts of the province were also present as visitors ; very great interest being universally felt relative to pending matters, and the result of the deliberations of Conference.

During a part of the year before the Conference there had been serious differences between Mr. Ryan and Mr. W. Chamberlayne, Superintendent of Bay of Quinté Circuit. Mr. Ryan had preferred charges, or caused them to be preferred, against Mr. Chamberlayne, and by a Committee selected by himself, had suspended him. When the matters of complaint against Mr. Chamberlayne were brought up in Conference, they were found to consist of the veriest trifles, and the whole affair was dismissed from the Conference. Mr. Chamberlayne had also preferred a series of charges against Mr. Ryan, and had sent them in a letter to Mr. Ryan by one of the preachers, who informed Mr. Ryan, on delivering the letter to him, that it was from Mr. Chamberlayne. On Mr. Ryan's name being called in the examination of character, Mr. Chamberlayne said that he had preferred charges against Mr. Ryan, and was now prepared for their investigation. Mr. Ryan then rose, and, with some apparent surprise, said, " Charges ! charges ! I know nothing about Mr. Chamberlayne's charges. I never received any from him." Mr. Ryan added, " Some time ago, Brother —— put into my hand a letter, saying it was from Mr. Chamberlayne. Supposing it to contain some of his usual invectives, or abuse, I put it in my pocket and never read it." Mr. Chamberlayne was then called upon to read his charges, but he had kept no copy of them, and had none to read. He requested Mr. Ryan to produce them, but Mr. Ryan again replied, " I say I know nothing about your accusations, and if I had my pocket full of them I would not read them for you. It is for you to find and read your own charges." The presiding bishops decided that Mr. Chamberlayne must produce and read his own charges; at which

Mr. Chamberlayne seemed confounded, and looked foolish, while the members of the Conference all laughed. The matter, however, was "laid over," and time allowed Mr. Chamberlayne to furnish himself and Mr. Ryan with the Bill of Complaints. When the matter again came up before the Conference, Mr. Ryan objected that he had not had the timely notice which the Discipline required, and that he protested against being "twitched" up before the Conference in that manner without proper previous citation. At this stage of the proceedings the Bishops and Dr. Bangs interposed their good offices, and so far succeeded in reconciling differences and conciliating parties as, outwardly at least, to settle the dispute, and in a measure to heal the wounds. Mr. Ryan's character then passed.

It was not considered desirable by the Bishops and their advisers to appoint Mr. Ryan again as Presiding Elder, but Mr. Ryan was unwilling to take a Circuit; and arrangements were therefore made to designate a certain region of country situated between the upper waters of the Chippewa River and the lower part of the Grand River, a "Mission," and Mr. Ryan was this year appointed "Missionary to the Chippewa and Grand River and the destitute settlements in those parts." He accepted this appointment, his family residing on his own farm a few miles north of Chippewa River.

The Rev. Thomas Madden was appointed Presiding Elder on the district; and as **Mr.** Ryan **and** he had been warm friends and fellow-labourers in the ministry for many long and toilsome years, it was hoped now that all things would go on pleasantly and peacefully, and that unity would be restored to the Church. But unfortunately it was not the case. Only a few months passed before differences arose between these aged ministers, which towards the close of the Conference year produced a total estrangement between them, and culminated in mutual criminations, until at last they preferred charges against each other. These charges were brought up for investigation at the Conference held at the Fifty Mile Creek, near Grimsby, the 14th of September, 1825. The time of this Conference was much occupied in listening to the disputes, etc., between Messrs. Ryan and Madden. At length matters were finally adjusted so as to afford some ground of hope that peace and quietness. might once more be enjoyed, at least among the preachers. **Mr. Ryan,** according to his request, received a superannuated relation. During this year Mr. Ryan was most of the time travelling through the country, visiting the people and holding meetings in various places—trying to create a belief in the minds of the people that he was a persecuted man; that the itinerant preachers were combined against him, seeking to destroy him; that the Bishops of the American Methodist General Conference would never set off Canada; that the postponement of the measure from 1824 to 1828, for consideration, was a mere ruse for the purpose of gaining time preparatory to stifling the thing altogether; that if ever the Societies in Canada were set off, they would have to set themselves off.

There also appeared in print this year an anonymous "circular," or pamphlet, which was extensively circulated among the Societies throughout the country. This circular-pamphlet professed to give a true account of the difficulties between Messrs. Ryan and Madden, and the proceedings of the Conference in relation to them. It made gross attacks upon the character of Mr. Madden and his family; that the preachers threw a cloak over the falsehoods of Mr. Madden and irregularities of his family, and, indeed, that most of the travelling preachers were no better than Mr. Madden himself.

The author of this pamphlet-circular also accused the Conference of malpractices and tyranny, and of sacrificing to selfishness the interests and welfare of the people.

The Conference of 1826 met in the township

of Hamilton, north of Cobourg, Newcastle District, August 31st, under the presidency of Bishop George. The preachers generally were greatly troubled and dissatisfied, owing to the anonymous pamphlet-circular and general conduct of Mr. Ryan; but more because several of them sympathized with him, secretly abetting his doings, and some of them openly apologizing for many things he did, and which could not be defended. Still no one seemed to know, or felt able to suggest, any plan by which the evils could be remedied.

The authorship of the incendiary pamphlet-circular could not be positively proved, nor the mode and agency of its circulation be certainly ascertained; although, perhaps, *no one* had any doubt that to Mr. Ryan belonged both the authorship and the circulation. Still nothing respecting the matter was done during this Conference; and Mr. Ryan was again returned as "superannuated;" and for another year he derived more or less of his support from the Church which he was now labouring to destroy.

In the course of the following year another pamphlet-circular made its appearance—more insolent and libellous than its predecessor. It attacked the Bishops, and referred to several other preachers by name, impugning their motives and charging them with downright immoralities.

Among the preachers named were Messrs. Case, Madden, William Ryerson, and others ; the whole Conference, with very few exceptions, were held up to reprobation and scorn.

There were some things in the matter and style of the pamphlet that clearly identified Mr. Ryan as its author, and many strong circumstantial evidences clearly proved that he had been concerned, if not chief agent, in its circulation. All these circumstances, together with the uneasiness, heart-burnings, and schisms they caused, induced Mr. Case to prefer charges against Mr. Ryan at the next Conference, which was held in Hamilton, Gore District, commencing the 30th of August, 1827—Bishop Hedding presiding. Dr. Bangs also attended. Mr. Case charged Mr. Ryan before the Conference with the authorship and circulation of the pamphlet-circular in question. Mr. Ryan did not deny the one or the other, but called upon his opponents (as he styled Mr. Case and others) to prove their allegations, saying that every man was held to be innocent until he was proved to be guilty. After a very careful investigation of the whole matter, the Conference judged Mr. Ryan guilty of the allegations preferred against him, and directed that he should be reproved and admonished by the Bishop in presence of the Conference. The admonitory address of Bishop Hedding was in language and manner most kind and affectionate, but was received by Mr. Ryan with many marks of dissatisfaction and unsubmission.

Next morning a note was received by the Bishop from Mr. Ryan, announcing his withdrawal from the Conference. A Committee was appointed to wait upon him, to try and soften his feelings, and persuade him from his purpose of leaving the Church ; but he was quite inexorable, saying that he had not left, nor did he intend to leave, the Church ; he had only withdrawn from the Conference. He expressed a desire, however, once more to speak to the Conference, which request was readily granted. This interview made matters worse; for in his address he endeavoured to justify all that he had stated in the circular-pamphlet, contending for the right of any member thus to defend himself when persecuted and injured. Mr. Ryan then retired, and thus ended his connection with our Church.

But not so the sore troubles and schisms which he subsequently occasioned. We have already stated that Mr. Ryan had for years assiduously spread the belief that the General Conference of the Methodist Episcopal Church in the United States would never set off as an independent Church the Canada connection, and now he harped upon this string more than ever. The domination of Republican Methodism, the tyranny of Yankee Bishops, the fallen state and corrupt character of the preachers in Canada, were the themes of his story, and the subjects of his laments in public and private. Had not the American General Conference, at this time, amicably set off the Canadian Conference and Methodists as an independent Church, no doubt the schism would have been extensive, and Mr. Ryan might have found himself at the head of a large body of followers. As it terminated, all his plans in this respect were defeated.

At the Canada Conference of 1827, it being the last previous to the meeting of the American General Conference to be held in Pittsburg, State of Pennsylvania, May 1st, 1828, five delegates were elected to constitute the proportion of the Canada Conference to the General Conference. The following were chosen—namely, Samuel Bolton, W. Chamberlayne, John Ryerson, William Ryerson, William Slater. A memorial was sent to the General Conference from Canada, petitioning for a separation from the Methodist Episcopal Church in the United States. The Canadian delegates were instructed to use their best endeavours to obtain the organization of an independent Methodist Church in Canada in fraternal connection with the Church in the United States. This subject was most carefully considered, and lengthily and earnestly debated by Drs. Bangs,

Fisk, Capers, Early, Winings, and several others, besides two or three of the Canadian delegates. Ultimately, by a vote of about two-thirds of the General Conference, the measure was carried, authorizing the Canada Conference to form itself into a separate independent Church. One or more of the Bishops was directed to ordain any one as Bishop of the Canadian Connexion who might be elected by the Canada Conference for that office. This intelligence having been officially conveyed to Mr. Ryan, he appeared greatly confounded, and for a time remained apparently undecided as to what course he would pursue. The ministers were encouraged to hope that he would reconsider the course of his proceedings, retrace his way back to the Church, and again become as useful as formerly. But these flattering expectations were doomed to painful disappointment. Only a short time elapsed before Mr. Ryan was again traversing the country, everywhere declaring that he was a member of the Methodist Church ; that he had never withdrawn from it, but had only separated from the preachers of the Conference, by whom he considered that he had been most basely treated, and cruelly persecuted ; that for his conduct and character he was responsible to the Church, and that if he could have a fair trial by its membership, he would abide by their decision whatever it might be.

All he wanted was a full investigation and a fair trial. In order for this, he proposed that there should be a Convention of lay members held on each of the two districts—namely, the Niagara and Bay of Quinté Districts. The Conventions were to be composed of delegates from the several Circuits, to meet in some convenient place in each district. Many of the members of the Church entered into Mr. Ryan's views, by acquiescing in his proposal. One of these Conventions was appointed to meet in Copetown, in the Gore District, and the other was to meet in Hallowell (now Picton), in the District of Prince Edward.

These Conventions were wholly illegal; and the Presiding Elders and most of the preachers opposed them; but a considerable number of very respectable and influential members in a majority of the Circuits (who had known Mr. Ryan in former years) had been induced to favour them; so that they were convened. After carefully considering the matter in all its bearings, it was thought advisable for J. and E. Ryerson to attend the Convention at Copetown. I was the Presiding Elder on the District, and E. Ryerson (his Superintendent having died) was then the minister in charge of the Circuit which embraced Copetown.*

* *Note by E. Ryerson.*—This Convention was presided over by the late Hugh Willson, Esq., of Saltfleet (an

It was perfectly clear, from the commencement of the proceedings of this Convention, that instead of Mr. Ryan being on his trial, it was his object to try and get a verdict against the Conference, and especially against certain of its members, bringing up many and grievous charges against them.

We attended closely every day, and allowed no allegations or statements of an injurious or false character against the Conference or preachers to pass unexamined, however painful the affair might be. The result proved very beneficial to the interests of the Church, in preventing any

old friend of Mr. Ryan, but a true member of the Wesleyan Methodist Church), brother of the late John Willson, Esq., once Speaker of the House of Assembly, and formerly member of the Wesleyan Methodist Church, but who had become dissatisfied and withdrew from the Church, and obtained grants from the Government to assist Mr. Ryan.

The Convention at Copetown lasted *eight* days, and decided *unanimously* against Mr. Ryan's statements and proceedings, and in vindication of the Conference and preachers impeached.

· The late Ebenezer Griffin, of Waterdown, though immersed in the business of his mills, devoted the whole of eight days as Secretary of this Convention. Like his father, the late Smith Griffin, of Smithville, and like his distinguished son, the Rev. W. S. Griffin, he was a true man to the Church, and a liberal supporter of its institutions.

considerable schism, and in maintaining its unity and peace. The Convention decided *unanimously* against Mr. Ryan, and in perfect approval of the proceedings of the Conference respecting him.

This was a terrible blow to Mr. Ryan, to be condemned after eight days' investigation of all the matters of his complaints and accusations, and that by a Convention of laymen of his own getting up, and composed of his own chosen friends. Such a defeat would have discouraged most men; but Mr. Ryan's extreme self-willedness and indomitable resolution when he undertook anything, propelled him on, notwithstanding the entreaties of his friends to return to the Church, and become again useful and beloved as he had been many long years before he commenced this unhappy war upon his brethren.

The Hallowell (or Picton) Convention was appointed some two or three weeks after the Convention at Copetown. By the advice of Mr. Case and myself, Mr. E. Ryerson was instructed to proceed to Hallowell, although it cost him a long journey of some three hundred miles on horseback, at an inclement season of the year.*

* *Note by E. Ryerson.*—Elder Case, the acting Superintendent of the Church, was then at Toronto, and gave me directions to inform him without delay of the result of the Copetown Convention. At the close of the eighth day of the Convention, I got a copy of its decision, and

The proceedings and results of this Convention, which lasted nine days, were similar to those of the Convention at Copetown.

It was now thought that Mr. Ryan would desist from further agitation, and retire quietly into private life, or make his way back into the Church. Alas! this was not the result; he turned round upon the members of his own lay Conventions with as much or more bitterness of spirit than had marked his conduct before against

proceeded about nine o'clock at night on horseback, and reached Toronto about eight o'clock next morning. When Mr. Case read the decision of the Convention he was greatly affected, and thanked God, with many tears, for His providence and goodness to His servants in the ministry and membership of the Church.

I urged the appointment of the late Rev. F. Metcalfe (then stationed minister in Toronto) to meet Mr. Ryan at his second Convention at Picton; and went to bed, exhausted with the unceasing and painful labours of the previous eight days, and the preceding night's journey on horseback. When I awoke in the afternoon, I found that my horse had been shod, and that it had been decided that I must proceed to Hallowell. From my rule of duty, and ordination vows, to "reverently obey our chief ministers," and "submit to their godly judgments," I obeyed orders, but I could not refrain from tears at the hardness of my lot, and in view of the great fatigues and terrible contest that awaited me, especially unaided by the counsels of my ever trusted brother, the late John Ryerson. When I arrived at Hallowell, I

the Conference and its members—impugning
their motives by saying that they had been
bought, and that money had blinded their eyes,
and that justice would be avenged on them for
the sins which they had committed against him
and the truth. He called upon the true Methodists and good people to join with him in reclaim-
ing the fallen Church, and saving the country
from political and religious ruin. The Rev. Isaac
found the whole community in a state of excitement,
and that Mr. Ryan had assembled a Convention of his
friends, and most of them his countrymen, who were so
vehemently hostile to the Conference, that during the
first four or five days of the Convention, when I rose to
defend the Conference, Elder Case, Mr. Madden, etc.,
against the accusations of Mr. Ryan and his right-hand
man, James Jackson, a majority of the members of the
Convention turned their backs to me ; but I took no
notice of this treatment, and proceeded calmly with the
cause I had in hand, until about the fourth or fifth day
of the Convention I observed a manifest change in the
feelings of its members, several of whom came to me
and asked pardon, with deep feeling, for the manner in
which they had treated me. This Convention lasted nine
days, and at the close decided in the strongest language,
and unanimously, against Mr. Ryan's statements and
proceedings, and in favour of the Conference and its
accused members.

Thus by two juries of laymen, of his own selection, and
each consisting of upwards of twelve men, were Mr.
Ryan's statements and conduct condemned, and the
objects of his accusations vindicated.

B. Smith (Mr. Ryan's son-in-law, but between whom and Mr. Ryan there had been variances for many years) and the Rev. James Jackson joined with him in exertions to create dissatisfaction and discord amongst the members of the Church.

A considerable number of Methodists now left the Church, and connected themselves with Mr. Ryan and his friends; so that before very long Mr. Ryan called another Convention for the purpose of organizing (as he said) a reformed and pure Church. At this Convention a constitution of Church government was adopted, providing for lay delegation, elective presidency, etc. After this, the work of making inroads into and dividing Methodist societies was pursued more systematically, but not more successfully than heretofore. This party (which was now called "Ryanite") employed several itinerant preachers, and during Mr. Ryan's life, and perhaps for a short time after, went on with some success, in some places. A few years, however, only elapsed when they began to dwindle and grow weaker and weaker; and had it not been for their becoming united with the "New Connexion Methodists" in England, they would probably ere this (1866) have been among the things which had been.

ESSAY X.

EPISCOPAL DIVISION.

By the late Rev. John Ryerson, written March, 1865, at Brant-
ford ; with Notes and an Appendix by E. Ryerson.

NOW proceed to give some account of the
origin and separation from the Wesleyan
Methodist Church of the party which constituted
themselves into a separate organization, taking
the name of "The Methodist Episcopal Church
in Canada." The resolutions adopted at Hallowell in 1832, proposing a union with the English
Conference, were generally, yes, it may be said
with the utmost truth, *universally*, approved.
Not a murmur or whisper was heard from any
quarter, but quite the contrary. Several local
preachers, who afterwards became leaders in
Episcopal schism, were present at Hallowell (now
Picton), and heard the discussions and resolutions
of Conference ; among whom was Mr. John
Reynolds, who was appointed first bishop of the
party. Mr. Reynolds, then and afterwards,
declared his entire approval of what the Con-

ference had **done,** and **expressed** a pleasurable **hope of** soon witnessing a union with the English Conference, and the relinquishment **of** Methodist Episcopacy in Canada.

The proceedings of the Conference of **1833,** held in Toronto, over which the **Rev. George Marsden** presided, when **the** articles **of union** (which had been agreed **to by** the English **Con**ference) were ratified, were, with equal unanimity, approved throughout the Connexion. During the succeeding year, **no dissent was** heard **from** any quarter until **after the** Conference **held in** June, 1834.

This Conference **was** presided over by **the** Rev. Edmund Grindrod, **having for his** associate the Rev. Mr. (afterwards **Dr.) Alder. At this** Conference some measures **were adopted for the** better regulation **of** several **matters connected** with local affairs [as is **the case in** every Conference]. Among others, some **rules** were adopted for amending and **improving the** regulations regarding local preachers, **called "The** Local Preachers' Resolutions." **There were two things** in these **rules that were** objected **to by** certain parties, namely, **the** discontinuance **of local** preachers' Conferences, and the ordination **of local** preachers. Several **took umbrage at this, among** whom was Mr. Reynolds; and a convention **was** called **(by** whom **I** know **not), to** meet in Belleville (where **Mr.** Reynolds resided) late in the autumn of 1834. This convention consisted of twelve **or** fifteen persons, who adopted certain resolutions **condemning** the "local preachers' resolutions" **of** the Conference, and also expressing disapprobation **of the** union with the British Conference altogether, **out of** which, they said, **the evil they** deprecated had grown. This meeting **of local** preachers **was** held seventeen or eighteen months **after** the union between the English and Canadian Conferences had become ·an accomplished fact, **and two** years and a half after the resolutions proposing the measure to the English Conference had been passed by the Canadian Conference. So that those local preachers with whom originated the so-called Methodist Episcopal Church in Canada, were members of the Wesleyan Methodist more than one year and a half subsequent to the superseding of Episcopacy **by an annual** presidency in our Church, and the completion of the union with the English and Canadian Conferences.

This perfectly agrees with what the Rev. John Reynolds said a little while before the meeting of the local preachers: "The **day** is not far distant when I shall *cease* to be a member of the Wesleyan Methodist Church."

During the spring, **or** early in the summer after this **meeting,** there came together four or five persons, for the purpose, as they stated, of organizing a *General Conference* of the Methodist Episcopal Church in Canada. This meeting consisted of John Reynolds, a local preacher; Joseph Gatchel, a superannuated preacher; and Daniel Picket, who had been a preacher, but was at this time not a member of any Church, with one or two others—all, with the exception of Picket, were members of the Wesleyan Methodist Church. From this little party, the organization of the *General Conference* of the so-called Methodist Episcopal Church in Canada took its rise —thereby causing schism, which for many years disturbed the peace of our Church. This party of separatists became intensely political, boasting of their high reform principles, and accusing the Wesleyans of High Church Toryism, of seeking and obtaining Government support, of selling themselves for money, indeed, of sacrificing everything dear to the religious and political rights of the people to ambitious selfishness; calling upon the Methodists and people everywhere to come out and separate from this Babylon, lest they should become partakers of her sins and involved in her ruin.

Politicians, seeing that the agitation might be turned to some political party purpose, took up their cause with great zeal, and certain political papers teemed with articles on the tyranny,

18

despotism, and political depravity and religious apostacy of Wesleyan Methodism. Indeed, it would seem that for a long time the Episcopal party were impressed with the belief that the destruction of the Wesleyan Methodist Church was an indispensable desideratum to the continuance of their party as a separate body.

The *pseudo* Episcopals, as they were properly styled, made no pretensions at their commencement, nor for a good while after, to be the continuers of the old Methodist Episcopal Church. Thus, their pretence was an *afterthought*.

No pretensions to be owners of the Church property were made until 1836; on the contrary, they made it a matter of boasting and self-congratulation that they had forsaken all, and " come out from among them."

Some three years after the union between the English and Canadian Conferences, they claimed to be *the* Methodist Episcopal Church, (i. e.) the very Church that was separated from the M. E. Church in the United States in 1828; that they never belonged to the W. M. Church in Canada; that some of them remained in the house, but they never belonged to the household; that the Methodist Episcopal Church had always continued, and that the Wesleyan Methodist Church were separatists from them! Monstrous as these assumptions were, the Episcopal party made them, and their confidence seemed to increase as their false assumptions multiplied, and, by frequent reiterations, some of them were doubtless brought to believe the truth of what they so often asserted.

Then followed the pretension that they (the Episcopals) were the legal owners of the Church property, that all the churches and parsonages belonged to them, and that they would take possession of them. This they first attempted by violence, or surreptitiously. Several church doors were forced open, and forcible possession was attempted to be taken of them. Others were entered by stealth, and detention was sought in this way. In the winter of 1836 I had an appointment to hold a missionary meeting in the Switzer Church, Ernesttown. At the close of the services on Sunday, when the people had nearly all gone, I noticed some persons sitting near the door. As I passed them, they hung down their heads, and looked suspicious, as though some ulterior object was the cause of their remaining. With several of them I was well acquainted, and knew they had left our Church and joined the Episcopals. Meeting two or three trustees outside of the church, I communicated to them my suspicions, and advised them to go back and there remain until these persons should leave. It appeared that it was the intention of these individuals to remain until all the people had gone, then to take possession of the church, put a new lock on the door, and, by thus securing it, to possess and occupy it. The trustees, as advised, went back, and requested the persons in question to leave, but they refused to do so; so that they, with the trustees, remained all night, *watching*, certainly, if not praying. On the following morning the Episcopals quietly left, and returned no more to disturb the peace of the society of Switzer Church.

About the same time the Waterloo Church, situated about four miles north of Kingston, was entered by several desperate men, professing to be Episcopal Methodists, who took the lock off the door, put another lock on, and in this way barricaded it against the Wesleyan trustees. After careful deliberation, it was considered best not to attempt forcible entry into the church, but to have recourse to the law to displace the intruders. A writ of ejectment was consequently taken out, and a civil action was commenced. The cause was tried at the Court of Assizes in Kingston, before Judge Macaulay, who charged the jury strongly against the prosecution. The judge—a high churchman and Episcopal successionist—held that Episcopacy being of God, no power on earth could do it away; that if only

one individual in the case before him had continued in his adherence to the Methodist Episcopacy in the Church, all its rights should centre
in him, and if all had gone from Episcopacy,
the Church was gone. He consequently charged
the jury in favour of the defendants, as at least
the most probable owners of the property. The
verdict of the jury (which consisted mostly, if
not entirely, of the political party of defendants)
was according to the charge of the judge, in
favour of the defendants. Judge Macaulay had
little or no knowledge of Church history, especially of the Methodist Episcopacy, or of the
nature of ecclesiastical constitutions adopted for
the government of different Churches; he was
himself a High Church Episcopalian, as far as
he knew anything about such matters, and held
that the Episcopal form of Church government
was ordained of God, and therefore could not
be lawfully superseded. Thus far he acted consistently with his principles.* And certainly the
authorities of the Methodist Church were very
blamable in not seeing that proper information
was given at the time of the trial respecting

* *Note by E. Ryerson.*—On the appeal to the Court
of King's Bench, after Judge Macaulay had examined
the documentary evidence on which the appeal was
found, he declined to re-assert the views he had expressed to the Kingston jury.

the nature and character of Methodist Episcopacy, and of the power given to the General
Conference, by the constitution of the Church,
to control, modify, or even do it away ; and that
the Canada Conference had done nothing more
than the constitution and laws of the Church
freely authorized them to do, and that they had
carefully observed every legal particular in their
proceedings.*

An appeal was made from the judgment of
the Court at Kingston, to the higher Court of
King's Bench at Toronto, which set aside the
verdict of the lower court, and ordered a new
trial. It is only necessary to say at this (second)

---

* *Note by E. Ryerson.*—I think the fault was rather
with legal counsel employed at the trial than with the
" authorities of the Church," who were prepared to give
every explanation and needful authority on the subject ;
but their counsel, Mr. Hagerman—afterwards Attorney-
General, and after that judge—said the case was so plain
that no explanation was necessary, and introduced the
case without a word of remark for the ejectment of a
party who had clandestinely and unlawfully trespassed
upon the property of the trustees, who were plaintiffs in
the case, leaving to the Judge alone, without a single
word or document, the exposition of the doctrine of
Episcopacy, irrespective of the sentiments of the Methodist Church in England, the United States, and Canada,
respecting the rule of Episcopacy and the authority of
the American General and Canadian Conferences in
respect to it.

trial, as also that respecting the Belleville Church
property case, in which the Episcopals were the
plaintiffs, the whole matter was ventilated,*
and the result was, the legal decision of the
highest judicial tribunal of the land confirmed
the Wesleyan Methodist Church as the rightful
owner of the church property, it being the true
representative and successor of the original Methodist Episcopal Church in Canada. These legal
litigations extended over more than two years ;
and the friends of Zion and of peace greatly
rejoiced when they were brought to a just and
final settlement.

* *Note by E. Ryerson.*—I was directed to collect and
prepare documentary and other evidence for this case.
In addition to early editions of the Discipline and other
documents, I travelled as far as Baltimore, U.S., to
consult the old preachers who were members of the first
General Conference in the United States, and had to
do with the organization of the Episcopal government
of the Methodist Episcopal Church. I also consulted
leading ministers of the Church of a later age—such
as Bishop Hedding, Dr. Fish, and others. The answers
of these venerable men, from 1784 to 1837, to the
questions proposed to them, are as follows :

Question. "Has the General Conference power, under any
circumstances whatever, by and with the advice of all the
Annual Conferences, to render the Episcopal office periodically
elective, and to dispense with the ceremony of ordination
in the appointment thereto ? "

The Episcopals, though utterly defeated in their endeavours to obtain our Church property, and also some legal recognition as a Church, if not *the* Methodist Church, still continued to reiterate their claims to being the Methodist Episcopal, which had been set apart from the Methodist Episcopal Church in the United States in 1828.

Answers.

By the Rev. Samuel Luckey, D.D., Editor of the official periodicals of the Methodist Episcopal Church in the United States :

"In my opinion the General Conference undoubtedly has this right. This is evident from the fact that the Discipline provides for the possibility of their doing so—as it is explicitly enumerated among the things which the General Conference shall *not* do without the recommendation of the Annual Conferences, plainly implying that it *may* do it with such recommendation."

By the Rev. Elijah Hedding, D.D., the second senior Bishop of the Methodist Episcopal Church in the United States :

"I believe our Church never supposed the ceremony of ordination was necesary to Episcopacy ; that is, that it could not in any possible circumstances be dispensed with,—nor that it was absolutely necessary that one man should hold the Episcopal office for life."

"We concur in the opinion of Bishop Hedding, expressed above.

(Signed)　　　　　"THOMAS MASON,

"GEORGE LANE,

"Agents of the General Conference for the Publication of "Books for the M. E. Church."

It was not, however, until 1844, that a formal application was made to the General Conference of the M. E. Church in the United States, as *the* Methodist Episcopal Church in Canada, and as a regular or legitimate branch of the Wesleyan family.

In 1844 they sent to the General Conference in the United States a fraternal address, in which they expressed their earnest desire for recognition,

Questions addressed by **E.** *Ryerson* **to Rev. Dr.** *Fisk, President of* *Wesleyan* **University,** *Middletown, Ct.*

"1st. Is Episcopacy held by you to be a doctrine or matter of faith, or a form or rule of Church government, as expedient or not according to times, places, and circumstances?

"2nd. Has the General Conference power, under any circumstances whatever, by and with the advice of all the Annual Conferences, to render the Episcopal office periodically elective, and to dispense with the ceremony of ordination in the appointment thereto?

"And as you were present at the British Conference in 1836, as the representative of the Methodist Episcopal Church in America, I would beg to propose a third query—

"3rd. Do you consider the ordinations performed under the direction of the British Conference to be Scriptural and Methodistical?"

Dr. Fisk's Reply.

"First, in reference to the Episcopal form of government.

"I, as an individual, believe, and this is also the general opinion of our Church, that Episcopacy is not 'a doctrine or matter of faith'—it is not *essential* to the existence of a Gospel Church, but is founded on expediency, and may be desirable and proper in some circumstances of the Church, and not in others.

etc., appointing as their representatives the Rev.
Messrs. P. Smith, David Culp, and John Bailey.
The Wesleyan Methodist Church was also repre-
sented at this Conference by the Rev. John
Ryerson and the Rev. A. Green.

"Next, as to the power of the General Conference to
modify or change our Episcopacy.

"On this subject our Discipline is explicit, that 'upon
the concurrent recommendation of three-fourths of all the
members of the several Annual Conferences who shall be
present and vote on such recommendation, then a majority
of two-thirds of the General Conference succeeding shall
suffice' to 'change or alter any part or rule of our government,
so as to do away Episcopacy *and* destroy the plan of our
itinerant General Superintendency.' Of course with the
above described majority the General Conference might make
the Episcopal office elective, and, if they chose, dispense with
ordination for the Bishop or Superintendent.

"I was a delegate from the Methodist Episcopal Church
to the Wesleyan Conference in England, in 1836. At that
Conference I was present at the ordination of those admitted
to orders, and by request participated in the ceremony. I
considered the ordination, as then and there performed, valid;
and the ministers thus consecrated, as duly authorized ministers of Christ."

I likewise waited upon and proposed similar queries
to the only ministers then living who were in the ministry
in 1784—the Revs. Ezekiel Cooper, Thomas Morrell,
Thomas Ware, and Nelson Reed—four of the finest
specimens of matured piety and undecayed mental vigour
in old age that I ever beheld. From these replies were
received, generally coincident with those already given.
The limits of space prevents our giving them in full.

When the address of the Episcopals was presented, the delegates from the Wesleyan Methodist Church objected to its being received, on the ground of its false assumptions, professing to emanate from the Methodist Episcopal Church in Canada, whereas there was, in reality, no such Church in Canada; and that the party from whom the documents proceeded were a number of local preachers, who, from dissatisfaction, had separated from the Wesleyan Methodist Church, in which they had endeavoured, and not without success, to make schism. They had subsequently organized themselves into some sort of Church order, under the name of the Methodist Episcopal Church in Canada.

After some deliberation on the subject, the General Conference appointed a committee, consisting of nine of its leading members, to whom the address of the Episcopals was referred. The Episcopal and Wesleyan representatives met the Committee, when the latter reviewed the history of the Episcopal schism from its commencement, showing that the petitioners were separatists from the Wesleyan Methodist Church, and that the schism was not commenced on the ground of the Canada Conference superseding Episcopacy by an annual presidency in their mode of Church government, or of their union with the British Conference, but for reasons which had no con-

nection with either; that the men who had commenced the division were local preachers in the
Wesleyan Methodist Church many months after
the relinquishment of Episcopacy for an annual
presidency, and the union between the English
and Canadian Conferences had been consum-
mated. The real cause of the schism was the
discontinuance of the ordination of local preachers
by the Canadian Conference, and, of course, the
ambition of a few to be something greater than
they were, and to be at the head of something,
however diminutive that something might be;
that the meeting of the local preachers, when
the mischief commenced, was held in the year
1835, eighteen months after the union between
the British and Canada Conferences was finally
settled; that what was called their first General
Conference consisted merely in three men getting
together—one a local preacher, one a superannuated preacher, yet a member of, and receiving
support from, the Canada Conference, and the
third no preacher or member of any Church—
these three men getting together and constituting
themselves a *General Conference*, and electing a
local preacher, one of their own number, to be
their Bishop, were doings so monstrous as not
to be thought of without the most profound
contempt and the deepest sorrow.

The above-mentioned, and other facts bearing

on the questions under consideration, were fully established before the Committee of the American General Conference by evidence, the truth of which could not be questioned. The representatives of the Canada Conference also reminded the Committee of the persecuting and aggressive proceedings of the Episcopal party throughout, and of their unscrupulous efforts to destroy the character and usefulness of the Wesleyan ministers—to sow the seeds of discord among, and divide the societies of the Wesleyan Methodist Church; that the worst of motives had been imputed to the preachers, and even vile attacks made upon their moral character, as well as on their official proceedings.

The delegates of the Canada Conference observed that if the Episcopal party had come there in their own real character, as separatists from the Wesleyan Methodist Church in Canada, to solicit the friendship and good-will of the Methodist Episcopal Church in the United States, no one would have objected. But it was quite a different thing when they came *declaring themselves to be the original Methodist Episcopal Church in Canada*, which, in consequence, implied that the Wesleyans were schismatical separatists from the said Church, and which they had the assurance to assert hundreds of times.

The representatives of the Canada Conference

insisted that the application of the Episcopal party should not be granted—that they should not be recognized in any way as constituting a regular branch of the Wesleyan family.

The substance of the above statements, and proved facts, was embodied in the report of the Committee of the American General Conference, and resolutions, founded upon the report, were, after some directions, almost unanimously adopted by the said Conference, declaring that certain preachers from Canada, representing what they called the " General Conference of the Methodist Episcopal Church in Canada," could not be received, nor their request be granted; and that in the opinion of the General Conference the said party should not be recognized as a regular branch of the great Wesleyan family.

Thus ended this unpleasant and painful business, so far as the proceedings of the American General Conference on the application of the Episcopal party is concerned. Of the subsequent proceedings of the Episcopals I have nothing more to say, having pointed out their origin and early doings, as connected with the history of the Wesleyan Methodist Church.

Note by E. Ryerson, *1880*.—It is due to the memory of the late Bishop Richardson to say that he had nothing to do with these calumnies against the ministers of the Wesleyan Methodist Church, as he was a member and minister of that Church, and Chairman of a District, three years after the union took place between the English and Canadian Conferences, in 1833. Early in 1836 the House of Assembly appointed a select Committee to inquire into the question of Government grants to religious bodies, which, among others, summoned the Rev. Messrs. Case, Richardson, and Evans, as witnesses. The following is an extract of the proceedings of this Committee :

"WEDNESDAY, 30th March, 1836.

"Committee met.

"The Rev. James Richardson was called and examined.

"Question 100.—'Are -you a member of the Methodist Conference in this Province, formerly known as the Conference of the Methodist Episcopal Church in Canada ? ' Ans.—' I am.'

"Question 101.—' By what title is the Conference now distinguished ? ' Ans.—' The Conference of the Wesleyan Methodist Church in Canada.' "—*Index to the Journals of the House of Assembly* of Upper Canada, 2nd Session, 12th Parliament, Vol. 1II., p. 10, No. 108.

Note by E. Ryerson.—This Committee, of which W. L. Mackenzie was Chairman, employed every possible means, by cavilling and disingenuous questions, to make out that the Conference of the Wesleyan Methodist Church was a recipient of one of the Government grants to religious bodies ; but utterly failed. Mr. Richardson's evidence was honest and straightforward ; Mr. Evans' evidence was acute and exhaustive, parrying and exposing every attack and insinuation of the Committee ; Mr. Case was exceedingly severe on the Seventh Report of the Grievance Committee of 1835 (written by Mr. W. L. Mackenzie), for its misrepresentations and falsehoods against the Conference and ministers of the Wesleyan Methodist Church in Canada.

Bishop Richardson was a faithful and devout labourer through a long life, and died in the harness of work for his Master. The example and spirit of Bishop Richardson had a salutary influence in abating the acrimony of the Episcopal party in after years. The writer of these essays visited him a few days before his decease, and rejoiced to see his countenance radiant with hope, and find his heart full of love ; and after his departure for his heavenly home, his son, Dr. J. H. Richardson, requested, in accordance with his father's wish, that Dr. Ryerson would be one of the pall-bearers at his funeral—a request readily complied with, whereby the writer had the satisfaction of paying his last respects to the venerable man who had been his first superintendent in the Methodist ministry.

ESSAY XI.

FIRST DIVISION AMONG **THE** METHODISTS **OF** UPPER
CANADA **CAUSED** BY THE **LONDON** WESLEYAN MIS-
SIONARY COMMITTEE, **FROM** 1817 **TO** 1820 ; SETTLE-
MENT **OF** DIFFERENCES **AND** RECOGNITION OF **THE**
TRUE WESLEYAN PRINCIPLES OF METHODISTIC
ONENESS BETWEEN THE ENGLISH **AND** AMERICAN
CONFERENCES ; **INTENDED** VIOLATION **OF THOSE**
PRINCIPLES BY THE LONDON WESLEYAN **COMMITTEE,**
UNDER THE INFLUENCE **OF HIGH** CHURCH **REPRE-
SENTATIONS AND** PROMISED **PECUNIARY GRANTS IN**
1832.

*By the late Rev. John Ryerson ; with Notes by his brother,
Egerton Ryerson.*

*I*NTRODUCTORY *Remarks by E. Ryerson.—*
The late Rev. John Ryerson entered the
Methodist ministry in 1820, while the writer of
these Essays entered it in 1825. Mr. J. Ryerson's
early connection with all Methodist affairs, and
his personal acquaintance with the late Bishop
Emory and other chief ministers of Methodism in
America; his tenacious recollection of the most
minute facts which came to his knowledge ; his
careful accuracy and inviolable integrity in his
statements, qualified him for narrating what came

within his own personal observation, or of which he had been informed. When, as the senior member of the deputation to England, with the late Dr. Green, in 1847, he was introduced by Dr. Bunting to address the Conference Committee on Canadian affairs, Dr. Bunting observed that the Committee might rely with perfect confidence upon the strict accuracy of every statement that Mr. John Ryerson might make to them.

Mr. John Ryerson never wrote a line on any subject of controversy, ecclesiastical or civil; he was an able preacher, and confined himself wholly to the work of the ministry and the general affairs of the Church; he thought and formed his opinions for himself on all subjects, irrespective of friends or adversaries. For no one, perhaps, did he entertain a warmer affection than for myself; yet he scrutinized my acts with rigour, and reproved or remarked upon what he thought was wrong with severity, as will be seen in the following paper:

In 1866 he furnished me with upwards of 200 pages of closely written manuscript, carefully transcribed, containing historical recollections of Canadian Methodism, embracing the most interesting account I have yet read of the Methodist divisions, caused by Mr. Ryan, the Episcopals (given in Essays IX. and X.), and the London Wesleyan Missionary Committee, as also a brief but comprehensive account of the origin and early progress of the various institutions of Canadian Methodism, such as the Missionary Society, Upper Canada Academy (now Victoria University), Domestic Missions, Indian Missions and their agents, the Book Room, Superannuation Fund, Contingent Fund, etc., etc. My brother's historical recollections will, doubtless, at a future day be published in their entirety, with explanatory notes. In the meantime, instead of writing an account myself of the schisms and divisions in Canadian Methodism, I think it best to avail myself of what my late brother John has written on these subjects, supplying some omissions, and adding explanatory notes.

The thirty years' history of Methodism, from 1816 to 1846, its relations to the American and British Conferences, its defence of its religious and civil rights, its schisms and divisions, embraces the least understood, yet most important, period of Canadian Methodism, and must be thoroughly discussed in order to be understood, —not from any party standpoint, or resting on individual statements, but on the authority of documents which were first published from sixty to forty years ago, at the times the events referred to transpired, summarized by the late Rev. John Ryerson in the narrative which follows in this and the next ensuing essay.

Historical Account by the late Rev. John Ryerson.

In the year 1832 a determination was come to, and arrangements made by the Wesleyan Missionary Committee in London, England, to send British missionaries into the Province of Upper Canada. The Rev. Robert Alder (afterwards Dr. Alder), one of the secretaries of the Society, was appointed a deputation to conduct a company of twelve missionaries, who were appointed to take up stations in Upper Canada.

In order to a clear understanding of this matter, it will be necessary to go back to the years 1817 and 1818, and briefly review the proceedings of the London Wesleyan Missionary Committee in regard to this country. It has already been stated that Methodism was introduced into Canada by preachers from the United States. In 1812, just at the commencement of the American war with Great Britain, several of the American preachers who had been appointed to Canada declined coming, as they feared the approaching troubles. The same spirit influenced American preachers in this country—namely, Roads and Densmore, who applied to the Canadian Government for permission to return to their own country. Mr. Ryan, who was left in charge of the work, immediately called out and sent into the field other labourers, by

whom all the circuits were supplied, and the
work maintained in its integrity. After the close
of the war, a few restless spirits sent communications to the Wesleyan Missionary Society in
London, requesting the appointment of British
missionaries in Canada, stating that the preachers
then in the country were American republicans,
enemies to the Government, etc.* The London

*Note by E. Ryerson.—This representation to the
London Wesleyan Missionary Committee was perfectly
untrue in every respect. It has been shown in the first
number of these essays that the first Methodist preachers
came to Canada in its destitution because they were
Loyalists, and the first members of the Church were the
first Canadian Loyalists ; and when, after a few years,
two or three preachers of the New York Conference
volunteered to come into the Canadian work, not from
partiality to British institutions, they declined to accept
appointments to Canada on the eve of the American
war in 1811, and the only time preachers in Upper
Canada of American sympathies—Messrs. Roads and
Densmore—obtained, on application to the Canadian
Government in 1812, permission to return to the United
States ; so that there was not a Methodist preacher in
Upper Canada, during and at the close of the war in
1815, who was not as loyal to the Throne and Government of England as any member of the London
Wesleyan Missionary Committee. It was stated in the
evidence before the Select Committee of the U. C.
Legislative Assembly, in 1828, that no less than four
of the Methodist preachers volunteered their services
in the extremity of their country's danger, and fought

Committee, without having any consultation with
the authorities here, resolved to act on the petitions of the very few individuals who had memo-
rialized them, and forthwith sent missionaries to
Cornwall, Kingston, York, Niagara, and a few
other places. The result of the labours of these
missionaries can easily be conceived, for they
entered not a place where our Methodist preachers

in several battles, in which two of them were wounded.
And, as a witness before the same Committee, the late
Hon. William Dextler, of the District of Niagara, the
theatre and field of the chief battles of the war—himself
a High Churchman—testified that "the Methodists as
a religious sect prompted and encouraged their hearers
in defence of the Province, and in repelling invasions in
that part of the Province where I resided." In the face
of these indubitable facts and testimonies as to the true
loyalty to the Throne of the ministers and members
of the Methodist Church in Upper Canada, the London
Wesleyan Committee, on the *ex parte* representations
of the enemies of Canadian Methodism, without inquiry
as to the truth of the representations, determined to
send missionaries into Upper Canada — not to the
heathen aborigines or the destitute settlements of the
country, but to the principal places where the Canadian
Methodist preachers had visited the people in the destitution and infancy of such places, had formed societies,
and erected places of worship. This first mission of
the London Wesleyan Missionary Committee to Upper
Canada was, therefore, like the two which followed,
wholly political—a war upon the Methodism of the
Province on the false representations of High Churchism.

had **not** laboured before, **and** where societies
had not been formed. These circuits were at
once everywhere disturbed, societies divided, and
all the evils of schism inflicted **on the people.**
Thus things continued, growing worse **and** worse,
until 1820, **when the** General Conference **of the**
Methodist Episcopal **Church in** the United States
resolved **to send a** deputation to **the** British Conference respecting these troubles. **The Rev. John**
Emory (subsequently Bishop) **was appointed on**

So glaringly **unjust and** anti-Methodistic **was this**
proceeding, that, on the representation of the American
Methodist General Conference to the British Wesleyan
Conference in 1820, the latter agreed forthwith to withdraw **their** (political) missionaries from Upper Canada,
while the former agreed to **leave Lower Canada to the**
sole care of the London Wesleyan Missionary **Committee**
and its missionaries, like the provinces **of Nova Scotia,**
New Brunswick, and Newfoundland. **This agreement**
was founded **upon** the **principle laid down by Mr.**
Wesley, and formally avowed **by both** the British and
American Conferences in 1820, **that the** Methodists
were one body (or Church) throughout the world, **and**
were determined to remain so. But Methodism, though
wholly self-supported, **advanced more** rapidly **in Upper**
Canada, and **obtained a** wider **influence than in any**
other province of British America.

This arrangement continued from 1820 to 1832, during
which time a Canadian Conference **was established (in**
1824), **and** the Methodists in Canada were formed into
a separate connexion **from that in the United** States
(in 1828).

this mission. Suffice it to say, that the negotiations of Mr. Emory resulted in an arrangement by which the English Conference agreed to withdraw all their missionaries from Upper Canada, and the Methodist Episcopal Church agreed to withdraw theirs from Lower Canada. This agreement was carried into effect the following year, with the exception of the missionary at Kingston, who, it was supposed, influenced the Missionary Committee in London to refuse (as far as Kingston was concerned) to carry into effect the arrangements agreed upon by the two branches of what both declared to be one Church throughout the world.*

* *Note by E. Ryerson.*—The resolutions of the English Conference, held in Liverpool, August, 1820, and signed by "Jabez Bunting, President," and "George Marsden, Secretary," anticipated by sixty years all that the Methodist Œcumenical Council, to be held in London in 1881, can say on the *oneness and unity* of the Methodist Church throughout the world. I give the following extracts of the resolutions of the English Conference and instructions of the London Wesleyan Committee, from the pen of the noble-minded Richard Watson, who, had he been Missionary Secretary for Canada in 1840, instead of Robert Alder, no separation between the British and Canadian Conferences would have taken place. The resolutions of the English Conference, adopted August 20th, 1820, are as follows :

"On the subject of the unpleasant circumstances which have occurred in the Canadas between the Amer-

This satisfactory adjustment between **the Eng-**
lish and American Conferences again **restored**
unity and concord to the **Church,** which **nothing**
occurred to disturb until **1831,** or early in **1832,**

ican preachers **and our missionaries,** referred **to the**
Conference **by the Missionary** Committee in **London,**
with their **opinion that Upper** Canada shall **be** left **in**
possession **of the** American brethren, **and** that **our**
missionary exertions shall **be** confined **to the Lower**
Province, the **Conference adopted the** following principles .
and arrangements :

" 1. *That as the American Methodists and ourselves*
are but one body, it would be inconsistent with our unity
ana dangerous to that affection which ought to charac-
terize us in every place, to have different societies and
congregations in the same towns and villages, or to allow
of any intrusion on either side into each other's labours.

" 2. That this principle shall **be the rule by which**
the disputes now existing in **the Canadas, between our**
missionaries, shall **be terminated.**

" 3. That the simplest and **most effectual manner of**
carrying **this** rule into effect appears to us to be to accede
to **the** suggestions **of the** American Conference, that
the American brethren shall **have** the occupation of
Upper **Canada and the British** missionaries **that** of
Lower **Canada, allowing** sufficient **time for carrying this**
arrangement into effect, **with all possible tenderness to**
existing prejudices **and conflicting interests on both**
sides ; the arrangements **to be completed within a period**
to be fixed as early as possible **by the Missionary Com-**
mittee.

" 4. That if hereafter it **shall** appear **to any of our**
brethren there, either British missionaries or American

when, as above stated, the Wesleyan Missionary Committee in London again resolved to send missionaries to Upper Canada. I was at that time President of the Canada Conference Mis-

preachers, that any place on either side of the boundary line needs religious help, and presents a favourable opportunity for usefulness, the case shall be referred by the Canada District Meeting to the General Conference, or by that body to the Canada District ; and if either shall formally decline to supply the place on their own side of the boundary, then the other shall be at liberty to supply the said place, without being deemed to have violated the terms of this friendly compact.

" 5. That it shall be explicitly understood in this arrangement that each party shall be bound to supply with preachers all those stations and their dependencies which shall be relinquished by each of the Connexions, that no place on either side shall sustain any loss of the ordinances of religion in consequence of this arrangement.

" 6. That the Missionary Committee be directed to address a letter to the private and official members, trustees, etc., under the care of our missionaries in Upper Canada, informing them of the judgment of the Conference, and affectionately and earnestly advising them to put themselves and their chapels under the pastoral care of the American preachers, with the suggestion of such considerations, to incline them to it, as the Committee may judge proper.

" 7. That the Bishops of the American Connexion shall direct a similar letter to the private and official members, trustees, etc., under the care of the Methodist preachers in the Province of Lower Canada, requesting

sionary Society, and of course of the Missionary
Board, whose meetings were held in York, which
was also my circuit. In the month of May,
1832, I received a communication from the Rev.

them to put themselves and their chapels under the care
of the British missionaries."

The following extracts of a letter of instructions from
the Missionary Committee in London, signed "Joseph
Taylor, Richard Watson, Secretaries," and dated "Wesleyan Mission House, 77 Hatton Garden, London,
23rd August, 1820," furnish a clear exposition of the
application of the above avowed principles to the case of
Upper Canada :

"*Extracts of a Letter of Instructions from the Missionary Committee in London to the Rev. Messrs.
R. Williams and the other British Missionaries in
the Provinces of Canada.*

" Dear Brother,—Herewith we transmit you copy of
resolutions passed at our late Conference, on the subject
of the disputes which have unhappily existed between
our American brethren and us, relative to our missions
in Canada.

" We have given you the resolutions in full, that you
may see that we have recognized the principle *that
the Methodist body is one throughout the world*, and
that therefore its members are bound to cordial affection
and *brotherly union.*

" The resolutions of this Committee, passed some time
ago, and forwarded for your guidance, prohibiting interference with the work of the Canadian brethren, would
show you that the existence of collisions between us
and them gave us serious concern, and that the Com-

Mr. Alder (afterwards Dr. Alder), informing me
that the Wesleyan Missionary Committee in
London had determined to resume their work in
Upper Canada, and that he, with twelve mission-
aries, would, in the course of a few days, sail from
England on this mission.

mittee were anxious to remove, as far as they at that
time were acquainted with thé circumstances, every
occasion of dispute.

"Certainly the case of the Montreal chapel was one
which we could never justify to our minds, *and the Committee have, in many instances, had but a partial knowledge of the real religious wants of Upper Canada, and
of its means of supply.* The *only reason* we could have
for increasing the number of missionaries in that Province was the *presumption of strong necessity, arising
out of the destitute condition of the inhabitants, the total
want, or too great distance, of ministers.*

"On no other ground could we apply money, raised
for missionary purposes, for the supply of preachers to
Upper Canada. The information we have had for two
years past has all served to show that the number of
preachers employed there by the American brethren was
greater than we had first supposed, and was constantly
increasing.

"To us, therefore, it now appears that though there
may be places in that province which are not visited,
they are within the range of the extended American
itinerancy ; and that Upper Canada does not present to
our efforts so fully and decidedly missionary as the
Lower Province, where much less help exists, and the
greater part of the population is involved in Popish
superstition.

It will be necessary for me here to show both the ostensible and real cause of this movement. The controversy respecting the Clergy Lands, called the "Clergy Reserve Question"—involving the equal rights and privileges of the religious denominations—had been going on for

"We know that *political reasons* exist in many minds for supplying even Upper Canada, as far as possible, with British missionaries ; and however natural this feeling may be to Englishmen, and even praiseworthy when not carried too far, it will be obvious to you that this is a ground on which, as a Missionary Society, and especially as a society under the direction of a Committee which recognizes as one with itself the American Methodists, we cannot act.

" 1. Because, as a Missionary Society, we cannot lay down as a principle that those whose object is to convert the world shall be prevented from seeking and saving souls under a foreign Government ; for we do not thus regulate our own efforts.

" 2. To act on this principle would be to cast an odium upon our American brethren, as though they did not conduct themselves peaceably under the British Government, which is, we believe, contrary to the fact.

" 3. That if any particular exceptions to this Christian and submissive conduct were, on their part, to occur, we have not the least right to interfere, unless, indeed, the American Conference obviously neglected to enforce upon offending parties its own discipline. Upon any political feeling which may exist, either in your minds or in the minds of a party in any place, we cannot therefore proceed. Our objects are purely spiritual, and our American brethren and ourselves are one body of

several years. The *Christian Guardian* had taken a leading part against the exclusive claims of what was called the "High Church party." Indeed, the *Guardian*, and the Methodists its supporters, formed the principal, if not the only, serious barrier to the success of the exclusive

Christians, sprung from a common stock, holding the same doctrines, enforcing the same discipline, and striving in common to spread the light of true religion through the world.

"In conformity with these views, we have long thought it a reproach, and doing more injury, by disturbing the harmony of the Connexions, than could be counterbalanced by any local good, that the same city or town should see two congregations, and two societies, and two preachers professing the same form of Christianity, and yet proclaiming themselves rivals to each other, and, in some instances, invading each other's societies, and thus producing party feelings.

"The Committee, previous to the Conference, went with the representative of the American General Conference fully into the discussion of the disputes in the Canadas, and recommend those principles of adjustment which the Conference, after they had been referred to a Special Committee during the time of its sitting, adopted, and which we now transmit to all the brethren in the Canadas.

"You will consider these resolutions as the fruit of very ample inquiry and serious deliberation.

"None of the principles here adopted by us do indeed go further than to prevent interference with each other's labours among the American and British missionaries, and the setting of *altar against altar, in the same city*,

and monopolizing claims of the High Church
party. Every possible effort was, therefore, made
by the High Church party and their friends to
break down and level to the ground this great
mountain of Methodism, which stood so frown-
ingly in the way of their success. Strenuous
exertions were used to destroy or weaken the

town, or village; but knowing that circumstances of
irritation exist, and that too near a proximity might,
through the infirmity of human nature, lead to a violation
of the union which the Conference has deemed it a
matter of paramount importance to maintain, we have
thought it best to adopt a geographical division of labour
of each, and that Upper Canada should be left to the
American brethren and Lower Canada to you.

"Feel that you are one with your American brethren,
embarked in the same great cause, and eminently of
the same religious family, and the little difficulties of
arrangement will be easily surmounted; and if any
warm spirits (which is probable) rise up to trouble you,
remember that you are to act upon the great principle
sanctioned by the Conference, and not upon local prejudices.

(Signed) " JOSEPH TAYLOR and RICHARD WATSON,
" Secretaries."

Remark by E. Ryerson.—Had Richard Watson (the
author of the above truly Wesleyan and patriotic resolutions and instructions) been 'Missionary Secretary in
1839 and 1840, instead of Robert Alder, not a ripple
of dissatisfaction would have disturbed the tranquil unity
of the British and Canadian Conferences, much less a
separation between them, and all the evils of schismatic
divisions in Upper Canada.

influence of Methodism; every seceding party,
however trifling, was encouraged. Ryanism was
openly patronized by Churchmen, who utterly
hated everything connected with Methodism.
Mr. Ryan and his friends received direct pecuniary assistance from Dr. Strachan and his friends.*

But in spite of all, the circulation and influence
of the *Christian Guardian* (then the leading
newspaper in Upper Canada) increased daily; the
number and power of the Methodist Church grew
more and more every year; so that the greedy few
felt that their prey was in great danger of being
lost. For their protection, justice was out of the
question; and every scheme and effort to divide
and defeat the friends of right and truth having

---

* "The Conference of 1827 was held at Hamilton,
and commenced its session on the 30th of August,
Bishop Hedding presiding. The Rev. Henry Ryan
withdrew from the Church. Mr. Ryan having now
severed all connection with the Church, set to work
to more perfectly arrange the plans which he had for
some time been forming, of effecting such a division
in the Church as should eventuate in a general disruption. To this course he was urged by the counsel,
and encouraged by the aid, of parties who, high in
authority, were still, as ever, the bitter, unscrupulous
enemies of Methodism, and judged this one of the best
methods of retarding its progress in the country. Among
those who thus urged Mr. Ryan on were the Hon.
John Wilson, the then Speaker of the House of Assembly, who had formerly been a member of the M. E.
Church, but who had become dissatisfied; and Dr.

failed, they knew not what to do or on whom to call for help.

One thing, however, remained to be done, which was to try again the plan of 1817 (to divide the Methodist Church by sending English missionaries into Upper Canada), which had been defeated by the measures entered into between the English and American Conferences in 1820. The Government and Church party (for they were but one party, under the control of the Archdeacon of York), therefore, lost no time in mastering a plan to induce the British Conference again to undertake the occupancy of Upper Canada as missionary ground, and forthwith to send missionaries into the province for that purpose. A correspondence was opened between the head of the Canadian Executive Government, Sir John Colborne, and the Wesleyan Missionary Committee, on the subject of the new missionary enterprise into Upper Canada.

Strachan, Mr. Ryan's former opponent, who took this opportunity of manifesting his contempt for, and hatred of, the Methodist Bishops, and of that form of Methodism which had accomplished so much for the Canadian people by its opposition to the establishment of a State Church, by sending Mr. Ryan the sum of $200 to assist in what he professed to consider the praiseworthy effort to break up and destroy those Yankee Methodists."—*Webster's History of the M. Church in Canada*, chap. xvii., pp. 200, 201.

ESSAY XII.

CONDITIONS AND WORKING OF THE UNION UNTIL 1838;
RE-ELECTION OF EGERTON RYERSON AS EDITOR;
HIS EDITORIAL PROSPECTUS, DEFINING THE OBJECTS
OF HIS ELECTION AND HIS INTENDED COURSE OF
PROCEEDING; THE FIERY TRIAL COMMENCING.

*By the late Rev. John Ryerson; with Notes by his brother,
Egerton Ryerson.*

THE Canadian Government had stated that
Methodism in this Province was republi-
canized by the labours and influence of Yankee
preachers, the majority of whom were enemies to
British institutions and government; that by
their power the connection between the Colony
and the Mother Country was not only weakened,
but actually endangered; and that if their influence was not reduced, and their democratic
course checked, they would endanger the integrity
of the United Empire, and throw the Province
into the hands of the United States; that it was
indispensable for the British Conference to send
without delay British missionaries to every principal place in Upper Canada.

These *disinterested patriots* [headed and directed by the Archdeacon of **York**] enforced their reasonings by the *golden* argument "That **in** case of compliance on the part of **the London** Wesleyan Committee, there would be granted out of the *casual and territorial* revenue of the Crown [not Clergy Reserve revenue] **the sum** of one thousand pounds sterling per annum towards the support of such Canadian Missions." By these arguments and considerations the London Wesleyan **Committee** was convinced that **it** was their duty **to** consider the call from Canada **as** *providential,* **and** therefore came to the **conclusion to** re-occupy the Province **of** Upper **Canada as** *missionary ground.*

Of this **we were advertised, as before stated,** by Dr. Alder's letter. This announcement **of the** London Wesleyan Missionary Committee, and **the** appointments they had absolutely made, **were to us** like thunder-claps. **For** eight or nine years our Church had been wading through deep **waters** of **affliction, and enduring** fightings without and **fears within,** while **contending** for **right to** hold property **on** which **to** erect **places of** worship and **in which** to **bury our dead, the** right to solemnize matrimony, against **the Clergy Reserve** monopoly, **and for** equal rights **and** privileges **before** the law with **the Church of** England, **in** effecting **[by mutual** consent] **our** separation from the Methodist Episcopal Church in the United States and our organization into an independent Church, preceded and followed as it was by the tumults and schisms of Ryanism. And now, when peace and quiet had apparently returned, and when expectations of increased prosperity were beginning to cheer us, to receive such an announcement was disheartening and crushing beyond what can be expressed. It was easy to predict what would be the result of rival Methodist congregations in every town and principal neighbourhood, and the rival congregations served by able ministers from England.* Oh! the darkness in the future! What a cloud seemed to spread over the whole Methodist family in Upper Canada!

My sadness was very great; for many days I ate little and slept less. My consolation and hope was in God only; and in this state I gave myself to fasting and prayer. One day, while walking along Bay Street, pondering in my mind

* This Mission was in direct violation of the principles avowed by the English Conference and instructions of the London Wesleyan Missionary Committee, as previously quoted. But Richard Watson was no more, and his successor was more of a High Churchman than Wesleyan in Canadian affairs, and at length left the Methodists altogether, obtained orders in the Church of England, and died several years since as Canon in the Cathedral of Gibraltar.—*Note by E. Ryerson.*

what would be the result of pending matters, and that if there was any possible way by which the impending evil could be averted, it came into my mind suddenly, as though some supernatural power had suggested it, whether or not some arrangement could not be entered into by which the two Conferences could be united, and thus mutually help and strengthen each other, instead of devouring one another, as the enemies of Methodism were seeking that they should do, and thus prevent the further schemes and evils of divisions. The more I thought of this, the brighter the streak in the cloud seemed to grow; and I resolved to suggest the matter to the Editor of the *Christian Guardian*—then the only minister in the town of York besides myself. At the earliest convenience I mentioned the matter to him, in which, after some consideration, he concurred. After several interviews and conversations on the subject, we agreed upon the outlines of a plan of pacification, or one to *prevent* strife. I visited and conversed with the several members of the Missionary Board and all the leading members of the Church within my charge. The time approached for Dr. Alder's arrival, and it was agreed upon among us, that after he came I should call a meeting of the Missionary Board and invite Dr. Alder to attend, when the whole matter should be discussed, and finally to propose our plan to him. In a few days Dr. Alder arrived, accompanied by two or three missionaries. The Missionary Board met; the whole matter was considered; and the proposals, previously agreed upon among ourselves, were made. Dr. Alder requested time to consider the matter, and, after various conversations, provisional arrangements were come to; articles of settlement were agreed upon, substantially such as those that received the sanction of both the British and Canadian Conferences, and became Articles of Union between them from 1833 to 1840. At the request of our Missionary Board, Dr. Alder consented to remain in Canada, and meet our Conference, to be held in the town of Hallowell (now Picton) on the 18th of the following August. After long and careful consideration, the Conference, by a large majority, agreed to adopt the Articles of Settlement which had been proposed by the Missionary Board at York. The Rev. E. Ryerson was appointed representative to the British Conference for the purpose of accomplishing the final settlement and definitely arranging the whole matter.*

Note by E. Ryerson.—I think there is very little reason to doubt that Dr. Alder and his High Church friends in Toronto (with whom he was in constant consultation) supposed and assumed that placing the Canadian Missions and Conference in connection with, and

During the session of the British Conference which was held in Manchester, August, 1833, the Articles of Union between the British and Canadian Conferences were satisfactorily settled, and the Rev. George Marsden was appointed first President of the Canadian Conference, and the Rev. Joseph Stinson was appointed Superintendent of Canadian Missions. Thus ended the great matter of settlement by which threatening danger was avoided, the foundation was laid for conserving the peace and unity of the Church, and for promoting its usefulness.

After a few years, however, another dark cloud came over our Church, and she was again doomed to pass through a fiery ordeal and to drink deeply the waters of affliction. "The Clergy Reserve Question" has been mentioned; and for several years the British Conference and their representatives in Upper Canada cordially co-operated with the *Christian Guardian* and the Conference in defending and maintaining the equal rights and liberties before the law of all

in subordination to, the British Conference would paralyze, if not lead to the suspension altogether of the exertions of the Canadian preachers against the establishment of Church-of-England supremacy and monopoly in Upper Canada. How their policy and expectations were defeated and disappointed will appear in subsequent notes.

religious persuasions, and in opposing the pretensions and claims of the High Church party
to the power and revenue of a dominant Church.
And it is more than possible that they would
have continued to do so but for the troubles in
the country in 1837, called the " Insurrection," or
"the Mackenzie rebellion." These political and
civil disturbances greatly agitated the country;
and when they were over, the "Family Compact"
(*i.e.*, Dr. Strachan and his supporters) endeavoured
to make High Church capital out of them, by
representing that the whole mischief had grown
out of the opposition of the pretenders and advocates of equal rights and liberties, but who were
really opponents of the British constitution and
government. After aiding to suppress the rebellion, and when the heat of it was over, the
Christian Guardian resumed the discussion of
the Clergy Reserve question, and insisted that
it should now be settled; that this bone of
contention should now be taken out of the
way; that equal religious and civil rights should
now be established for all Christian denominations; and that sectarian monopoly and exclusive
party government should be *bygones forever*. But
nothing was further from the thoughts of Dr.
Strachan and his friends, together with Sir George
Arthur, the Governor, than such an equitable
settlement. They bitterly contended that any

mooting of these questions at the present time was evidence of the disloyalty of the parties who, they alleged, were endeavouring to despoil "The Church" of its lawful rights. The Editor of the *Guardian* was threatened with personal violence, with prosecution, and banishment.

Yet still the *Guardian* kept on the even tenor of its way; and in proportion to the fury of the monopolists did the Editor of the *Guardian* increase his exertions to wrest from them their unjust gains. Then the opposers of equal rights, seeing that nothing else would do, called in requisition the old craft, to divide the Methodists, or at least, by means of a new party, to *coercively control* them. Sir George Arthur [the amanuensis of Dr. Strachan in these matters] wrote to the Wesleyan Missionary Committee in London of the evil and disturbing doings of the *Christian Guardian* and its supporters, and calling on them for their interference. Such an appeal was, of course, flattering to the vanity of the Committee, from whom Sir George Arthur received a very complimentary and *encouraging* reply. The Committee also wrote to the Rev. Messrs. Harvard, Stinson, and Richey, and directed their interposition in arresting the unjustifiable course of the *Christian Guardian.* The matter [or rather *pretext*] of complaint was not so much that the *Guardian* discussed the settlement of the Clergy

Land question, but that it had become *party political;* that its course was disquieting to the country and disreputable to Wesleyan Methodism, which had always been reputed for its loyalty and conservatism. It is not to be denied that the course of the *Guardian* at this time was very political for a religious journal, the organ of a Church, and many of its best friends thought it ought in this respect to modify its manner of proceeding.* But the Editor was firm and

---

* It is true, as my late brother has intimated, that the *Guardian* was "intensely political," because the Editor was intensely in earnest on the great object for which he had been elected by his Conference. Some of his friends thought he should be more conciliatory, and compromise ; but the times of his former proposed conciliations and compromises were now past. He felt the awfulness of the crisis and the responsibility of his position. The reform party had been crushed by the Rebellion of 1837, and the reform press silenced ; there was in fact no reform party. The High Church party thought their day of absolute power and ecclesiastical monopoly had dawned. It had been agreed by W. L. Mackenzie and his fellow-rebels in 1837 to hang Egerton Ryerson on the first tree they met with, could they apprehend him. He alone stood above successful calumny by the High Church party, and backed as he was by his Canadian brethren, he determined to defend to the last the citadel of Canadian liberty, by whomsoever or from whatsoever quarter assailed. He knew that as in a final struggle for victory between two armies, when victory was trembling in the scales,

unyielding, contending "that **all** the political questions then pending **had a** direct or indirect bearing **on** the *great question;* that in warfare, belligerents were not expected to be exceedingly nice **in** regard to the instruments they employed **in** making a breach into **the** enemy's camp and pulling down his bulwarks; that he employed no illegitimate **means, but that he** would not be turned aside **from** the great object **until it was**

the wavering **of** a single battalion on either **side might** animate and decide victory **in** favour **of the** enemy; so a compromising sentence or ambiguous word **from the** Editor might rouse the High Church **party to increased** confidence and action, and proportionably weaken **the** cause of civil and religious liberty **in Upper Canada.** The Editor of the *Guardian* had no fear, as **he evinced** none. **He had** studied and **learned the principles of** British **constitutional** government, **not from party news-** **papers or politicians** (for he **knew none); but, before** he was twenty years of age, or **knew** any political man, he had studied *Paley **on** Political Philosophy,* especially on the *British Constitution;* and *Blackstone's Commen-* *taries on the Laws of England,* especially on the Rights of the Crown, of Parliament, of the Subject, etc.; besides *Locke on* **Government,** *Bingley's* **British Characters,** etc., and he has **been through** life swayed **no more by** poli- tical than by religious parties, but has written and acted in public affairs, irrespective of sect **or party, according** to the great principles of constitutional and **just govern-** ment which he had learned before **he knew anything** **of** political parties or party politicians.

attained; that the real object of the Government and the London Missionary Committee was not so much to prevent the introduction of politics into the *Guardian* as the discussion of the Clergy Reserve question itself, and the equal religious rights of the people altogether, so that the High Church party might be left in peaceable possession of their exclusive privileges, and their unjust and immense monopolies, without molestation or dispute." This latter statement of the Editor was doubtless *the truth;* and had he yielded to the dictation of Sir George Arthur's government and ꞏthe interference of the London Missionary Committee, *one-seventh* of the land of the Province might now be in the hands of the Church of England. But the course of the *Guardian* and the firmness of our Conference in this matter, however right, brought upon them calamities and sufferings of seven years' continuance.

The Government and the London Committee, however, were not to be diverted from *their* purpose; letters and verbal communications passed between the parties, which so far from settling differences only increased them, and matters every day became more and more complicated. In the spring of 1839 the Rev. Dr. Alder was sent to Canada [professedly] for the purpose of ascertaining the state of things and parties, and, if possible, of adjusting matters, that he might report to the Committee, "What of the night? what of the night?"

Soon after Dr. Alder's arrival there was published a pamphlet signed "M. Richey and J. Stinson," professedly giving a correct statement of the misunderstandings and controversy between the two bodies. An attempt was also made at arguing the subject; but it was a very lame and weak production, doing neither good nor harm. All parties looked upon it as a sort of weakling, that made its appearance out of due time. Still the friends of the Conference thought that Messrs. Richey's and Stinson's pamphlet should be answered and its fallacies pointed out. [An easy task, for however Drs. Richey and Stinson might excel in the pulpit, like Dr. Alder, they were feeble in argument and controversy, and Dr. Alder was not much better.] This was only three weeks before the meeting of Conference; but the Editor of the *Guardian* prepared and published an answer [including an answer to an elaborate letter from Dr. Alder, addressed to and published by the Editor], which was ready for distribution at the time of the meeting of the Conference. Dr. Alder attended the Conference [which was held in Hamilton, June, 1839]; during which all the subjects of dispute were carefully considered and earnestly discussed; the result of which was the reconciliation of parties and the [apparent] healing of the breach.

Appendix by Egerton Ryerson to the First Part of the foregoing narrative by the late Rev. John Ryerson.

Several circumstances of which my late brother was not aware, or to which he did not attach much importance, are omitted in the foregoing narrative.

1. Dr. Alder brought a letter to Sir George Arthur, signed by Dr. Bunting and the other Missionary Secretaries, condemnatory of the Editor of the *Guardian* and eulogistic of Sir George Arthur's Government. This letter was forthwith published in the *Patriot*, the organ of the Government. This letter was regarded by the High Church party as an extinguisher of the Editor of the *Guardian*, who, however, inserted and replied to the letter in the next number of the *Guardian*. Dr. Alder proposed to vindicate the Missionary Secretaries' letter, and to expound his own position, for which purpose the Editor of the *Guardian* offered him the use of its columns. Dr. Alder availed himself of the offer, and was replied to by the Editor.

2. Dr. Alder attended the Conference at Hamilton, June, 1839, and introduced resolutions expressive of his views, to which he insisted upon

the concurrence of the Conference. The resolutions were discussed for some three days without the Editor of the *Guardian* saying a word; until Dr. Alder complained that Mr. Egerton Ryerson had not condescended to make any statement or explanation. Mr. E. Ryerson said he would speak when he thought it expedient; and the following day discussed, in a speech of upwards of two hours, the whole of Dr. Alder's statements and position. Dr. Alder acknowledged the argumentative power of the defence, but attempted no reply, and seemed to despair of success. His resolutions were rejected by the Conference by a majority of fifty-five to five. Mr. E. Ryerson was re-elected Editor of the *Guardian* by an almost unanimous vote of the Conference.

Dr. Alder appeared disappointed and depressed; and after the close of the Conference I said to him, as nearly as I can recollect, in the following words: "Dr. Alder, you see how inapplicable your views are to this country—how entirely you have mistaken the state of Canadian society, the views and feelings of the Methodist people and of our Connexion. Now, I do not wish that you should return to England with the stamp of a defeated and disgraced man. I will tell you what I propose to do. I purpose to write a short editorial for the *Guardian*, stating that the differences and misunderstandings which

had arisen between the London Wesleyan and
Canadian Conferences, after having been carefully considered and fully discussed, were adjusted
in an amicable spirit and the unity of the Church
maintained inviolate."

Dr. Alder appeared delighted and thankful
beyond expression at such an announcement. I
prepared the editorial article and read it to him
before giving it to the printer.

Dr. Alder used and interpreted this editorial
article as a part of the report of his mission,
on his return to England, to show that the
Canadian Conference and its Editor had acceded
to all his demands, and that he had been completely successful in his mission to Canada, when
every member of the Canadian Conference knew
that neither the Conference nor its Editor had
receded one iota from their position or course
of proceeding. The London Wesleyan Committee adopted resolutions complimentary to Dr.
Alder for the ability and success with which
he had executed his Canadian mission, while the
Editor of the *Guardian* smiled at this little
by-play for the gratification of Dr. Alder, when
published in the London *Wesleyan Watchman*,
but did not imagine that Dr. Alder's fictitious
representation of the results of his mission would
be made the authority or ground of charges
against himself.

In the meantime the discussion on the question of a dominant Church monopoly and party absolution and proscription in the Government waxed hotter and hotter. A Royal Commission had been appointed to investigate the state of things in Canada; the constitution of Lower Canada had been suspended; rumours prevailed of a change of Government in Upper Canada; the High Church party felt that this was their time, and perhaps their last chance, to confirm their absolute power and Clergy Reserve monopoly; the elections of 1836 and the rebellion of 1837 had crushed the Reform party, silenced or rendered powerless the Reform newspaper press, and the High Church party were completely in the ascendant until the arrival of the Earl of Durham as Her Majesty's High Commissioner, and the superseding of Sir George Arthur by the appointment of the Right Hon. Poulett Thompson, afterward Lord Sydenham.

To enable the reader to understand the nature and the importance of the crisis then approaching, and the circumstances under which, and the purposes for which, I was elected Editor of the *Guardian* to meet it, it will be necessary for me to go back a little and state the following facts:—

From December, 1835, to March, 1837, I was in England, at the request, even command, of

21

the English President (Rev. Wm. Lord), who had
got into financial difficulties with the Wesleyan
Committee, which had dishonoured his bills of
exchange to the amount of £1,800 sterling, and
during which time I relieved Mr. Lord of his
difficulties and obtained a Royal Charter and
grant of £4,000, besides private subscriptions, in
behalf of what is now Victoria University. On
my return to Canada in the spring of 1837, I
was urged to resume the editorship of the *Guardian;* but I had promised our people in Kingston,
from whom I was suddenly removed in the
autumn of 1835, that I would remain with them
at least a year on my return to Canada. I will
here quote the account of the whole affair, and
of the conditions and objects of my ultimately
resuming the editorship of the *Guardian,* as
published in 1841, in London, in my vindication
against the attacks of the London Wesleyan
Committee, the soundness of which has never
been questioned :

"I was solicited to accept the editorship of
the *Guardian* in June, 1837, but I refused, and
begged my friends to retain the then Editor.
In the course of that year I was reduced to
the alternative of treating the most earnest entreaties of the principal preachers with indifference, resisting the appointment of the Conference,
or accepting the editorship of the *Guardian*

[which I disliked, delighting in the ministerial and pastoral work]. And amongst the most earnest of those preachers with whom my remonstrances were unavailing, was the Rev. **Mr. Stinson**, the London Wesleyan Committee's Superintendent in Upper Canada, with whom also agreed the **Rev. Mr. Richey**, the Committee's Assistant Superintendent here. It was their opinion, as well as that of others, that High Church domination required a more decided opponent, and Methodist rights and religious equality a more energetic advocate, than the then Editor. This will appear evident from the extract of a letter addressed by **Mr. Stinson** to a leading preacher (**Rev. John Ryerson**), a few weeks before the Session of the Conference at which I was elected Editor. It is dated **April 7th, 1838.** The extract is as follows:

"'I am quite of your opinion, that Brother Egerton (Ryerson) ought to take the *Guardian* next year. *There is a crisis approaching in our affairs,* which will require a vigorous hand to wield the defensive weapon of our Conference. There can be no two opinions as to whom to give that weapon. *We now stand on fair grounds to maintain our own against the encroachments of the oligarchy, and we must do it or sink into a comparatively uninfluential body. This must not be.*'

"It will therefore be seen, that my appointment as Editor was not only promoted by the representative of the London Wesleyan Committee, but with the express view of resisting the 'encroachments of the oligarchy'—that is, of the High Church party. Messrs. Stinson and Richey had not at that time received instructions from Dr. Alder to support the pretensions of the High Church party in Canada.

"As the justification of the Committee's hostile proceedings turns, in a great measure, and the Committee's charges against me depend entirely upon the conditions on which, and the objects for which, I was appointed Editor of the *Guardian* in June, 1838, it is important that I state them.

"Here, then, let the following things be noted : —1. Messrs. Stinson and Richey voted for me as Editor. 2. Previously to my election, I stated at large to the Conference my intended course in regard to the religious and civil affairs. 3. I then embodied in an editorial prospectus the substance of what I had stated to the Conference. 4. When I published that exposition of my views and intended editorial course, it was objected to by no party or individual that I ever heard of, but seemed to satisfy our own preachers and societies generally—even those who have since been drawn away from us—and was never objected to by Dr. Alder or his colleagues in London. The following extracts from my editorial prospectus, published in the *Guardian* of the 11th of July, 1838, will show whether I concealed my sentiments, and subsequent events are my witness whether I have not consistently, firmly and honourably maintained the views and purposes I then stated and avowed. The extracts are as follows :—

(From the Canada Christian **Guardian,** *July 11, 1838).*

"'In respect to the ecclesiastical affairs of this Province, notwithstanding the almost incredible calumny which has in past years been poured upon me by antagonistic party presses, I still adhere to the principles and views upon which I set out in 1826. I believe the endowment of the priesthood of any Church in this Province will be an evil to that Church as well as impolitic in the Government. I have never received one personal favour nor one farthing for my own gain from the Government or public treasury, or from any political man or party whatever ; and by the grace of God, I will not rob myself, nor allow myself to be robbed, of that ground of glorying, whatever may be my views of general measures. In accordance with the declaration put forth by several principal ministers of the Methodist Church, in January

last (called and presided over by the Rev. Wm.
M. Harvard, at that time President of the Canadian Conference, by the appointment of the
British Conference), I believe that the appropriation of the Clergy Reserves to educational purposes will be the most satisfactory and advan-
tageous disposal of them that can be made. If
in the way of such a disposal of the Clergy
Reserves insuperable obstacles should be thrown
in the way (although I believe nothing is politically impossible with the Earl of Durham in
these Provinces), I think the next best settlement of that question will be to divide the
proceeds of the Clergy Reserves among the
different religious denominations (according to the
plan proposed by several Methodist ministers,
last winter) in proportion to what is raised by
each; leaving to the discretionary disposal of
each religious body its own apportionment. In
connection with such a possible adjustment of
the question, I think proper to observe that
in the event of any part of the proceeds of
the Clergy Reserves being apportioned to the
Methodist Church, it has been determined to
apply that amount—1. To educational purposes,
that the means of education may be brought
within the reach of youth as much as possible.
2. To assist the members and friends of the
Church in the erection of churches and par-

sonages; **but** not a farthing of it to be for the endowment of the clergy in any way whatever.

" ' To the very natural and important inquiry, in relation to *civil affairs,* ' Do you intend to be neutral ?' I answer, No, I do not; and for the simple reason, I am a man, and a British subject, am a professing Christian, and representative of a British community. At one period, in Greece, Solon enacted a law inflicting capital punishment upon all neuters. The present is an epoch in the affairs of this Province in which no man of intelligence or consideration can be safely or justifiably neutral. *The foundation of our Government is being laid anew; the future character, and relations, and destinies of the country are involved in pending deliberations; the last whisper of rebellion is to be silenced in the land.* My decision, however, is not one of party, but of principle—not one of passion, but of conviction—not of partial proscription, but of equitable comprehensiveness. To be explicit as well as brief, *I am opposed to the introduction of any new and untried theories of government.* As the organ of the Methodist Church, I assume that the doctrines and discipline of that Church are true and right. I take them for granted as far as the members of that Church are concerned, and expound, and recommend, and act upon them accordingly. So in civil affairs, I assume that this country is to remain a portion of the British empire, and view every measure, not in reference to every or any abstract political theory, however plausible that theory may be, but in reference to the well-being of the country in connection with Great Britain. As in Church affairs I take my stand upon the constitution of the Church in its doctrines and rules, as expounded by its fathers and ablest theologians, and illustrated by general usage; so, in civil affairs, I take my stand upon the *established constitution* of the country, as expounded by royal despatches, and illustrated by the usages of the British Parliament, British Courts of Justice, and the common law of England. Nothing more is wanted to render this Province happy and prosperous than the practical and efficient application to every department of our government, and to our whole system of legislation, of the principles and instructions laid down in the despatch of the Earl of Ripon, addressed to Sir John Colborne, dated 8th November, 1832, and the despatch of Lord Glenelg, addressed to Sir F. B. Head, dated 15th December, 1835.

" 'If past partizanship and party combinations be forgotten—if the great body of the inhabitants will unite as one man to lay the foundation and erect the superstructure of an impartial and popular Government, a few years at most will bring about what His **Excellency** the **Earl** of Durham has avowed it to be the great object of his mission to accomplish—to lay " the foundation of such a system of government as will protect the rights and interests of all parties, allay all dissensions, and permanently establish, under Divine Providence, the wealth, greatness and prosperity of which such inexhaustible elements are to be found in these fertile countries."

" ' In conclusion, it is but just that the readers of the *Guardian* and the public should know that the foregoing article contains a mere summary of what I avowed before the late Conference, in a lengthened address of some hours, previous to being elected to my present office by a ballot vote of forty-one to sixteen. I feel, therefore, strongly sanctioned in those principles, and views, and purposes ; but I am deeply sensible of my fallibility. I pretend to no exemption from the ordinary errors and infirmities of humanity ; I confess myself liable even to imprudences. In promoting, therefore, the varied objects of the *Guardian*, I must crave the indulgence and forbearance of its readers, as well as hope for their confidence and support—depending primarily, ultimately and entirely upon the favour of Him without whose blessing nothing is wise, or good, or strong.

(Signed)   " ' EGERTON RYERSON.'

"I will appeal to every candid man in England whether I could have been more frank and explicit in the expression of my sentiments, and in the avowal of my intended course of proceeding.

"A few months after, it was found that Sir George Arthur, late Lieutenant-Governor of Upper Canada, had thrown himself into the hands of the 'oligarchy' on the question of the Clergy Reserves—would not consent to have them applied to any other purpose than the support of the clergy, and was anxious to get them reinvested in the Crown. When Sir George Arthur's views and plans were brought before the Provincial Legislature, I opposed them. The Wesleyan Committee in London interposed to support Sir George Arthur on that question, and sent a letter to Sir George disclaiming all participation in the views of the Canada Conference advocated by me—and sent a letter to Mr. Stinson instructing him to oppose me and support a Church Establishment in this Province. Messrs. Stinson and Richey turned round, and from that day forward supported the 'oligarchy' which they had elected me to oppose. However, Her Majesty's Government subsequently set aside the proceedings of Sir George Arthur upon the very grounds on which I had opposed them ; but that

made no difference in the feelings of Dr. Alder
and his colleagues.

"At the Canada Conference of June, 1839 (held
at Hamilton), Dr. Alder was present, when I
vindicated the consistency and expediency of the
course I had pursued, was sustained by the
Conference, and stated that I should feel it my
bounden duty to pursue the same course again
in like circumstances. Lord Durham's mission
had terminated, and the report of his mission
had been laid before Parliament; and the latest
intelligence then (June, 1838) received from England informed us that, in accordance with Lord
Durham's urgent recommendation for the immediate adjustment of Canadian affairs, a Bill for
their settlement would be proposed during that
session of Parliament.

" In those circumstances, I stated to the Conference that the moment those questions affecting
our constitutional and just rights as British
Canadian subjects, and as a religious body, were
adjusted, we ought to abstain entirely from any
discussions in reference to civil affairs. While
Dr. Alder's resolutions were rejected by our
Conference, one prepared by myself was unanimously agreed to by our Conference, which,
though it disclaimed any intention ' to interfere
with the merely secular party politics of the day,'
avowed its ' *determination to maintain its senti-*

ments on the question of an ecclesiastical estab-
lishment in this Province, and our constitutional
and just p, ivileges."

The seven years' fiery trial on which the Methodist Church in Canada was now entering will
be the subject of the two next Essays, including
the change of views and feelings which came
over the Wesleyan Methodists in England in
regard to their status as a Church and relations
to the Church Establishment both in England
and Canada, the repentance of Dr. Alder for the
wrongs he had done his Canadian brethren, Dr.
Bunting's change of views and feelings in regard
to Canada, the reunion of the British and
Canadian Conferences and happy results.

ESSAY XIII.

EVENTS WHICH PRECEDED THE SEPARATION OF THE ENGLISH AND CANADIAN CONFERENCE IN 1840 ; OFFICIAL CHARGES OF THE LONDON WESLEYAN MISSIONARY COMMITTEE AGAINST EGERTON RYER-SON ; HIS TRIAL BEFORE THE CANADIAN CONFER-ENCE ; HIS ACQUITTAL AND JUSTIFICATION.

By the late Rev. John Ryerson ; with Notes and Supplement by his brother, Egerton Ryerson.

THE last essay closed with some account of the proceedings of the Canadian Conference held at Hamilton, June, 1839 ; the rejection of Dr. Alder's Resolutions after three days' discussion (the minority consisting of only five) ; the expressed determination of the Conference to maintain its rights on the question of the Clergy Reserves and a Church Establishment in Upper Canada, and the apparent acquiescence of Dr. Alder.

The late Rev. John Ryerson proceeds thus with his narrative.

"From this Conference [held in Hamilton, June, 1839,] the preachers departed to their various Circuits, satisfied and full of hope. But alas! bright hopes were again doomed to prove illusive, and cheerful expectations disappointed. Only a short time elapsed before signs of uneasiness and trouble ahead again approach. One party resolved that the clergy land question should cease to be discussed in the *Guardian,* while the other party insisted that it should be discussed until the question should be settled by righteous adjustment. Unfriendly correspondence and disputatious conversations ensued; and at the Belleville Conference of 1840, a communication was received complaining of the political character of the *Guardian,* declaring the intention of the ·English Conference to withdraw from the Union with the Canadian Conference. Our Conference then passed resolutions declaratory of their firm adherence to the Articles of Unicn; of the fact that they had never, in anything, or in any degree, infringed or violated those Articles; that they protested against the unjust and unlawful assumption of the London Wesleyan Committee, or the English Conference, in claiming the right to with draw from the Union in direct violation of those Articles, which had been drawn up, ratified and signed by the two contracting parties, and which could not be annulled, or renounced, but by the same parties who had enacted and subscribed to them.

"At the same time the Canada Conference appointed the Revs. William and Egerton Ryerson a deputation, or representatives, to the English Conference. The efforts of these representatives, it is painful to say, amounted to nothing. Neither party was in a suitable frame of feeling for kindly adjusting the differences between the two connexions. Proceedings were brought to an abrupt conclusion, much to the dissatisfaction of the Canadian representatives. The English Conference, however, appointed a large Committee to meet in London, who had power further to consider this matter.* The Canadian Representatives did not meet this Committee, but previously to their leaving London [in three days] prepared and published an historical argumentative account of the whole affair [giving the official documents on

* *Note by E. Ryerson in 1880.*—In this my brother, the late John Ryerson, was mistaken. The Committee of the Newcastle Conference, 1840, adjourned to meet at Manchester, to deliberate and decide upon the whole Canada matter. This was the Committee at which the Representatives of the Canadian Conference should have been notified and invited to attend. This Committee, in the absence of the Canadian Representatives, deliberated and decided upon all matters in reference to the separation of the English from the Canadian Conference, and their future operations of division and schism in Upper Canada ; and then appointed a Sub-Committee in London to carry into effect their purposes ; and then invited the Representatives of the Canada Conference to meet his Executive Sub-Committee of war against the Canada Conference and its congregations.

both sides]. Yet the pamphlet produced no effect on the public Wesleyan mind in England. [The authors did not advertise it, left England on the day of its publication, and brought most of the edition to Canada with them.] On the return of the Messrs. Ryerson a special session of the Canada Conference was called, which met in Toronto the 29th of October [1840]. This Conference declared its approval of the proceedings of its representatives, and passed a resolution of thanks to them for their services, and for the firmness with which they had maintained the rights of the Methodists and of the people generally of this country."

(Thus ends the narrative of the late Rev. John Ryerson down to this point. The rest of his narrative will be given in a succeeding Essay.)

Supplement to the foregoing narrative, by Egerton Ryerson, in 1880—taken from the pamphlets published in England in 1840, by the Revs. W. and E. Ryerson, in reply to the publication by the Committee of the English Conference :

" A few weeks after this session of our Conference [held at Hamilton, June, 1839], arrivals from England brought us the intelligence, firstly, that Sir George Arthur's Clergy Reserve Bill had been disallowed, and that the question had been referred back again to Canada ; secondly, that the

Queen's Ministers had abandoned the idea of passing a Bill for the future government of this country through Parliament that session, but would introduce one, and send it out to Canada for consideration and discussion until the next session of Parliament.

"The English reader, however little he may know of Canada affairs generally, will be able to judge, from what has been above stated, of the position in which I found myself placed, the duties which devolved upon me, both in harmony with long avowed and universally admitted principles, as a colonist, and as a guardian of the constitutional and just rights of a large Christian community. In such circumstances every Englishman of common sense will see that I could not have been silent on a measure (of Lord John Russell) which proposed a new and entirely different constitution for the government of the country from that under which I had been born and sworn allegiance, without sacrificing what is dear to every British subject—my public character as a man, and the very principles on which I had been supported by the religious public of the country.

"Here was the length and breadth of my unconstitutional doctrines. In the extract from the *Christian Guardian* of the 11th of July, 1838 (given in the last essay), the reader has seen the official exposition of my opinions on the civil government of Canada. At the English Conference held in Newcastle-upon-Tyne in August last (1840), I challenged any one of my accusers to produce a single passage in all that I had ever written, containing doctrines or sentiments at variance with those stated in the above extract. I repeat the challenge. I leave any candid English reader of any party, after reading the extract, to say whether my doctrines, as Editor of the *Guardian*, were not as loyal and constitutional as they were just. Their capital error with the Wesleyan Committee is, *that they do not recognize a Church Establishment in Upper Canada* [as will be shown hereafter in their own words]; although their own agents, Messrs. Stinson and Richey, then voted for me as editor with the express view of resisting the High Church 'oligarchy.'

" But the real character of the Wesleyan Committee's conduct, and the attacks of their writers, will appear still more obvious by what follows. As soon as Lord John Russell said that the press and people of all parties in Canada unanimously rejected his Bill, and were much dissatisfied at being kept any longer in suspense, the Right Hon. C. Poulett Thompson (now Lord Sydenham) was sent out to Canada as Governor-General. After a few months' residence and inquiry in Canada, his Excellency sends home a draft of Bill for the

future government of Canada—that Bill, with
some modifications, is passed by Parliament in
1840, but does not contain the clauses to which
I and various others had objected in Lord John
Russell's first Bill of 1839; and even after this,
the Wesleyan Committee and their writers make
war upon me for having objected to a Bill which
has long since been abandoned by the Government, and superseded by another Bill on which
I have never made a remark.

"Again: when his Excellency Mr. Thompson
(now Lord Sydenham) arrived in Upper Canada,
in the autumn of 1839, after having explained
his general views and intentions, he desired my
co-operation and assistance towards restoring
peace and harmony, and establishing good government in the province. I consented, and aided
to the best of my humble ability to put down
party spirit, and to promote confidence and unity
where there had been distrust and division, and
to carry out those important measures with which
his Excellency had been entrusted by her Majesty's Government, and which have since been
brought into operation in Canada. The objects
which the Governor-General desired to secure,
and towards the accomplishment of which I
rendered what aid I could, were threefold: 1.
The consent of the United Legislature to the
Union of the Canadas. 2. The settlement of

the Clergy Reserve question. 3. The preparation of the public mind for an improved state
of things, by abolishing party hostilities and distinctions, and encouraging a spirit of forbearance,
unity and enterprise, for the common interests
and happiness of the country.

" Having thus, from November, 1839, to April,
1840, in the most eventful crisis of Canadian
affairs, performed a patriotic duty to my Sovereign
and native country [without one farthing's pecuniary reward], and seeing the great objects in
progress of accomplishment on account of which
I had been urged even by the London Wesleyan
Committee's agents, in 1838, to resume the editorship of the *Guardian*, after three years' retirement from it, I formally took leave of public
discussions, and in a few weeks, on the assembling
of Conference in June, 1840, retired from the
editorship of the *Guardian*, as I had always
declared my intention of doing at the moment
of settling the Clergy Reserve question. Since
that time, April, 1840, I have not written a line
on civil affairs, nor in any way interfered with
them.

" It might be reasonably supposed that by such
a six months' conclusion of my editorial career,
in which I had given great satisfaction to the
Government, and to my brethren and friends in
Canada, my retirement would not be interrupted

from England. Yet within four days of the assembling of the Canada Conference, in that very month, June, 1840, I was accosted with the London Wesleyan Committee's grave and criminating charges.

"' Charges by the London Wesleyan Missionary Committee against Mr. Egerton Ryerson, dated 77 Hatton Garden, Wednesday, 29th of April, 1840.

"' I. That just grounds of complaint exist against the Rev. Egerton Ryerson, particularly on the following points:

"' 1. That Mr. Ryerson, as it appears to this Committee, in his recent communications with the Governor-General, and on other occasions, has virtually and practically superseded the Rev. Joseph Stinson, the regularly appointed President of the Upper Canada Conference, and therefore the Official Agent and Representative of the Wesleyan Body in Upper Canada, during the interim of its sittings ; and has thus acted with great and culpable irregularity.

"' 2. That in the judgment of this Committee, Mr. Ryerson has discovered an utter want of ingenuousness and integrity in thus attempting to gain the possession, on behalf of the Canadian Conference, in whole or in part, of the grant made by the Crown to the Wesleyan Missionary Society, and that he has in this matter committed a flagrant violation of the obligations arising from the Union between the two Conferences.

"'3. That the *Christian Guardian*, of which Mr. Ryerson is the Editor, instead of being conducted according to express stipulation and promise made to Dr. Alder, and the direction of the Canada Conference, as a religious paper, has become more than ever a political and party organ.

"'II. That the Committee are far from implicating the whole or any part of the members of the Upper Canada Conference in these unjustifiable proceedings of Mr. Ryerson, and cannot but hope that they will utterly repudiate them at their next annual sitting, and mark the sense which they entertain of such a dishonest attempt to deprive the Wesleyan Missionary Committee of their just and righteous claims on the plighted faith of the British Crown and Government, by partial, clandestine, and unauthorized representation, in such a manner as the nature of the case requires; and that they will place the *Christian Guardian*, if it must be continued a newspaper at all, in such hands as will at least secure the fulfilment of the oft-repeated promise, that it shall be exclusively a religious publication. The Committee are the more encouraged to hope that the Conference will adopt this course, from the

Report of Dr. Alder, that various members of that Body had expressed to him the deepest grief at the political course pursued by Mr. Ryerson in conducting the *Christian Guardian,* and their earnest desire to maintain unimpaired, on just and proper principles, the Union which now exists between the two Conferences.

"' III. If, however, this reasonable expectation should be disappointed, and a majority of the Canada Conference, at their next sitting, should be found to support and encourage such proceedings as those of which the Committee complain, it will be their painful duty to recommend to the next British Conference to dissolve the Union which at present subsists between the two Connexions, and to adopt such measures for the maintenance and extension of the Indian Missions in Upper Canada as may appear to be necessary.'"

The proceedings and answer of the Canada Conference in regard to the foregoing accusations and resolutions of the London Wesleyan Missionary Committee are as follows, in the words of the official and printed Minutes:

Extracts from the Journal of Conference of the Wesleyan Methodist Church in Canada, assembled in Belleville, June, 1840.

"*Friday Morning, June 12th.*—Resumed the question in relation to the examination of character.

" On the name of Egerton Ryerson being called, the President of the Conference presented certain documents from a Committee of the British Conference. The documents were read, headed as follows, viz. :

"'Extract of a letter from R. Vernon Smith, M.P., Under Colonial Secretary, addressed to Dr. Alder, 15th April, 1840.

"'A copy of a letter addressed to the Governor-General of Canada, by the Rev. E. Ryerson, dated Toronto, 17th January, 1840. (For this letter see following essay.)

"'Copy of the Resolutions of a Committee appointed by the British Conference in 1839, to decide finally on all matters relating to the Union existing between the British Conference and the Upper Canada Conference, and the Indian Missions in Upper Canada, 77 Hatton Garden, Wednesday, 29th April, 1840.

"'Resolved, that these documents be taken into consideration Monday morning, the 15th instant.'

" *Monday, June 15th.*—Proceeded to take up the documents transmitted from the Committee of the British Conference in England in relation to Egerton Ryerson.

" The Assistant Secretary read the before-mentioned documents.

" Mr. Richey appeared as the accuser in behalf

of the London Committee. After a lengthened address, Mr. Richey moved, seconded by E. Evans, that it be

"Resolved—'That this Conference has heard, with great surprise and regret, of Brother Egerton Ryerson's attempt to deprive the British Wesleyan Committee of the annual grant received by them from the Imperial Government, to enable them to extend their Missions in this province; and that they utterly repudiate such proceedings on the part of Mr. Ryerson, not only as irregular and unauthorized, but directly opposed to a resolution adopted by this Conference at its last session, rescinding the *second*, *fifth* and *sixth*, passed by this Conference in June, 1837, on the subjects of the grants in question, because those resolutions were represented by Mr. Alder as interfering with the usages of the British brethren, and calculated materially to retard their interests.'

"*Tuesday, June 16th.*—Resumed the consideration of the documents relative to E. Ryerson.

"The Memorial of the Rev. Joseph Stinson, President of the Conference, and the Rev. Matthew Richey, Superintendent of Toronto City Circuit, to his Excellency the Right Honourable Charles Poulett Thompson, Governor-General of Canada, on the subject of the Clergy Reserves, was read."*

---

* This Memorial was unknown to the Members of the Conference until then read. Mr. E. Ryerson had heard

"Mr. E. Ryerson proceeded to address the Conference, and continued his address in the afternoon session.

"*Wednesday, June 17th.*—The Conference resumed the consideration of the Resolutions of London Committee.

"After considerable discussion, the Resolution introduced by Mr. Richey was put, and was negatived by a majority of fifty-one.

"*Friday, June 19th.*—After most mature consideration of the several subjects referred to in the Resolutions of the Committee of the English Wesleyan Conference, it was Resolved—

"'I. That we cannot recognize the right on the part of the Committee to interfere with the Canada Conference in the management of our own internal affairs (except as provided for by the Articles of Union), and especially with our views and proceedings on the question of the Clergy Reserves; as we are precluded by the Articles of Union with the English Conference from all claims upon its funds, and as our own uncontrolled action and interests have always, been reserved and admitted in relation to the question of the Clergy Reserves.'

from the Governor-General of the existence of such a Memorial and of the purport of it, but did not know its wording, and insisted upon its being produced and read before proceeding with his defence.

"'II. That, as the Articles of Union between the English and Canadian Conferences expressly secure to the Canadian Preachers all their rights and privileges inviolate, we consider it at variance with the letter and spirit of those Articles, and an anomalous and alarming precedent, for the Committee in London to accuse and condemn a member of this Conference, and then to enjoin upon us to carry into execution their sentence on pain of a dissolution of the Union.'

"'III. That whilst we have always maintained, and are resolved to maintain, to the fullest extent the dignity and authority of the office of President, as provided for in our Rules and in the Articles of Union, we are impelled by an imperative sense of duty to decline acceding to the claim of the Committee in London, that the President appointed in England is to be regarded by virtue of his office as the "Agent and Representative of the Wesleyan body in Upper Canada" in the transaction of affairs with the Government, in which the interests of our Church are involved; as we have always, in anticipation of such transactions, appointed a Committee or Representative to guard and represent the views and interests of our Church; especially as this Conference, at its last session, appointed the Rev. Egerton Ryerson as its Special Representative to confer with the Government on matters affecting our civil

and religious rights and interests; and **we** can
discover **no** good reason **for** departing from an
established and proper usage.'

"'IV. That it appears to this Conference that
a proper regard to the rights and interests of the
Wesleyan Methodist Church in Canada rendered
it the imperative duty of the Rev. Egerton Ryer-
son to confer with his Excellency the Governor-
General of Canada on our financial affairs; and
we fully concur in the exposition which Mr.
Ryerson has given of the financial relations
between the English and Canadian Conferences
in his letter to the Governor-General, dated
Toronto, January 17th, 1840. And whilst denying any wish to interfere with the legitimate
claims of the Wesleyan Missionary Society upon
the faith of Her Majesty's Government, **we learn**
with feelings of gratitude that the rights and
interests of the Wesleyan **body in** this Province
have been brought under the consideration of Her
Majesty's **Secretary of State for the** Colonies **by**
his Excellency the Governor-General, **and we** are
prepared to submit to the decision of **the proper**
authorities respecting **them.'**

"'V. That in reference to the last Resolution
of the **Committee in** London, declaring their intention, **under any circumstances, to** claim, and,
if possible, to secure the possession of the Indian
Missions in Upper Canada; this Conference, con-

sidering that those Missions, with two or three exceptions, were established by our exertions prior to 1833 (when the Articles of Union were agreed to), and that they have, in a great measure, been supported by funds obtained in this Province, and sustained chiefly by the ministrations and labours of Canadian preachers and teachers, we cannot regard it as reasonable, or our Providential duty, under any circumstances, to relinquish our pastoral connection with those Missions which were established previously to the Union.'

"' VI. That firmly believing, as we do, that the Resolutions of the Committee in London have been adopted upon erroneous impressions; and being satisfied that our fathers and brethren in England could not have intended, nor would intend, anything unkind towards the members of this Connexion, or unjust to its interests; and deeply anxious as we are to maintain inviolate and unimpaired the principles of the Articles of Union between the English and Canadian Conferences; and being disposed to do all in our power to prevent the dissolution of the Union, therefore Resolved, that a delegation be sent to the Wesleyan Conference in England, to lay all the matters of these Resolutions before that honourable body, and to use all proper means to prevent collision between the two Connexions.'

"Egerton and William Ryerson were duly elected.

"The Rev. Joseph Stinson was requested to accompany the delegation to England."

Such were the "deliverances" of the Canada Conference in reply to the assumptions, accusations and threats of the London Wesleyan Committee.

ESSAY XIV.

AGREEMENT OF THE ENGLISH CONFERENCE IN 1833
TO SUPPORT THE CANADIAN CONFERENCE IN THE
MAINTENANCE OF ITS RIGHTS AND IN OPPOSITION
TO A CHURCH ESTABLISHMENT IN UPPER CANADA,
AND ACTED UPON BY THE REPRESENTATIVES OF
THE ENGLISH CONFERENCE DURINGS IX YEARS;
BUT VIOLATED IN 1839, WHICH CAUSED THE SEPA-
RATION OF THE TWO CONFERENCES IN 1840.

TO enable the reader to understand fully this
crucial epoch of Canadian Methodist history, which involved nothing less than the union
and separation of the British and Canadian Conferences, and the character of individual members of them, I will subjoin to the foregoing
statements: first, extracts from the Memorial of
Messrs. Stinson and Richey to the Governor-
General, January 3rd, 1840, which led His
Excellency to investigate the financial relations
between the English and Canadian connexions;
I will next give the letter of Mr. Egerton Ryerson to the Governor-General, dated January
17th, 1840, on which the charges against him
were made; then the correspondence which
showed the objects of Mr. Ryerson's letter, and

his writing it at the Governor-General's request; and lastly, the vindication of it, in a letter to Lord John Russell, in answer to a letter of Dr. Alder to his Lordship. I will present these facts, as far as possible, in the language of the Pamphlets published in England at the time by Dr. Alder and by Messrs. William and E. Ryerson:

In the letter of Messrs. Ryerson to Lord John Russell, in reply to Dr. Alder, occurs the following statement of the circumstances under which Messrs. Stinson and Richey addressed their Memorial to the Governor-General:

"On the 2nd of January, 1840, Messrs. Stinson and Richey had an interview with the Governor-General, during which they informed His Excellency that the Union between the English and Canadian Conferences was expected to be dissolved (a measure the most remote from the thoughts of the members of the Canadian Conference), and desired His Excellency so to frame his Bill as to secure that portion of the proceeds of the Clergy Reserves, to the control of which the Conference of the Wesleyan Methodist Church in Canada would be entitled, *to the control of the Wesleyan Conference in England*, for the benefit of those who should adhere to it on the dissolution of the Union with the Conference. On the day following Messrs. Stinson and

Richey embodied their views in a Memorial to
His Excellency, enclosed, marked B. [See below.]
In that Memorial it will be seen that the Wesleyan *Conference in Canada* is superseded by the
Wesleyan *Conference in England*, and that when
one of the Articles of Union between the two
bodies provided that the former should have no
claim upon the funds of the latter." . . .

The following are extracts from the Memorial
of Messrs. Stinson and Richey to the Governor-
General:

"Sustaining, as we do, an intimate and responsible relation to the Methodist Church in this
Province in connexion with the British Wesleyan
Conference, we deem it imperative upon us to
lay before your Excellency an explicit statement
of our views and wishes in reference to the Clergy
Reserves. . . .

"The Church of England being, in our estimation, the Established Church of all the British
Colonies, we entertain no objections to the distinct
recognition of Her as such ; and had the Reserves
been exclusively appropriated to Her, according
to the original intention of His Gracious Majesty
George the Third, we should not have interfered
with the matter; but as the disposition of them
has been referred to the Colonial Legislature, we
confess we are entirely at a loss to conceive why
the Wesleyan Methodist Church should be placed

in any degree inferior to the Church of Scotland.   .   .   .

" In any settlement of this important question,
we regard it of vital importance to the permanent
peace and prosperity of the Province, as a British
Colony, that the sum to be appropriated to us be
given to the Wesleyan Methodists who are now,
or who may be hereafter, connected with the
British Wesleyan Conference.

(Signed)
  " J. STINSON, *President of the Conference.*
  " M. RICHEY, *Superintendent.*
Toronto, January 3rd, 1840."

It will be seen that this Memorial was official,
professedly presented on behalf of the Wesleyan
Methodist Church in Canada, and, according to
the assumption of the London Wesleyan Committee, the only official communication that
could be made to the Government in regard to
the Canada Conference or the Methodist Church
of Upper Canada; yet it is in direct opposition
to what the Methodist Church in Upper Canada
had constantly professed and demanded for nearly
twenty years. Messrs. Stinson and Richey professed that the Church of England was not only
the Established Church of England and Ireland,
· but "*the Established Church of all the British
Colonies*"—contradicting not only Blackstone in

his Commentaries on the Laws of England, but
the history of the old British Colonies for a
hundred and fifty years—contradicting what was
avowed in the Report of a Select Committee
(with the late Mr. Huskisson as Chairman) of
the House of Commons on the Civil Government
of Canada in 1828, and by the first statesmen of
the day, as well as by the decision, in a year or
two afterwards, of the Judicial Committee of the
House of Lords. This Memorial, though affecting
the vital rights and interests of the Canada Conference and Methodism, was unknown to a single
Member of the Conference or Members of the
Methodist Church in Canada for five months,
except its authors, and might therefore be called
"clandestine." The peculiar mode of its presentation and the extraordinary character of its
contents, together with the verbal communication
of Messrs. Stinson and Richey the day before,
that the Union between the British and Canadian
Conferences was not likely to continue, excited
the curiosity of His Excellency, and induced him
to inquire into the relations of the two bodies,
and the origin and objects of the Government
Grant. Immediately after the interview with
the Governor-General, His Excellency sent his
Private Secretary to the residence of the Rev.
Egerton Ryerson, requesting his presence at the
Government House, and stating the object of it.

Mr. E. Ryerson obeyed the summons, gave a brief account of the Grant, and then, at His Excellency's request, reduced his statement to writing in the evening of the same day. His letter was as follows:

"TORONTO, January 2nd, 1840.
"May it Please Your Excellency,—

"In accordance with your Excellency's request, I recapitulate in writing the leading facts relative to the Government Grant to the British Conference. I know not that I can do it more satisfactorily than by making the following references:

"I refer your Excellency to the Earl of Ripon's letter to Lord Glenelg (dated Carlton Gardens, 4th April, 1836), and Lord Glenelg's despatch to His Excellency Sir F. B. Head (dated April 15th, 1836), for a statement of the circumstances under which the Grant was originally made, and subsequently revived. These documents are contained in the printed paper that I left with your Excellency.

"The only material point is, as to whether the Grant is made in aid of the funds of a body in England or in Upper Canada.

"On this point I beg to direct your Excellency's attention to the following documents: 1. Mr. Secretary Rowan's letter to 'The British and Canadian Conferences,' dated 'Government House, March 15th, 1833.' * 2. Letter from Mr. Secretary Rowan to 'The Wesleyan Methodist Conference,' dated 'Government House, Toronto, July 4th, 1834.'† 3. Letter from the Rev. Joseph Stinson to His Excellency Sir John Colborne, dated 'City of Toronto, July 7th, 1834.'

"As to the light in which this Grant has always been viewed by the Conference of the Wesleyan Methodist Church in this Province, see Resolutions adopted in 1837, in the accompanying printed Minutes, pp. 24-28.

"As to the relation in which the Conference in Canada stands to the Conference in England and its funds, see the Articles of Union between the two bodies in the accompanying book, entitled

---

* This letter, dated March 15th, 1833, announced a Grant of £900 stg. to the British Wesleyan Conference, and £600 to the Canadian Wesleyan (or Ryanite) Conference, to enable them to build Churches and Chapels.

† This letter, dated July 4th, 1834, announced a Grant of £550 for the same purpose. The letter was sent by mistake to the Rev. James Richardson, who sent it to Dr. Stinson, who acknowledged its receipt on behalf of the British Wesleyan Conference, and informed His Excellency that it would be applied to the erection or repairing of Chapels and School-houses, and in *defraying the general expenses of the various Mission Stations in our charge.*

' Doctrines and Discipline of the Wesleyan Methodist Church in Canada,' pp. 137-142.

     " I have the honour to be, &c.,

        (Signed)   " EGERTON RYERSON."

It is seen that the above letter was written in obedience to the Governor-General's request, and consisted wholly of references to official documents.

I have no doubt in my own mind that Lord Ripon had the most benevolent objects in view in devoting a part of the Crown revenues to assist in "building chapels and parsonages" in poor and needy places in Upper Canada; but I have as little doubt of the accuracy of the late Mr. John Ryerson's statements, that the object of the local High Church party in recommending these Grants was to buy off the opposition of the religious parties against the high pretensions to supremacy and monopoly of the proceeds of the Clergy Reserves, until they could be secured in the possession of their supremacy and monopoly.* But their policy did not succeed ac-

---

* That this was the case so far as the Methodists were concerned is obvious from the facts that the first avowed object of Mr. Alder's first mission to Upper Canada was, by aid of the proposed Government Grant, to bring twelve Missionaries, not to go to the Indians or destitute settlements in Upper Canada, but to the principal cities and towns, in order to divide Societies and break down the Methodism of the Canada Conference.

cording to their expectations. Much had been
expected by the High Church party from the
Union between the British and Canadian Conferences in favour of their policy, which, however,
was counteracted by the arrangement which the
Representative of the Canada Conference was
enabled to effect with the British Conference in
negotiating the Union in 1833. After discussing
and agreeing upon the principal Articles of Union,
Dr. Bunting introduced the question, by way of

And when Mr. Ryan seceded from and arrayed himself against the Conference of the Wesleyan Methodist
Church, Archdeacon Strachan not only gave him fifty
pounds to aid him in his crusade against the Conference, but a Government Grant was made to Mr. Ryan's
party in 1833, through Mr. John Wilson, of the sum of
£666; and in 1834, of £388.

The following Grants were also made : 1833—Rev. J.
Strachan, £333 8s. The Archdeacon of Kingston, same
amount. The Clergy Corporation, £3880. Roman Catholic Bishop, £555. Church of Scotland, £1205. Presbyterian Synod of U. C., £388. Roman Catholic Clergy,
£1111. For R. C. Schools and Churches, £823. R. C.
Bishop of Quebec, £200. There were similar large
sums paid in 1834, including £611 paid to the Wesleyan
Missionary Society, and £388 paid to the Canadian
Wesleyan Methodists.

Remarks by E. Ryerson, 1880.—The above items are
copied from the Returns of the Government, in compliance with an Address of the House of Assembly. I am
unable to state what Grants were made after the year
1834. The above Returns show how largely the Casual

inquiry, as to the alleged interference of Canadian Preachers with politics. I think Dr. Bunting was prompted to introduce this question by Mr. Alder, who evidently expected that some apology or concession would be made on the part of the Representative of the Canadian Conference, who, however, seized the long-desired opportunity to bring the whole subject before the senior and leading Members of the British Conference. "He expressed his pleasure at having the opportunity of answering for his Canadian brethren and him-

and Territorial Revenue in Upper Canada (a revenue arising from fines and sales of public lands at the disposal of the Crown) was absorbed by this general subsidizing of the Clergy of different religious persuasions (of which the Clergy of the Church of England had the lion's share), which, though it silenced the individual recipients of it, had no influence upon the country at large in weakening, much less paralyzing, the opposition to a dominant Church Establishment and the Episcopal monopoly of the proceeds of the Clergy Reserves. The Canada Conference received not a farthing of these Government Grants from the Casual and Territorial Revenue; maintained, without wavering, its protests against and opposition to the Clergy Reserve monopoly and dominant Church Establishment in Upper Canada, though assailed by the High Church and Ryan party on the one side, and by the misrepresentations and hostility of the Episcopal party on the other side, together with their republican confederates of the W. L. Mackenzie party, which culminated and collapsed in the rebellion of 1837.

self before the Fathers of the British Conference
to the oft-repeated charge that the Canada Conference interfered in politics. He avowed at once
that the Canada Conference had interfered with
what their adversaries called politics, the whole
field of which those adversaries sought to reserve
to themselves for the purpose of establishing a
Church supremacy and monopoly inconsistent with
the just rights and privileges of the Methodists
in Upper Canada. He stated that before the year
1818 there were but four settled Ministers of the
Church of England in all Upper Canada, whilst
the labours of the Methodist ministers extended
back to before the year 1790, and to the establishment of societies, congregations and places of
worship in every district of Upper Canada ; that
the Clergy of the Church of England evinced no
interest in the religious instruction of the people
of Upper Canada when the settlements were new
and the people poor, until the Clergy Reserves
(one-seventh of the lands of the Province) began
to be valuable ; then an Ecclesiastical Corporation of the Church of England was obtained in
1818 for the sale of the Clergy Reserves and the
management of their proceeds. Then began the
pretensions of the high party (in fact, Government party) in Upper Canada, that the Church
of England was the Established Church of the
Province and of the Empire, and that all persons

opposed to its supremacy and emoluments were disloyal to the Crown—especially the Methodists as they were the most numerous and successful; they were characterized as *Yankee* and *Republican*, and calls were made upon the British Parliament and the Propagation Society for large additional grants in order to prevent Upper Canada from being overrun by Yankee Methodists and other denominations hostile to the Church of England. Four of these slanderous attacks were made by writers (two of them by dignitaries) of the Church of England upon the character of Methodist ministers before a line was written in their defence; but they were at length roused to defend themselves, and petitioned the Legislature to investigate the charges against them and the early religious history of the Province. The Legislative Assembly appointed a Committee to investigate the whole subject. The Select Committee did so, and examined no less than fifty-two witnesses, most of whom were professed members of the Church of England, and all of whom, with scarcely a variation, testified to the early and beneficial labours of the Methodist ministers, to their uniform loyalty, and even zeal in defence of the country in the American war of 1812-15 against Great Britain; that the Methodists were by far the most numerous religious body in Upper Canada, and were entitled to equal privileges with the Church of England. The House of Assembly, by a majority of more than two to one, passed an Address to the King, vindicating the character and usefulness of Methodist ministers, and deprecating the exclusive establishment of the Church of England, or of any one Church. In the same year, 1828, the House of Commons appointed a Select Committee (of which Mr. Huskisson was Chairman) on the Civil Government of Canada; which Committee reported against the exclusive claims of the Church of England in Upper Canada.

"In addition to these considerations of equity and authority, the Canadian Conference had other legal and moral grounds in justification of their claims and proceedings. Blackstone, in his Commentaries on the Laws of England, declared that whilst by the Act of Supremacy, 1st of Elizabeth, the Established Church was the Established Church of England and Ireland, it was not the Established Church of any of the British Colonies, except under one or more of three conditions —namely, by Royal Proclamation, if a Crown Colony; or by Imperial Enactment; or by Local Statute, as in the case of Virginia. On neither of these grounds could the Church of England claim to be *the* Established Church of Upper Canada. The Imperial Act 31 George the Third, passed in 1791, called in the Canadas 'The Constitutional **Act,'** which **formed Upper** Canada **into a separate** Provincial Government **from** Lower **Canada, set apart** one-seventh of the public lands of the Province for the support of 'a Protestant Clergy' (in contradistinction to the Roman Catholic clergy, who **were endowed in Lower** Canada), **but no Church as** established **by law was** named, **and other** Protestant **clergy than those** of the **Church of** England **were named in** the Act, and **regarded by the ablest** statesmen **and** lawyers, **both in** England **and** Canada, as comprehended **in the provisions of the Act.** The [then] present **Secretary of State for the** Colonies, Lord **Stanley [afterwards Lord Derby],** said, in supporting the **Report of the House of Commons on** the **Civil Government of** Canada, '**That if any exclusive privileges were** given **to the Church of** England, **not only** will **the measure be repugnant** to every **principle of sound legislation, but** contrary to the **spirit and intentions of the** Act of 1791, under **which the Reserves were** made **for the** Protestant **clergy.'**

"**There was another and** equally unanswerable **ground on which his** Canadian brethren **and himself justified** their claims to equal rights and **their opposition to the exclusive** pretensions of the Episcopal Clergy, **namely,** the composition of **Canadian** society. **Now, only a** small minority **of the people of** Upper **Canada** were even nominal members of the Church of England; and a large majority of even the laity of that Church, both in and out of the Legislative Assembly, were supporters of the claims of the Methodist and other denominations to equal rights and privileges before the law.

"When his Canadian brethren commenced the defence of their character and rights against the attacks and aggressions of Episcopal Church dignitaries, they had no law to enable them to hold land on which to worship God and in which to bury their dead, much less for their ministers to solemnize matrimony; in the course of five years they had obtained laws to hold Church and burying grounds, and for their ministers to solemnize matrimony; and they were determined to persevere until in all respects they were recognized by the Legislature of the country as second to no other religious persuasion in it."

The apparently spontaneous reply (embracing so wide a field) of the Representative of the Canada Conference to an unexpected question, seemed to excite surprise, elicited frequent cheers in the course of delivery, and at the conclusion was followed by a round of applause from the large Committee and various other members of the Conference present, and the venerable men exclaimed (without a dissenting voice) from all parts of the audience room, "The Canadian brethren are right, and ought to be sustained in the contest for their rights."

Thus were the intrigues or counsels of the leaders of the High Church party in Toronto defeated, and the moral influence and support of the British secured to the Canada Conference in the struggle for equal civil and religious liberty.

To show the accuracy of the foregoing statements, and the utter falsity of the representations to the contrary of a pretended historian of Methodism in Canada (Webster), I will quote the Report of the Representative of the Canada Conference to the British Conference in 1833, when the first Union was formed between the two bodies. That Report was prepared on shipboard during the author's return from England; was submitted to and concurred in by the Rev. George Marsden, Representative of the British Conference, and first appointed British President of the Canadian Conference, and by the Rev. Joseph Stinson. The Report, after having been read to the Canada Conference in the presence of the English Representatives, and concurred in by them, was printed by its authority in the *Christian Guardian* of the 16th October, 1833. In its two concluding paragraphs are the following words:

" The last topic to which I would avail myself of this occasion to refer, is our constitutional and

just rights as a body of Christians and as Canadian
British subjects. To attain these to that extent
which we firmly and conscientiously believe are
guaranteed to us and to all classes of Protestants
by law, as well as by equity, and to refute those
shameless misrepresentations which ignorance
and pride, selfishness and cupidity, have originated and doggedly persevered in against us, this
Conference addressed His Majesty's Government
about two years ago; and two or three other
addresses of the same nature have been approved
and promoted by many of us, as individuals, in
our different fields of labour. I am happy to be
able to state that, during my late visit to England,
I was favoured with an opportunity of bringing
this whole subject again under the consideration
of His Majesty's Government, and to state at
large the legal, religious and political grounds on
which we, in common with the House of Assembly and the great body of the inhabitants of
the Province, resist the introduction of a dominant Church Establishment into Upper Canada,
and maintain our claim to the enjoyment of
equal privileges, advantages and immunities with
all other classes of His Majesty's Canadian
subjects.   .   .   .

"It is likewise a ground of thankfulness and
congratulation to be able to add, that when this
subject was introduced as a matter of enquiry by

Mr. Bunting, before a large and most respectable and intelligent Committee at the Wesleyan Conference, the statement and explanation which I gave of it, and the authorities I adduced, fully satisfied the Committee, not only of the reasonableness and legality of our claims, and of the injustice of the various slanderous reports and insinuations against us, but also of the propriety and expediency of the measures which we, as a body, have been induced to adopt in respect to them; so that Mr. Bunting afterwards remarked to the Conference on this point, that although he deprecated political intermeddling with merely party and secular politics amongst professing Christians, and especially amongst Christian ministers, and considered it unworthy of their character and calling, he believed the part the Canadian Conference had taken was a laudable maintenance of their rights, sanctioned by the highest authority and the opinion of members of His Majesty's Government; and that the Canadian brethren, as a body, any more than individuals, were not bound to submit silently to unjust exclusions, or to desist from maintaining in a constitutional and Christian manner their claims to privileges and advantages, to the possession and enjoyment of which they are so justly and legally entitled. I can, therefore, assure the Conference that we may rely upon the cordial and powerful co-operation of the Missionary Secretaries in support of our rights and interests with the parent Government. This is one of the many great advantages which I anticipate from the union of the two Connexions, and which encourage me to hope and believe that the proposed Articles of Agreement will receive the concurrence of this Conference with the same cordiality and unanimity as they have been already adopted by the English Conference.

(Signed)   " EGERTON RYERSON."

Four successive Representatives of the British Conference, appointed as Presidents of the Canada Conference, acted in the spirit of the foregoing Report, acted in harmony with their Canadian brethren from 1833 to 1839, signed in their official capacity the resolutions and addresses adopted from time to time by the Canada Conference in the maintenance of their civil and religious rights, and against a dominant Church Establishment in Upper Canada.

ESSAY XV.

RESOLUTIONS AND ADDRESSES OF THE CANADIAN CON-
FERENCE IN SUCCESSIVE YEARS AGAINST A CHURCH
ESTABLISHMENT AND THE CLERGY RESERVE MO-
NOPOLY IN UPPER CANADA, SIGNED AND ENDORSED
BY THE REPRESENTATIVES OF THE ENGLISH CON-
FERENCE, WITH PORTENTOUS WARNINGS, BY THE
"GUARDIAN," DURING THE EDITORSHIP OF THE
REV. E. EVANS.   IN THE REBELLION OF 1837 NO
MINISTER OR MEMBER OF THE WESLEYAN METH-
ODIST CHURCH WAS IMPLICATED, OR EVEN SUS-
PECTED OF SYMPATHISING WITH IT, THOUGH BOTH
MINISTERS AND LAITY WERE ALL ADVOCATES OF
EQUAL CIVIL RIGHTS IN UPPER CANADA.   TER-
GIVERSATIONS AND UNFAITHFULNESS TO THEIR
PROMISES OF MANY MEMBERS ELECTED TO THE
LEGISLATIVE ASSEMBLY IN 1836.   RE-ELECTION OF
EGERTON RYERSON AS EDITOR OF THE "GUARDIAN,"
AND ITS OBJECTS STATED.   FIRST AVOWED OPPO-
SITION OF THE LONDON WESLEYAN MISSIONARY
COMMITTEE AND THEIR CANADIAN AGENTS TO THE
EQUAL CIVIL RIGHTS OF METHODISTS AND OTHER
CLASSES IN UPPER CANADA.

THE last Essay closed with an extract from
the report by the representative of the
Canadian Conference to England in 1833, in
which the latter was assured of the support of
the English Conference in its defence of Meth-

odist rights, and the struggles for **equal** civil and religious privileges before the **law in Upper** Canada. It was **then added,—"Four successive** representatives of **the** British Conference, appointed as Presidents of the Canadian Conference, acted in the spirit **of** the foregoing **report,** and in harmony with their Canadian brethren from 1833 to 1839, signed **in their** official capacity the resolutions and addresses adopted **from** time to time by the Canadian Conference in maintenance **of** their civil **and** religious rights, **and** against a dominant **Church** Establishment **in** Upper Canada."

I **now** proceed to remark **that it is needless** to give extracts from **these addresses and** resolutions **in** succession. **I will confine myself** to four years—1836, **1837, 1838, and 1839.** I select first 1836, because **I was not present** at that Conference, being **detained and** labouring in England **from** December, **1835, to** March, **1837.** The Canada **Conference of 1836** adopted two addresses, **one to the Lieutenant Governor,** and **the** other **to the** King, both expressing the sentiments **of the** Conference **on the question** of the Clergy Reserves and **Church** Establishment. I will quote **from** that addressed **to the** King, abounding in expressions of loyalty **to the** throne and constitution, and **connection with** the Mother Country, stating **the** numbers **of the min-**

isters, congregations and adherents, and stating
their claims to equal rights and ·privileges, in the
following paragraphs :

" We also beg most humbly to represent to
Your Majesty, *that we, together with the great
majority of your loyal and devoted Canadian
subjects, are conscientiously and firmly opposed to
the recognition of any Church Establishment
within this Province.* It is, therefore, with extreme regret we have learned that during the
past year fifty-seven rectories have been established and endowed out of lands set apart for
·the support of a Protestant clergy ; notwithstanding the wishes of Your Majesty, most
graciously made known through the Earl of
Ripon, that the disputes which had arisen respecting the disposition of those lands should be
settled according to the wishes of its inhabitants,
so often constitutionally expressed by petition,
and through their representatives in the House
of Assembly.

" We should not discharge the duty we owe
to Your Majesty in the present posture of the
affairs of this Province, did we not most humbly
and respectfully convey to Your Majesty our full
conviction, *that nothing could tend more directly
to weaken the attachment of the people of this
country to the Parent State, than the continuance of this system of exclusive patronage to any*

*one Church ; **nor** could any **measure** more happily conduce to allay existing agitation **and** dissension, **and to** produce **a more** affectionate **and enthusiastic** devotion **to** Your Majesty's Government, than an assurance **that** this system **will be no longer** pursued.*

" We devoutly **pray** the Great **Disposer of** events **to** guide **us in** all **the** affairs of Your Majesty's Councils, **to throw** over your **Majesty,** at all times, **the** shield of **His divine** protection, **and to render Your Majesty's** reign **long, feli-** citous, and prosperous, **and productive of the** happiest results throughout **every part of your** widely-extended dominions.

" Signed by order, **and on behalf of the Con-** ference,

. (Signed) **" WILLIAM LORD, *President.*** **" WILLIAM CASE, *Secretary.***

" Belleville, **Upper Canada, June 13th, 1836."**

The **Canada Conference never employed more** decisive **and energetic language** against a **Church** Establishment **in** Upper Canada, **and against** delay and **the** danger **of not** settling **it than in** the above quoted address **to the King, prepared** by the Rev. E. Evans, and signed **by Mr. Lord,** the representative of the British **Conference, and** by the venerable William **Case, as Secretary of** **the** Conference, **and** transmitted **to the Rev.**

Egerton Ryerson, then in England, to be laid, in the usual way, before the King. The editorials in the *Guardian*, by Mr. Evans, during the years 1836, 1837, and the first part of 1838, were in harmony with the Conference address above quoted. It is plain, from the language of the Conference, that the public mind was becoming more and more impatient and chafed at the delay in settling the Clergy Reserve, or Church Establishment question, and at the arbitrary and partial system of grants to the clergy of certain religious bodies out of the Casual and Territorial Revenue—these grants now amounting to $7,400 per annum.

At its annual session in June, 1837, the Canadian Conference again took up the subject, and adopted eleven resolutions on the subject of the Reserves, and of the Government Grants made to the clergy of certain religious bodies. The great object of these resolutions was, of course, to urge the immediate and just settlement of Clergy Reserve, or Church Establishment questions ; but their immediate design was to protect and vindicate the members of the Canada Conference from the persistent misrepresentations made against them. The Canadian preachers suffered severely on account of the Government Grants to the London Missionary Committee, not only in their influence, but in their means of support, their adversaries representing that they were individually recipients of the grant made to the Wesleyan Missionary Society, and were not, therefore, entitled to support from the members of their congregations.

The resolutions, after the most mature consideration, were *unanimously* adopted by the Conference, including the Representatives of the British Conference and of the London Wesleyan Missionary Committee, and were never objected to by that Committee for two years, when, in June, 1839, Dr. Alder objected to the second, fifth and sixth, as interfering with the relations between the Committee and the Government, and requested the Conference to rescind them. His request was readily acceded to. The original objects of them had been accomplished.

But the *eight* out of the eleven resolutions were never rescinded, nor objected to—a fact showing that, even as late as 1839, the London Wesleyan Committee admitted and recognized the right of the Canada Conference to oppose the erection of a Church Establishment in Upper Canada.

The eleven resolutions, as *unanimously* passed by the Conference, were as follows :—

Extracted from the printed Minutes of the Conference assembled at Toronto, June, 1837, pp. 163-168 :

"GOVERNMENT GRANTS—CLERGY RESERVES.

"*Quest.* 21. What are the views which the members of this Conference feel themselves called upon, in the present peculiar and eventful crisis of the ecclesiastical and civil affairs of this Province, formally to embody and unitedly to avow, in regard to the great questions which relate to the religious instruction of the country, and our own rights and privileges as a Christian community?

"*Ans.* After a very lengthened and minute and comprehensive investigation of the whole subject, the following resolutions were UNANIMOUSLY adopted :—

"It having been represented that there are dissatisfactions in different parts of the Province on account of certain grants made by His Majesty's Government to the Wesleyan Missionary Committee in London for the religious instruction of the Indian tribes and destitute settlers,—also on account of the unsettled state of the Clergy Reserve question; and whereas vigorous and widely-extended efforts have been and are being made, under these pretexts, to excite prejudices against our Connexion, this Conference deems an expression of its views on these subjects due to its own character, and the feelings and interests of the Church of which it is the pastoral head; it is therefore Resolved,—

" '1. That at its last two annual meetings this Conference has expressly stated that no public grants have ever been made to this body, and that it desired no other support for its members than the voluntary contributions of Christian liberality.'

" '2. That the sum of £900 sterling was granted to the Wesleyan Missionary Committee in London, in 1833, and also a further sum of £550 in 1834, by order of His Majesty's Principal Secretary of State for the Colonies; which sums were granted (as appears by official documents) without any solicitation on the part of the Committee in London—similar grants having also been made by the Imperial Government to Committees of the Church, London (Congregational) and Baptist Missionary Societies, to promote the instruction and improvement of the destitute in other Colonies. That the sums which were granted by His Majesty's Government to the Wesleyan Missionary Committee have been expended (as may be seen by the printed reports of the Auxiliary Methodist Missionary Society in this Province) solely and entirely on the improvement of the long-neglected aboriginal Indian tribes and destitute settlers, and in no instance whatever, either to increase or make up the disciplinary allowances of the Circuit preachers; and there is every reason to believe that, had no grants ever been made by the Imperial Government to the Wesleyan Missionary Committee, either through the Treasurer in London or their agent in this Province, the personal interests of no preacher or Missionary would have been in the slightest degree affected.'

"'3. The correctness of this statement of the case is put beyond all possible doubt by the fact that no grant has been received from the Government by the Wesleyan Missionary Society during the years 1835, 1836 and 1837, and yet not a farthing of loss has been sustained by any member of this Connexion; although the field of Missionary labour may have been thereby circumscribed.'

"'4. That the members of this Conference, either collectively or individually, have no interest to promote in the religious and civil improvement of the aboriginal Indian tribes and destitute settlers, different from that of every friend of the cause of Missions throughout the Province.'

"'5. That this Conference, without any desire to interfere in engagements between His Majesty's Government and the Wesleyan Missionary Committee in London, cannot forbear to express its deep regret that, in consequence of the divided state of public sentiment, and of various

misrepresentations which have been circulated,
the several Government grants, commonly called
" Religious Grants," which have been made for
specific religious purposes (however benevolent
the intentions and the feelings which have dictated them, however noble and Christian the
objects for which they were intended), have
proved seriously prejudicial to the peace and
tranquillity of the Province; and especially as
the continuance of them in their present form
seems to have been made use of to embarrass
the settlement of the Clergy Reserves.'

" ' 6. That as the continuance of the aforesaid
grant to the Wesleyan Missionary Committee,
in aid of the Indian tribes, as a charge upon the
casual and territorial revenue, is one of the conditions upon which His Majesty's Government
has proposed to concede the control of the said
revenue to the Provincial Legislature; and as,
in a message from His Excellency the Lieutenant-
Governor to the House of Assembly, bearing
date the 18th of January, 1837, it is stated that
a claim is urged upon the same revenue by the
Wesleyan Society in this Province; and as the
alleged existence of such a claim has been represented as impeding the settlement of the
general question relating to the casual and territorial revenue, pending between this Province
and the Imperial Government,—this Conference,

with a view of correcting an impression so erroneous and injurious, *disclaims any demand upon the casual and territorial revenue,* and leaves it entirely to the unbiassed judgment of the authorities concerned, to decide whether any public aid can be properly and advantageously given towards the injured aboriginal inhabitants and owners of the colony, and, if any, to what amount, and through what agency.'

"'7. That it is the strong conviction and deliberate judgment of this Conference, that the interests of religion, the stability of the Government, and the welfare of the Province, require the earliest possible settlement of the long-agitated Clergy Reserve question, in accordance with the wishes and circumstances of the inhabitants; and that those interests have been very seriously sacrificed by the delays which have attended the proposed adjustment of that question, so frequently urged upon the attention of the Provincial Legislature by the Imperial Government.'

"'8. That while, as a body of Christian and Methodist ministers, and especially in view of the affectionate reverence we feel for the honoured memory of our venerable founder, Mr. Wesley, we would conscientiously abstain from all needless intermeddling with secular politics; yet, at the same time, this Conference has, heretofore,

as well by its addresses to His Majesty as
through its official organ, the *Christian Guardian*,
expressed its decided conviction of the inex-
pediency of the establishment of one or more
churches in this Province, with exclusive rights
and privileges,—however well suited such an
establishment may be to the condition of the
Mother Country, where it is distinctly recognized
by the constitution of the Government, is sanctioned by various legislative enactments, and
includes a majority, and is devised by the great
body of the nation; that, in this expression
of opinion, other religious bodies, and the
majority of the inhabitants of the Province,
through their representatives in the Provincial
Legislature, have concurred by repeated addresses
and petitions to the Imperial Government and
Parliament; and that the continued efforts of
certain members of the Church of England to
maintain, and the recent attempts of the convention of delegates of the Kirk of Scotland
to secure an ascendency over their Christian
brethren of other denominations, who ought to
stand on perfect equality with them, will, if
successful, be in direct violation of those principles of civil and religious liberty for the
maintenance of which this Conference still, as
formerly, contends, as being essential to the
peace, welfare, and good government of His

Majesty's faithful **and loyal** subjects **in** this Province.'

"'9. That this Conference cannot, without a dereliction of the duty which **it owes to** the members of the numerous congregations under its pastoral care and instruction, **and** without **a** wide departure **from** its often avowed senti- ments, sanction, even by its silence at the present **crisis, the** efforts which are employed **to** deprive **them of** those rights, and **of** that **equal** and **impartial** protection to which **their** numbers, **labours, and long-tried attachment to** His Ma- jesty's **Government give them an** indisputable 'claim.'   ·

"'10. That **should any adjustment of** the Clergy Reserve question be proposed and deter- mined on, which **would** contravene **the principles laid down in the** foregoing resolutions, **and by which individual** and collective effort can be com- bined **for the** religious and educational improve- ment **of the country, the** members of this Con- ference avow their determination not to receive **or apply any** legislative **aid for** their own pe- **cuniary support; or for** any **other** purpose **than the** religious and educa tional improvement **of the Province, in such a way as may be** in accord- ance **with the views of a majority of** two-thirds of the several Quarterly Meetings throughout the **Province; before** which the Chairmen **of the**

several Districts are directed to lay the subjec',
as soon as the Clergy Reserve question shall have
been settled by the Legislature.'

" ' 11. That this Conference, on the present
occasion, reiterates the expression of affection
and loyalty to our Most Gracious Sovereign ;
feels humbly grateful for the condescending and
liberal expression of royal favour to the efforts
of the Wesleyan Methodist Church and other
friends of Christian education in this Province ;
and resolves to continue its prayers and efforts
for the maintenance of the constitution as established by law, and the existing connexion
between this colony and the Parent State.'

" ' City of Toronto, June 24, 1837.

(Signed) " ' WILLIAM M. HARVARD, *President.*

" ' EGERTON RYERSON, *Secretary.*' "

It is obvious from the address of the Conference to the King, adopted June, 1836, and
from the eleven resolutions above quoted, adopted
by the Conference, June, 1837, that a wide-
spread dissatisfaction existed in Upper Canada
on account of the nonsettlement of the Clergy
Reserve and Church Establishment question, and
that a fearful crisis was approaching in the affairs
of Upper Canada ; and that the feeling of discontent was greatly intensified by the unfaithfulness
of many members of the Legislative Assembly
who had been elected with promises to support

the principles of equal civil and religious liberty
in Upper Canada, as well as the constitutional
prerogatives of the Crown and connection with
the Mother Country. The High Church party
appeared to subordinate their exclusive pretensions for the time being to the general interests
of the country; but no sooner were the elections
of 1836 over than the cloven foot of their old
exclusive, ecclesiastical pretensions reappeared;
the settlement of the Clergy Reserves was post-
poned; the transfer of the settlement to England,
by reinvesting the Clergy Reserves in the Crown,
was proposed, and a sufficient number of pur-
chasable members of the Assembly was found to
exchange, by a majority of one, their promises to
their constituents, for more or less than thirty
pieces of silver promised to them to rob the
people of Upper Canada of the disposal of one-
seventh of the lands of the province, and set over
them the Abimelech bramble of High Churchism; but the country at large were the more
disgusted at such betrayals of their elective
trust; the eleven resolutions of the Conference
of June, 1837, quoted above, were among the
public expressions of sentiment on the subject.
The W. L. Mackenzie, or republican section of
the Reform party, thought that no party would
now be found to support a Government so unjust
and untrustworthy; and, therefore, in November,

1837, unfurled the flag of rebellion, and attacked Toronto the 4th of December. But with the almost universal dissatisfaction of the people with the then existing partial and corrupt administration of the Local Government, there was an equally universal substratum of loyalty to law and authority; the country at large was loyal to the heart's core, and the rebellion was soon crushed. Not a minister or member of the Wesleyan Methodist Church was, directly or indirectly, implicated in that rebellious undertaking; all were loyal to law and legal authority to a man; and all were equally loyal to the principles of equal civil and religious liberty. But the High Church party were loyal to nobody but themselves, and to nothing but their own supremacy and monopoly, which, as Mr. John Ryerson states in his narrative, they sought in every way to turn to their own advantage, and to crush the Wesleyan Methodists as well as other loyalist reformers.

It was under these circumstances, and at this crisis, that the leading ministers of the Wesleyan Methodist Church, including the representatives of the British Conference, solicited Mr. Egerton Ryerson, from his seclusion, to resume the editorship of the *Christian Guardian*, in order to "resist the oligarchy," and place the law and government of the country upon the broad foun-

25

dation of equal civil liberty and justice to all
classes of the population. He knew the magnitude and difficulty of the task before him, but
he obeyed the voice of his brethren, and resolved
to do his best. It was not long, however, before
his worst fears were realized in the development
of a new element of opposition to the cause of
Methodist rights and of equal civil and religious
liberty in Upper Canada; the High Church
" oligarchy " of Toronto appealed for help to the
Hercules of the High Church " oligarchy " of
the London Wesleyan Missionary Committee,
whose opposition was more formidable than that
of the Toronto oligarchy, as it involved a defection within the Canadian Conference and
Church, the character and termination of which
will be the subject of the next essay.

ESSAY XVI.

CONTINUANCE OF THE CONFLICT OF THE ENGLISH WITH THE CANADIAN CONFERENCE ON GOVERNMENT GRANTS, AND A CHURCH ESTABLISHMENT IN UPPER CANADA.

IN continuing the subjects of my last essay, I will first give the letter addressed to the Governor by Mr. Egerton Ryerson, previously referred to, and on which the charges of the London Wesleyan Committee were based, and investigated and answered by the Canadian Conference. The letter is as follows:

TORONTO, Jan. 17, 1840.

" May it please your Excellency,—

" I proceed to state, in as few words as possible, the nature of the financial relations which exist between the British Wesleyan Conference in England and the Conference of the Wesleyan Methodist Church in Upper Canada. In the year 1784, the late Rev. John Wesley recommended the formation of the Methodist societies in America into a distinct and independent body, with the attributes and style of a Church—he having general superintendents, or bishops, to perform ordination, etc., among them. It was

by persons who had been ordained and appointed
by these American bishops, that the **Methodist
Church** was established in Upper **Canada.** Down
to 1833, the Methodist Church in **Upper** Canada
had **no more** ecclesiastical connection with the
Wesleyan **Conference** in England, than exists
between the Protestant Episcopal Church in the
United States and the Established Church **of
England.** In 1833 an arrangement **was** agreed
upon by the Wesleyan Conference **in** Upper
Canada and that in England, by which a co-
operation was to take place in the labours of the
two bodies in Upper Canada.   That arrangement
consists **of certain** regulations called ' Articles of
Union.'   These Articles **provide that** the Conference in England **may, when they see** fit, appoint
a person to preside over the **Canada** Conference,
the **same as the** Crown appoints a commissioner
to preside in the General Assembly of the Church
of **Scotland ; but that** the Canadian preachers
shall have no claims upon the funds of the
British **Conference.**

"It was also agreed **that the** British **Conference
should assume the** responsibility **of** supporting
the Indian missions, **which had been, or** might
thereafter be, established in Upper Canada.   **They
have also agreed to employ** Canadian preachers
on those missions ; **but the** Conference in Eng-
land is the judge of the amount to be expended

in each and every year; and the moment any preacher is disabled for the mission work, or ceases to be actively employed in it, he can receive nothing from the funds of the British Conference, but is entirely dependent upon the Canadian Conference.

" It will, therefore, be observed that there are two departments of the work in connection with the Wesleyan cause in Upper Canada, namely, what we call the regular, or circuit work, and the mission work. In carrying on the former, no claim can be made upon the funds of the British Conference ; in carrying on the latter, the British Conference has agreed to assume the pecuniary responsibility, and is the sole judge of the extent of it, and the amount of expenditure.

" The former embraces forty-seven regular circuits, and the latter embraces fourteen circuits, five mission circuits among the new settlements, and nine amongst the aboriginal Indian·tribes. On many of the regular circuits, the congregations are unable to pay more than two-thirds, and, in some instances, not more than one-half, of the disciplinary salary or allowance to the preachers. The loss of such deficiencies must be endured by the preachers concerned, unless, as in the case of Mr. Richey, they happen to be members of the British Conference, as we have not as yet any funds to supply them, and have no claims upon the funds of the British Conference for that purpose.

"The same remark applies to chapels that are in embarrassed circumstances, and also to places where chapels are needed, but where the inhabitants are not able to pay more than a part of what is necessary to build them.

"It may also be observed that, in addition to doing all that is done towards supporting the regular circuit work, and building all the chapels that are built in connexion with it, annual collections and subscriptions are made throughout all our congregations in aid of the funds of the British Wesleyan Missionary Society. These collections and subscriptions amount to from one thousand to fifteen hundred pounds per annum.

"It is, therefore, perfectly clear, that a government grant to the British Wesleyan Conference, and a grant to the Conference of the Wesleyan Methodist Church in Canada, are two very different things. That the latter is not in any way benefitted by grants to the former, will appear obvious from the following reasons :

"1. The Canadian Conference collects more than the sum necessary to support the five missions to the new settlements, and the nine Indian missions which were established previously to 1833, when the British Conference agreed to assume the responsibility of supporting them.

" 2. The government grants were discontinued for two or three years, but it did not in the least affect the Canadian missions; although if the society in England had had additional sums, equal to these grants, at their disposal those years, they would have extended their missionary operations in the other parts of the world in a corresponding ratio, as they are multiplying their various missions (except in Upper Canada) in proportion to the increase of their funds.

3. The government grants are not acknowledged in any reports of the Conference of the Wesleyan Methodist Church in Canada, but are acknowledged only in the annual reports of the Wesleyan Missionary Society in London.

"The annual appropriations for Canadian missions are made in June of each year, and should the dissolution of the union take place between the bodies, as intimated to your Excellency by Messrs. Stinson and Richey, the Conference in England would claim the missions in Upper Canada — notwithstanding their original establishment by the Canadian Conference, and the annual collections made by its ministers to support them. But I apprehend no disposition on the part of the British Conference to dissolve the union, unless they can get government aid, independent of the Canadian Conference, to prosecute their views.

"I conceive, therefore, that any grants intended to benefit the Wesleyan Methodist Church in Canada, ought, undoubtedly, to be placed at the disposal of the Conference of that Church.*

"I have, &c.,

"(Signed)   EGERTON RYERSON."

After the lapse of forty years, I cannot conceive a more accurate account of the financial relations then existing between the English and Canadian Conferences; yet it was on that letter that the charges of the London Wesleyan Missionary Committee were preferred against me in 1840, as quoted above, together with my trial before the Canadian Conference, the proceedings and decision of the Conference, and its resolutions

* *Note by E. Ryerson.*—When I wrote the foregoing letter, I had not the remotest idea that it would be laid before Her Majesty's principal Secretary of State for the Colonies, and therefore could not be an application to his Lordship on any subject. Mr. Vernon Smith had inadvertently attributed to me what was recommended by His Excellency the Governor-General of Canada. The recommendation was also spontaneous on the part of His Excellency, and flowed from his own sense of justice and sound policy, after the most thorough investigation of the subject. My letter was also dictated, to a considerable degree, by certain communications which Messrs. Stinson and Richey had made to His Excellency. (London pamphlet of Messrs. W. and E. Ryerson, p. 7, in a note.)

in reply to the assumptions and accusations of the London Wesleyan Missionary Committee, or rather the Alder-Canadian section of it. Dr. Alder wrote a long letter, and then a second letter, to Lord John Russell, against Mr. Egerton Ryerson's letter, and against Mr. Ryerson charging him with being a Republican, and trying to republicanize Upper Canada—a sentence of calumny, though read in the British Conference at Newcastle, August, 1840, omitted in the *printed* letter, but the substance of it was retained. In addition to the proceedings of the Canadian Conference on the subject, as given in a former essay, I give the introductory paragraphs of Messrs. William and E. Ryerson's reply to Dr. Alder, as it throws light upon the history of that epoch, and the justifiable proceedings of the Canadian Conference. It is headed, "Letter from Rev. W. and E. Ryerson to Lord John Russell, in reply to Mr. Alder, dated

'22 Cecil Street, Strand,
' Aug. 20th, 1840.

'My Lord,—We have the honour to acknowledge the receipt of Mr. Under-Secretary Vernon Smith's letter of the 29th ult., enclosing a copy of the Rev. Robert Alder's letter to your Lordship, dated 20th April last, purporting to be a reply to a letter from the Rev. Egerton Ryerson to His Excellency the Governor-General of Canada, dated January 17th, 1840, respecting the financial relations of the Wesleyan Conferences in England and in Canada.

'We beg, on behalf of the Conference of the Wesleyan Methodist Church in Canada, to express to your Lordship our sincere thanks for the opportunity which your Lordship has thus afforded us of discussing the several subjects of Mr. Alder's letter, and of vindicating the character and interests of the Wesleyan Methodist Church in Upper Canada, from the erroneous statements and imputations contained in that letter.

'As the circumstances under which Mr. Ryerson wrote to His Excellency the Governor-General of Canada the letter referred to, have been misunderstood, it may be worth while to state them. His Excellency having determined to undertake the settlement of the long-agitated question of the Clergy Reserves in Upper Canada, sent during the last week in December, and the first week in January last, for ministers and influential members of various religious denominations, in order to ascertain their opinions and wishes on the subject. Amongst others, he sent for Mr. Ryerson, and also for the Rev. Messrs. Stinson and Richey—the former President of the Upper Canada Conference and representative of the London Wesleyan Missionary Committee; the latter a member of the Wesleyan Conference in England, but temporarily connected with the Wesleyan Methodist Church in Canada by a special vote of the Canadian Conference.

'As the Governor-General proposed to transfer all the religious grants which had been paid out of the casual and territorial revenues, as first charges upon the Clergy Reserve Fund; and as these charges would for some years absorb the entire fund, Mr. Ryerson submitted to His Excellency the justice and reasonableness of making a grant to the Conference of the Wesleyan Methodist Church in Canada, in aid of the Upper Canada Academy, and of transferring that with the other religious grants to the Clergy Reserve Fund. His Excellency objected upon the ground that several hundred pounds per annum had already been granted in aid of the Wesleyan body in Upper Canada. Mr. Ryerson assured His Excellency that he was mistaken, and laid before His Excellency several documents, to satisfy him that the grant referred to had not been made to the Wesleyan body in Canada, nor in aid of its funds.

'His Excellency considered the matter of sufficient importance to require a thorough investigation, and requested Mr. Ryerson to recapitulate in writing the substance of what he had stated verbally. Mr. Ryerson did so, in a letter dated January 2nd, 1840, a copy of which is herewith transmitted, marked **A.** On the same day (January 2nd, 1840), Messrs. Stinson and Richey had an interview with His Excellency, during which they informed His Excellency that the union between the English and Canadian Conferences was expected to be dissolved (a measure the most remote from the thoughts of the members of the Canadian Conference), and desired His Excellency so to frame his bill as to secure that portion of the proceeds of the Reserves, to the control of which the Conference of the Wesleyan Methodists in Canada would be entitled, *to the control of the Wesleyan Conference in England, for the benefit of those who should adhere to it on the dissolution of the union with the Canadian Conference.* On the day following, Messrs. Stinson and Richey embodied their views in a memorial to His Excellency. In that memorial it will be seen that the *Wesleyan Conference in Canada* is superseded by the *Wesleyan Conference in England;* and that when one of the articles of union between the two bodies provided that *the former should have no claims upon the funds of the latter.*

'There is reason to believe that in the interview above alluded to, His Excellency gave Messrs. Stinson and Richey no reason to expect countenance from him to a proposition so obviously unjust and impolitic. Their views and statements furnished His Excellency with additional reasons for examining into all the existing relations and interests of the Wesleyan bodies in Canada and England. His Excellency examined all the despatches and other documents which related to the subject, and sought for information from official persons and from other quarters.

'The result of the investigation was a strong conviction in the mind of His Excellency that the Canadian Conference should alone be regarded as the head and representative of the Wesleyan Methodist Church in Canada ; that the grant which had been made to the London Wesleyan Missionary Committee, out of the Canadian casual and territorial revenue, operated injuriously rather than beneficially to the interests of the Conference of the Wesleyan Methodist Church in Canada, and was not distributed in a manner, and did not accomplish the objects contemplated by the Imperial Government when that grant was made, and ought to be distributed in a different manner hereafter. His Excellency, therefore, determined to write to your Lordship on the subject. His Excellency informed Mr. Ryerson of the result of his investigations and inquiries, and requested Mr. Ryerson to prepare a statement in writing of the financial relations between the Wesleyan Conference of the Wesleyan Methodist Church in Canada.

'In proof of the correctness of this statement

we refer your Lordship to the accompanying memorial of Messrs. Stinson and Richey to His Excellency the Governor-General; to His Excellency's despatch on the subject, addressed to your Lordship in February last; and to the following extract of a letter from Mr. Chief Secretary Murdoch, addressed to Mr. Ryerson in reply to applications which Mr. R. had made to His Excellency on the subject:

'Government House, Montreal,
'June 12, 1840.

'Sir,—I am commanded by the Governor-General to acknowledge the receipt of your letters of the 5th and 6th instant: the first endorsing a copy of certain resolutions adopted by the Committee of the British Wesleyan Conference on the 29th of April last with reference to your conduct; and the second respecting the grant for the support of the Wesleyan Missions in Upper Canada, which His Excellency addressed to Lord John Russell in the month of February last. These arrived during His Excellency's temporary absence from Montreal, the answer to them has been unavoidably delayed.

'His Excellency desires me to say, that he cannot gather from the resolutions of the British Conference that the despatch to the Secretary of State had been communicated to them, as you suppose, and as he has reason to think from other

circumstances that such a proceeding would not
have been adopted, it would be irregular in him
to furnish you with a copy of that despatch,
however much he may regret his inability to do
so ; because, had he been able to do so, it would
not only have fully explained his views, and the
grounds on which he is of opinion, that the grant
should be distributed in a manner different from
that which has of late been followed, but would
have afforded the most conclusive evidence on
some of the points noticed in your letter of the
5th inst. It would have shown, for instance, that
His Excellency's communications with the Secretary of State originated in an examination of the
whole of the circumstances of the Wesleyan body
in Upper Canada, and of the documents relative
to the Union between the British and Canadian
Conferences, which were submitted to him; and
upon this point I am directed to add, in reply
to your question, that this examination did not
proceed from any request of yours, and that the
letter drawn up by you in explanation of the
financial relations of the two bodies, was prepared
at His Excellency's request. It would also further
show, that it was from the Rev. Mr. Stinson, that
His Excellency first heard of the probable dissolution of the two societies.'

"(Signed)   T. W. C. MURDOCH,

'Chief Secretary.'

The above is the statement of the circumstances and object of **Mr. Ryerson's letter to the** Governor-General, in reply to Mr. Alder's letter to Lord **John** Russell. The principal subjects of this letter **have** been sufficiently disposed of by the Canadian Conference in the proceedings quoted on preceding pages. In the concluding part of the Messrs. Ryerson's letter **to Lord** John **Russell, in reply to Mr.** Alder, **the** following paragraphs may be quoted **as** presenting a new phase of the principal question discussed. The words of the Messrs. **Ryerson** are as follows:

" **Mr. Alder** dwells much upon the circumstance that both the **Canada Conference and Mr.** Ryerson had always admitted the exclusive right of the Missionary Committee **to the control of** the Grant. This is very **true, and** for two reasons: 1. Neither the Canada Conference nor **Mr.** Ryerson **was aware of** all the circumstances connected with the Grant **until** after the investigation of them by the Governor-General. 2. The Grant had always been paid out of the *casual and territorial* revenue, with the appropriations of which the Canada Conference had always declared it had no right to interfere, confining its discussions to *the question of the Clergy Reserves,* and its claims to whatever advantage might arise to the Wesleyan Methodist Church in Canada from an equitable settlement of that question.

" But now, my Lord, the affair assumes a very different aspect from what it has heretofore presented. It is supposed to relieve the casual and territorial revenue from the annual payment of this, as well as of other religious grants, and to transfer it as one of the primary charges upon the Clergy Reserve Fund ; an act which if it take place without varying the distribution and control of the grant in question, must, during the next fifty years at least, debar the ministers and members of the Wesleyan Methodist Church in Canada from the slightest benefit of the settlement of the Clergy Reserve question.

"The Wesleyan Methodist Church in Canada has not complained of the exercise of the Royal prerogative, though it has been altogether overlooked, in the distribution of the annual grants which have been made to the Wesleyan Committee in London, and to four other Christian denominations in Upper Canada ; but it will have just and permanent cause of strong dissatisfaction and complaint, should it be deprived of any advantages in the settlement of the Clergy Reserves in which other Churches in Upper Canada largely participate.

" We cannot but view with astonishment the efforts on the part of Mr. Alder and his friends, whose operations in Upper Canada are limited to the last seven years, to grasp every farthing of a

disposable *Canadian* revenue, from their brethren
in Canada, whose operations in that country reach
over the last half century, who have endured privations and labours unexcelled in any country or
in any section of the Christian Church during
that period, and who have contributed more than
any other one religious community to elevate
Upper Canada to its present comparatively advanced state of moral fruitfulness and religious
intelligence. We cannot persuade ourselves that
Her Majesty's Government can be induced to
countenance a policy so obviously unjust, unreasonable, and impolitic."

But Mr. Alder was not content with assailing
Mr. Ryerson individually in respect to his statements as to the relations of the English and
Canadian Conferences, but he denied the correct
ness of Mr. Ryerson's statements respecting the
early history of Methodism in respect to the
British Colonies, and these insinuations against
the General Conferences of the Methodist Episcopal Church in the United States were utterly
unjust and unfounded. These denials and statements were, of course, made to prejudice Lord
John Russell and the British Government against
the Canadian Conference as entertaining undue
leanings to the United States, and of the desire
of the American Methodist General Conference
to exercise a foreign influence over the ministers

and members of the Methodist Church in Canada, and are utterly unfounded insinuations and suspicions. The Canadian Conference never denied its immediate parentage, and did not hesitate to defend the American Conference as well as itself, against unjust statements and insinuations.

The Messrs. Ryerson replied to Mr. Alder's statements in his letter to Lord John Russell, in the following words:

" As to whether or not the late Rev. John Wesley intended the regulations which he adopted in 1784, in reference to the Methodist Societies in the United States, to extend to the British North American Provinces, it is not material to the objects of the present letter to decide. Respecting Mr. Alder's denial of the correctness of Mr. Ryerson's statements on that subject, three remarks may be made. 1. Mr. Wesley's address on that occasion was directed, not to the societies in the *United States,* but to the Methodist Societies in *North America.* 2. In 1787, Mr. Wesley, as well as Dr. Coke, recommended the setting apart *by ordination* of the Rev. F. Garrettson as superintendent or bishop over the societies in New Brunswick, Nova Scotia, and the West Indies, the same as he himself had, in 1784, set apart by ordination the Rev. Dr. Coke, as superintendent or bishop over the societies in North America. And at that period, during the life of

Mr. Wesley, preachers in the Provinces of New Brunswick and Nova Scotia, were stationed at Conferences in the United States. The early officially printed minutes of the Conferences of the Methodist Church in the United States, and the first volume of the history of that Church, by the Rev. Dr. Bangs, of New York, furnish ample evidence on this point. 3. In 1820, the English agreed with the American Methodist Conferences, to leave Upper Canada to be wholly supplied by ministers employed under the directions of the latter; which would not have been done, had it not been perfectly well known that such an arrangement was in accordance with the views and principles upon which Mr. Wesley had acted.

"Mr. Alder's statement that 'the General Conference of the United States endeavoured, with great tenacity, to retain their hold on the Methodist Society in Upper Canada,' is equally incorrect with the one just noticed. The ecclesiastical connection which formerly existed between the Methodist Church in the United States and in Upper Canada, down to 1828, never did exert any influence over the ministers or members of the latter, in relation to civil affairs, as is apparent from the fact, that during the war with the United States, and on all occasions which put their principles to the test, the Methodist

Church in Canada had always given the strongest proofs of loyalty. *The history of Upper Canada does not furnish an instance of a member of the Wesleyan Methodist Church being implicated in rebellion or in conspiracy against his Sovereign.* But the great majority of the ministers as well as members of the Methodist Church in that Province, being British born subjects, desired from personal feeling, as well as from deference to the understood wishes of the Government, to dissolve all ecclesiastical connection with the Methodist Church in the United States, and therefore applied to the General Conference of that Church in 1824 for a friendly *separation;* but the Representative of the British Conference, the Rev. Richard Reece, opposed the application, upon the ground that the Wesleyan body in Canada was too feeble and inexperienced to manage its own affairs; and stated to the American Conference, that if they complied with the application from Canada he should feel it his duty on his return to England, to recommend to the British Conference to send a sufficient number of Missionaries from England into Upper Canada to supply the whole work. At the next Quadrennial General Conference of the Methodist Church in the United States in 1828, the application for a separation on the part of the Methodist Conference in Canada was renewed, and readily granted;

after which time to 1833, when certain articles of
union were agreed to, the Methodist Church in
Canada existed as an independent body, established several Missions amongst the aboriginal
Indian tribes, had an accession of more than
6,000 communicants, and procured subscriptions
to the amount of nearly £6,000, towards the
erection of the buildings of the Upper Canada
Academy."

ESSAY XVII.

THE REPRESENTATIVES OF THE CANADIAN CONFERENCE
(REVS. W. AND E. RYERSON) BEFORE THE BRITISH
CONFERENCE; THEIR RECEPTION; THE PROCEEDINGS
AGAINST THEM AND THE CANADIAN CONFERENCE;
THEIR CONDEMNATION AND THE PROCEEDINGS
AGAINST THEM PUBLISHED; THEIR VINDICATION;
THEIR RETURN TO CANADA, AND APPROVAL OF
THEIR CONDUCT BY THE CANADIAN CONFERENCE.

IT has been seen that Messrs. W. and E.
Ryerson, were appointed by ballot by the
Canadian Conference, June, 1840, Representatives
to the English Conference, which was held at
Newcastle-on-Tyne, August following.

The reception of the Representatives of the
Canadian Conference was very peculiar. Before
ever having been heard, both the Canadian
Conference and its Representatives had been virtually condemned by the British Conference, or
rather by the Canadian Section of its Missionary
Committee. The Canadian Conference, instead
of being treated as a co-ordinate Conference of
Wesleyan Methodism, of equal standing with
any other Conference, were treated as inferiors to
even District Meetings of the English Conference

—the Canadian Conference was practically condemned as delinquent, and its Representatives as ecclesiastical criminals—receiving not the least indication of respect or recognition from the President and leading members of the British Conference.

The Representatives of the Canadian Conference say, in their reply to the Secretary to the British Conference :

" We came to England in accordance with the suggestion of the Committee of your Conference on Canadian affairs, which states that 'if the Canadian Conference should deem it to be its duty to send a Representative to the next British Conference, for the purpose of offering any explanations, or of making proposals with a view of perpetuating the Union ; or, should that be found impracticable, for the purpose of making such arrangements as may prevent unseemly and unchristian collisions between members of two divisions of the same great family ; the Committee assure the Canadian Conference, that such Representative will be received with cordial affection by the British Conference, and that every attention will be paid to his statements and representations.'

" The kind manner of our reception is familiar to you. We shall merely say, it was to us a new thing in Methodism ; and that up to the present moment, neither of us has been favoured with the honour or the courtesy of a salutation, either from Dr. Bunting or the President of your Conference, or any of the leading official members, with a few exceptions. If a Representative of your Conference to Canada, or to the United States, had never even been saluted by a shake of the hand, or a nod of the head, on the part of the presiding officers of the Conferences in those countries, we question whether it could be stated with truth, that he had been *received with cordial affection.*

" Into the further details as to our official reception we will not enter. For many expressions of kindness and attention on the part of individual members of your Conference, we cherish a grateful remembrance, and desire to record our heartfelt acknowledgments, especially for the unwearied and affectionate attentions of the Rev. William Lord, the President of the Canada Conference."

As to the mode of proceeding in the British Conference on the Canadian question, the Representatives of the Canadian Conference stated as follows, in a letter in reply to the Secretary of British Conference :

" It is probably known to you, that by notes to the President, and otherwise, we urged the early consideration of the subject of our mission, but that several days elapsed before the appointment

of a committee was proposed; that we objected
to the reference of the Canadian Address and
resolutions to a committee before they were read
and discussed in the Conference, as they were
addressed to the *British Conference*, and embodied
an appeal from the proceedings of its own Committee; that our objections were over-ruled, with
the assurance that we should have an opportunity of stating fully the whole matter to the
Conference. It will also appear by the Minutes
of your Conference, that the Committee thus appointed on Canadian affairs did not meet until
Saturday, the 8th of August—*eleven days* after
the commencement of the session, and within
three days of the then anticipated close of it.
It must be in your recollection, that when in
Committee we remonstrated against being interrupted at almost every stage of our remarks,
stating that we had not in any one instance
interrupted Dr. Alder in his four hours' statement, or Mr. Stinson in his statement in support
of the statements made by Dr. Alder, we were
informed by Dr. Bunting, in reply, that such was
your mode of proceeding in Committees—that
any statement was liable to be objected to the
moment it was made, and explanation demanded
at the time, that no credit was due to either of
us for not having interrupted Dr. Alder or Mr.
Stinson, as we might have done so if we had

chosen ; that when we came to speak in Conference we could proceed without interruption until
we had concluded.

"You are further aware, that the affair was
not reported to the Conference until Thursday
evening, the 13th instant, and not taken up until
the following day [Friday] a few hours before
the close of the session ; when, out of upwards of
three hundred (300) members who had attended
the Conference, the greatest number present
during the Canadian business was *seventy-two*
(a less number than there are members of the
Canadian Conference), the other two hundred,
or two hundred and fifty having left Conference
for their circuits ; that *then* we were told, that
as so much time had been occupied with the
investigation of the subject in Committee, and
as there was scarcely a preacher present who was
not either a member of the Committee, or had not
witnessed its proceedings, the further discussion
of the subject was inadmissible as well as unne-
cessary ; and that our remarks must, therefore, be
confined to the expression of our views respecting
the Report of the Committee."

"So as to the *mode* of your Conference proceedings in this affair. We have felt it our duty to
make these brief references to it, as it is several
times alluded to in the resolutions which you
have enclosed.

"In regard to the resolutions themselves, we cannot but express, in the first place, our surprise and regret at the manner in which the statements reported have been made, and the papers and documents, stated to have been read, are recorded in the report of the Committee, as we are persuaded it conveys a very erroneous impression of the proceedings of the Committee, and of the facts brought before it.

"The order in which the statements read is altogether different in the report, from what it was in *reality.* Why is this? The *dates* of some letters and documents read are given in the report; the dates of others are omitted. Why is this? A synopsis of some of the statements and documents read is given; the synopsis of other statements and documents is suppressed. Why is this? And in the synopsis of some of the principal documents those very points are omitted which constituted the leading features of those documents, and the points of difference between the two Connexions. Why is this? How is it possible for any reader to form a correct idea of the real nature and merits of a question, where the proceedings on it are thus reported?

"We will give some examples in illustration of these remarks." [The Messrs. Ryerson give several examples of the unfair manner in which the documents named by the Committee had been reported and printed. The following is the first example.] " In the enumeration of statements made and documents read in the Committee, three letters are mentioned, under the heads 9, 10 and 11 ; one from Dr. Alder to the President of the Canada Conference ; a second from the Missionary Secretaries to Sir George Arthur ; the third from the President of your Conference to the Rev. E. Ryerson (dated March 23, 1839). Now the reader would suppose, from the order and the synopsis given of these letters, that they were read to illustrate and establish the allegation that the organ of the Canada Conference had unjustifiably interfered with secular party politics ; yet the very reverse was the fact. Mr. E. Ryerson commenced his reply to Dr. Alder on Saturday evening and resumed it on Monday forenoon. Previously to resuming his remarks, he called for the reading of the letters referred to. Dr. Bunting and others objected to the reading of them, as irrelevant ; just thirty-five minutes discussion ensued before Mr. E. Ryerson was allowed to read the letters. Mr. Ryerson had shown, from documentary evidence, that when the Union was agreed to in 1833, and from that time to 1839, the question of the Clergy Reserves was left to the uncontrolled action of the Canadian Conference ; and that in its proceedings and views three successive Representatives of the British Conference had concurred and co-operated. He then proceeded to read the three letters in question, to prove : 1. That down to that period (1839) there was not the slightest complaint against him or the Canadian Conference on the score of interference in civil matters, as neither of these letters contained a word on the subject. 2. That each of these letters refers to *ecclesiastical* questions *only*, or questions of the Clergy Reserves (which phrases are synonymous in Canada, as no ecclesiastical questions have ever been discussed in Upper Canada besides the Clergy Reserves); thence stating the fact, that with the interference of the Missionary Secretaries in the question of the Clergy Reserves, contrary to the declaration of both the Representatives at the time the Union took place in 1833, and contrary to the administration of it for six years, commenced the misunderstandings between the English and Canadian Connexions. But what a totally different idea and meaning do these letters convey, from the order in which they are enumerated in the report of the Committee, and the partial and unfair synopsis which is given of them ? "

From the previous pages the *decision of the English Conference* may be anticipated ; but it may be advisable to give the resolutions them-

selves adopted by the Committee, recommended
to, and adopted by the seventy-two, out of some
400 members of the Conference, a few hours before the close of the Conference :

" I. That the three resolutions, or matters, contained in the resolutions of the Committee on
Canadian affairs, at their meeting on the 29th of
April last and forwarded by that Committee to
the Upper Canada Conference *are regarded as
fully proved ;* and that after seriously considering
the explanations and defence of the Rev. Egerton
Ryerson and the Rev. William Ryerson, the representatives of the Upper Canada Conference, on
these points, and giving them the full weight to
which they might be deemed to be entitled, the
Committee are decidedly of opinion, that the
representatives of the Upper Canada Conference
have entirely failed to establish a justification,
inasmuch as it appears that, notwithstanding all
that they have stated and explained, there existed :
1. A superseding of the Rev. Joseph Stinson as
President, by communicating with the Governor-
General, separately and without his knowledge,
and by acting without him, and without the
Committee of the Upper Canada Conference, of
which Committee Mr. Stinson was a member,
and Chairman *ex officio* on matters affecting the
permanency of the Government Grant to the
Wesleyan Missionary Society.

"2. A violation of the obligations arising from the Union, in not opposing but rather countenancing the payment of our grant in a certain contingency, not to us but to the Upper Canada Conference, for other reasons and different purposes. ·

"3. The decided and prominent political character of the *Christian Guardian*, in violation of the pledges given to us and to the Upper Canada Conference, from 1833 to 1839.*

"II. That after the most careful examination of the complicated and difficult subjects which have engaged the attention of the Committee appointed by the British Conference of 1839 to decide finally all matters relating to the Union between the British and the Upper Canada Conference, and to our Indian Missions in Upper Canada; and after having, in the course of a very protracted discussion had abundant proof of the wisdom, care, and kindness which the aforesaid Committee have manifested in relation to the ˋ affairs of Upper Canada, we are unanimously of opinion, that the members of the Committee in Upper Canada affairs, particularly in the resolutions adopted at their meeting in London, on Wednesday, April 29th, 1840, and transmitted

---

* *Note by E. Ryerson, 1880.*— No such pledges were ever given as thus stated; and no fault was found with the *Guardian* from 1833 to 1839, as shown previously.

to the Upper Canada Conference, have strictly adhered to those great principles which have always guided the Wesleyan body, and that they are, therefore, entitled to the thanks of this Conference for the important services which they have rendered to the common cause of Wesleyan Methodism.

" III. After a close consideration of the resolutions of the Upper Canada Conference of 1840, it was resolved :

" 1. That this Committee is most happy to perceive that one of the resolutions, which determines that the *Christian Guardian* shall cease to be a political paper, and shall be confined to purely religious and literary subjects and articles of religious intelligence, is to that extent satisfactory ; but that the unqualified reservation of the ' Clergy Reserve question ' — a reservation already so construed and abused as to be pleaded in almost unlimited discussion of great and general principles of ecclesiastical polity, held sacred by this body ; and the absence of adequate security for a more faithful observance of this resolution than has been maintained with respect to similar pledges given from 1833 to 1839, in connection with the fact that a direct negative was simultaneously given to another series of resolutions, which would have been more explicit and satisfactory on the several subjects referred to,

27

are circumstances which the Committee deeply regret, and cannot but regard with distrust and disapprobation.

"2. That on the other important topics embraced in the resolutions of our Committee on Upper Canada affairs, dated April 29, 1840, the resolutions of the last Upper Canada Conference appear rather to imply an acquiescence in the evils complained of, and an official adoption of them, than a cordial determination to prevent their future recurrence by substantial and efficient measures, and seem to evince that there is a decided difference between the two Conferences on the construction of the articles of union, in reference to fundamental principles essential to the working of the union, and which the Committee are of opinion that the British Conference cannot abandon, without compromising its own consistency and public reputation ; inasmuch as it cannot safely be identified in views and responsibility with any body, however respected, over whose public proceedings it is denied the right and power of exerting any efficient influences, so as to secure a reasonable and necessary co-ordinate but efficient direction, during the continuance of the union.

"IV. That in the judgment of this Committee, nothing has occurred, in the whole course of these investigations, to shake the confidence of the Con-

ference in the Rev. Joseph Stinson and the Rev.
Matthew Richey ; and that **the members of the**
Committee cannot but express their hearty esteem
and approbation **of the ability, fidelity and dili-**
gence with **which these** respected brethren have
performed **the duties** officially **confided to** them.*

* This special commendation **of** Messrs. **Stinson and**
Richey was **intended, of course, as a** corresponding reproach **to** the Canada Conference **and its** Representatives,
against whom Messrs. **Stinson and Richey now arrayed**
themselves **in** support **of** Mr. **Alder's** accusations. **The**
Annual Addresses of the Canada to the English Conference invariably referred to Messrs. Stinson **and Richey**
in the most respectful and affectionate terms. **They had**
been admitted members of the Canada **Conference by a**
special vote, though still retaining **their membership of**
the British Conference—a compliment **that was never**
reciprocated by the English Conference. **Even after they**
had informed the **Governor-General** that the Union would
probably **be** dissolved, and prayed to place the English
instead of the Canada Conference **as** the recipient of all
Canadian revenue that might **be** apportioned **to the**
Wesleyan **Methodist** Church in Canada ; **even after this,**
the Canada Conference, **in its address to the** English
Conference, **as** late as June, **1840, referred most** affectionately **to** Messrs. Stinson and **Richey,** without **even**
alluding **to their** defection **to the vital interests of the**
Canada Conference, **in their Memorial to the Governor-**
General. Mr. Stinson always admitted **the kindness and**
affection with which he **had been personally** treated by
his Canadian brethren, **both of the** ministry and laity.
Yet, on March 20, **1840, he wrote** a letter to the London

"**V.** That notwithstanding the ground of **grievance** and complaint on which the Committee **have felt it their duty to** express **so** strong an opinion,

Missionary Committee, **which was read** in the Committee of the Newcastle Conference, **in** which he says, "I have **lost all confidence** in **the men with whom I act; and if you** choose **to** degrade **yourselves any** longer by **a** connection with **such men, I hope you will** permit me **to** retire from the **Province."** "**Such were** Mr. **Stinson's words, as nearly as we could take them** down while **Dr.** Alder **was reading his letter.** [For copies of **the letters, and extracts of letters read, were not** furnished **to the Representatives of the Canada** Conference.] Yet, **a** short time after writing that letter, for perusal **and action in** *England,* Mr. **Stinson declared before** these **men in** Conference **assembled in** *Canada,* **that he conceived the** Canadian Preachers worthy **to stand, in every respect,** upon an equal footing with English **Preachers; that he** earnestly desired to perpetuate the connection **between the** two bodies; that he **would** consider it wrong **for the Government to pay the London** Committee the grant out **of the** Clergy **Reserve Fund, if** it should in the slightest **degree affect the** claims **or interests of the** Connexion in **Canada; that in the event of** the dissolution **of the Union, he** should **consider** it wrong for **the Committee** in London to attempt to retain **possession of those Indian** Missions **which** had **been** established **by the Canada** Conference prior **to** the Union. [Such, I believe, **were the real** sentiments **of** Mr. Stinson's judgment **and** heart; **but he had to** adopt different language for and **in** England, **or lose** his position with Dr. Alder and **the** Committee **misled by** him.] Relying upon such **professions and declarations,** the Canada Conference

they are aware of the desirableness **of maintaining** the existing **union** between the **two** bodies **for** reasons which **relate to the** general interests

requests Mr. **Stinson to accompany its** Representatives to England '*for co-operation and* **aid**.' He **comes to** England **and 'aids' and** 'co-operates **with' the Representatives of the Canada** Conference, by extracts **of such letters as we have above quoted, and by** kindred **verbal statements and** representations ; **and is** then thanked by **your Committee** and the remainder **of** your Conference ! **But resolutions** of **Committees or** **Conferences** cannot **alter** *facts*, **or make crooked things** straight, **or darkness light.**

"And these extracts of calumnious **letters against his** Canadian brethren, from Mr. **Richey, are read in your** Committee, and Mr. Richey **tells your Committee that** the 'ministerial character is **degraded' in Canada ; that** there is little 'chemical affinity' **in the connexion there** with British **Wesleyan** Methodism ; **and that** during his four years' residence in that Province **he was** treated (to use his own emphatic words) '*as a stranger, a foreigner, and an alien.*'"

"Mr. Richey was invited to Upper Canada as Principal of the Conference Academy ; **the Board of that** Institution applied **to** an American University **College to** confer **upon** him **the** honorary **degree of Master of** Arts, and **paid** his travelling **expenses while visiting** American Colleges **and in pursuit of a diploma ; paid him for** three years a salary **about twice as high as that** of any other Wesleyan Minister **in Upper Canada ; and** when it **was** not deemed **advisable [by the** Board **of the** Academy] to ask him **to continue in that** situation any

of our common Christianity *and to the continued connection of the Province with the* Mother

longer, he was stationed in the City of Toronto, the
City Road Circuit of the Canada Connexion. The Conference had requested him to prepare for publication a
volume of sermons, and directed its Book Steward to
publish them ; the Editor of the *Christian Guardian*,
Mr. E. Ryerson, wrote as encomiastic a notice of those
sermons as the warmest friendship could dictate ; and
although the Canada Conference could not approve of
Mr. Richey's views and conduct in reference to the
Resolutions of the London Committee, and his communications with the Governor-General, it possessed sufficient
judgment and charity to discriminate between a man's
views and proceedings in certain circumstances, and his
general character ; and, therefore, on Mr. Richey's departure for England, transmitted to the British Conference
a flattering letter of respect and affection in relation to
him. Mr. Richey comes to the British Conference and
tells you that he had been treated, during four year's
residence in Upper Canada, '*as a stranger, a foreigner,
and an alien;*' and you express your 'hearty esteem
and approbation of the ability, fidelity and diligence'
with which he had performed the duties officially confided to him. Thanks and eulogies thus obtained are
dearly purchased ; and whatever influence the representations of Messrs. Stinson and Richey may have had
upon your proceedings against the Canada Conference,
we are persuaded they will operate differently in Canada,
where the facts to which we have referred are well and
generally known." — (*Messrs. Ryerson's Reply to the
Proceedings of the British Conference, August 29, 1840,
published in London, pp. 94-97.*)

*Country.** Yet in their judgment, that union can be advantageously maintained only by the strict and undeviating adherence of our Upper Canadian brethren to the following principles and regulations :

* *Note by E. Ryerson, 1880.*—The insinuation implied in the words printed in italics was as offensive as it was unjust. There never was a more loyal body to the Constitution of Upper Canada and its connection with the Mother Country, than the Conference and members of the Methodist Church in Canada, as shown in the war of the United States against Great Britain in 1812-1815, and in the W. L. Mackenzie Rebellion in 1837, during both of which tests of loyalty not a minister or member of the Wesleyan Methodist Church in Upper Canada was found wanting in loyalty to their Sovereign and country—men who knew what loyalty was in the successive wars, and hundreds of whose fathers, brothers, and relatives had fallen or bled on the battle-field. Even one of the Canadian representatives had fought in two battles in the war of 1812-1815, together with two elder brothers in several battles, and a father in seven battles in two wars. For such men, and a whole community, to be impeached in their loyal character by a Committee in London, not one of whom had ever smelt powder on the field of battle, and knew nothing of the stuff of which true loyalty is made except to prate about it on occasions for partizan purposes, was unlike offensive and unjust.

After the lapse of two score years, and approaching myself my four score years, I can scarcely think of these imputations from such sources and for such purposes without a thrill of indignation pervading my whole being, or write about them in terms of moderation.

"1. That the continuation of the Government Grant to the Wesleyan Missionary Society be cordially assented to, and supported by our Upper Canada brethren, even if the payment should be ultimately transferred, as proposed by the Clergy Reserve Bill, lately passed by the Imperial Parliament, from the Casual and Territorial Revenue on which it is placed, to the Clergy Reserve Fund, in that Province; and that, as it appears that the payment of the grant has actually been again suspended, and it is at present withheld, to the great inconvenience and embarrassment of our Missions in Upper Canada, the Rev. Egerton Ryerson shall address a letter to Lord John Russell, disclaiming any intention or wish to deprive the Wesleyan Missionary Society of the grant of £700 per annum, secured to that Society as a fixed charge for Missionary purposes in Upper Canada, requesting that its regular payment may be continued; and assuring his Lordship that any other construction which may have been put upon his letter to the Governor-General, was founded in a misapprehension of his meaning.*

"2. That the *Christian Guardian*, or whatever newspaper or periodical may, in future, be recog-

---

* The requirement of this resolution was that Mr. Egerton Ryerson, without regard to consistency or character, should advocate what he knew to be wrong and to state what he knew to be false.

nized as the official **organ of the** Upper Canada Conference shall entirely **abstain from all** party political reasonings and discussions, confining **its** expression of opinions **to religious and** literary topics.

" 3. That **such** official **organ admit and main-tain all the** acknowledged **principles of the** Wesleyan Methodist Connexion ; **and that in** seeking for **a** proper **understanding on this point,** the Committee have special reference **to that principle of our body** which asserts **it to be the duty of civil** governments **to** employ **their in-**fluence and a portion **of their** resources, **for the** support of the Christian religion."

" The report above inserted, **was presented to** the Conference [a **few hours before its close,** when more than **four-fifths of its members had** left for their **circuits] and read in the hearing** of the Rev. Egerton and **Rev. William Ryerson,** representatives of the Upper Canada Conference. They **desired a copy of it, which was** accordingly handed to them ; **and they** examined its several parts. When **they returned they were again** heard at length **[but not permitted to go back** beyond the year 1839, **though the report extend-**ed back to 1833], and mutual explanations **were** made on several points to **which they demurred.** In the end, they frankly **and** explicitly declared it **as** their opinion that **the Upper** Canada

)

Conference would never be induced to listen to the views which are contained in the aforesaid report, and concerning which such serious misunderstandings have arisen; and that the maintenance of such views on the part of this body, would be regarded by the Canada Conference as a virtual dissolution of the union. Upon hearing this the Conference [one-fifth of its members being present, four-fifths having departed for their homes] was reluctantly led to the conviction, that a continuation of the more intimate connection, established by the articles of 1833 is quite impracticable. The Conference could not overlook the fact, that the pacific resolutions, which had already been proffered to the Upper Canada Conference of 1840, by some members, were negatived by a large majority ; and that from the statements of the Rev. Egerton and Rev. William Ryerson, just made, the same disposition evidently remains, and clearly precludes a further perpetuation of the union." (Extract from the *" Proceedings and Decision of the Conference on matters relating to the union between the British Conference and the Upper Canada Conference, and to our Missions in Upper Canada," Newcastle-on-Tyne, August, 1840, printed by the authority of the Conference, pp. 75-79.*

ESSAY XVIII.

SEVEN YEARS' DIVISIONAL OPERATIONS OF THE LONDON WESLEYAN COMMITTEE, IN UPPER CANADA, FROM 1840 TO 1847; RECONCILIATION AND RE-UNION OF THE ENGLISH AND CANADIAN CONFERENCES; ITS CAUSES AND RESULTS.

THE English Conference having determined to secede from the Union which it had entered into with the Canadian Conference in 1833, and to commence aggressive operations upon the Canadian Conference, and its societies and congregations, a special meeting of the Canadian Conference became necessary to meet this new state of things, to organize for resenting the invasion upon its fields of labour, and to maintain the cause for which they had toiled and suffered so much for more than half a century.

The prospects of the Canada Conference were gloomy in the extreme; their paucity of ministers, and poverty of resources in comparison to the English Conference, besides numerous other disadvantages; but the Ministers of the Canadian Conference with less than a dozen individual exceptions, had hearts of Canadian oak,-

and weapons of New Jerusalem steel, and determined to maintain the freedom of their Church, and the liberties of their country, whatever might be the prestige or resources of their invaders; and "according to their faith it was done unto them;" out of weakness they waxed strong. They sowed in tears, they reaped in joy. Their weeping seed-sowing was followed by rejoicing, bringing their sheaves with them.

The narrative of the state of things and of the work at this crucial and eventful juncture, is thus given by the late Rev. John Ryerson, who begins with the proceedings of the Special Conference held in Toronto, October, 1840 :—

"The Conference now proceeded to reorganize itself, and to make arrangements for carrying on the work committed to their charge as aforetime. The Rev. Thomas Whitehead was elected President and the Rev. John C. Davidson as Secretary. At the same time that the Conference was holding its sessions, the English Missionary District was being held in the Richmond Street Church, under the Presidency of the Rev. J. Stinson, who had been President of the Canada Conference up to this time.

"Ten of the Canadian ministers withdrew from the Canadian Conference and joined the English Missionary District Meetings. This was a heavy blow to the Canada Conference, but other preachers were employed, and all the appointments maintained as had been made at the commencement of the Conference year at Belleville. There were nine Indian Missions under the care of the Missionary Society; six of these remained under the superintendency of the Canada Conference; but three went to the Missionary District, the missionaries being two of the ministers who left the Canada Conference to join the British Conference.*

"The Canada Conference had no missionary funds independent of the Wesleyan Missionary Society; so that our Conference was left responsible for the support of the six Indian Missions and eight Domestic Missions without a farthing to support them.

"The deep and painful anxiety felt, in view of these sorrowful events, will never be known until the day of the revelation of all things. A short time after the adjournment of Confer-

* *Note by E. Ryerson*, 1880. – Among the ten who seceded from the Canada Conference to the London Wesleyan Committee, was the venerable William Case, who took no part in the crusade against his old Canadian brethren, but who wished to live in peace and quietness, with the supply of his wants assured him in his old lonely Indian Mission at Alnwick (once called Aldersville), near Cobourg, isolated alike from the white inhabitants and from other Indian tribes, where he continued until his decease.

ence, the Revs. A. Green, **J. Ryerson**, J. Scott
and E. Ryerson, with as many lay members of
the Church, met in an upper chamber at Mr. J.
R. Armstrong's, to consult respecting the present exigency, and to devise means for the support of the Indian and Domestic Missions. It
was finally concluded to commence a subscription
among ourselves, and then, that the Rev. J.
Ryerson, and the Rev. Peter Jones, should be
a deputation to visit and hold Missionary Meetings (as far as possible) in all the circuits and
stations throughout the Connexion. These brethren were enabled by the 'good hand of God
upon them,' to perform the onerous duty committed to them, during a tour of four months'
continuance. They visited all the circuits
situated between London and Bytown (now the
City of Ottawa), preaching every Sabbath, from
one to three sermons, and holding from three
to six missionary meetings during the week,
besides travelling many long and tedious jour-
neys.

"The people gave liberally, in most places
bountifully, and in some instances munificently;
so that at the close of the year, it was found
that *upwards of one third more had been
contributed in the Province for Missionary
purposes, than had ever been contributed before
in any one year.* Thus did the Lord provide,

and the hands of His servants and people were strengthened."

I have stated above that the English Missionary District was held in Toronto, at the same time as the Canada Conference. They were enabled to send preachers and missionaries to most of the principal places in the country, and supply their Indian Missions by employing the ten preachers, who had left our Conference, besides Messrs. Stinson, Hashard, Lang and Redney, and one or two others whom the London Missionary Committee had sent to Canada. Several other preachers were immediately in the field. Thus were the societies again divided, and sections were made in Kingston, Belleville, Peterboro', Toronto, Barrie, Hamilton, Brantford, London, Goderich, Guelph, and several other places. Every year during the six succeeding ones of the disruption, the Missionary District was increasing the number of its preachers, and enlarging the sphere of its operations. The work of discord and confusion increased in proportion, and even Indian Missions shared in the strife, and disputations arose amongst these helpless children of the woods.

"The sympathy of the great body . of the people in Canada was with the Canada Conference. But the prestige of the English *name* [especially with the lately-arrived emigrants], the

patronage and countenance of the Provincial
Government, and the ample funds of the Wesleyan Missionary Society in England, were with the
District Meeting. The schisms and heart-burnings from the large societies, down to the
domestic circles, were distressing beyond expression, and most painful to every lover of peace
in the family of Christ. But enemies of the
truth beheld this unnatural strife and disreputable discord with exultation and delight, virtually exclaiming, " So would *we* have it ; this is
what we have longed for, and have long sought
to effect. We have divided, let us now devour."*

Note by E. Ryerson, 1880.—I will quote on this subject the 1st, 7th, 8th, and 9th " Resolutions of the Special
Committee appointed by the Conference, October, 1840,
to protect the rights and interests of the Wesleyan
Methodist Connexion in Canada, adopted at a meeting
held in the City of Toronto, Canada, the 10th and 11th
of May, and afterward unanimously affirmed, by the
Conference, June, 1841, in reference to certain resolutions which had been adopted and published by a Special
Committee of the Wesleyan Conference, held in London,
England, the 8th and 9th September, 1840."
" I. That this Committee regrets to observe that so
large a portion of the *fourteen* lengthened resolutions of
the Special Committee of the English Conference on
Canadian affairs, is occupied with personal references to
the late representatives of the Canada Conference. This
Committee especially regrets to witness, in the resolutions of the London Committee, the repeated and suc-

But certainly the state **of** the Church during
these six years of divisive conflict **was** not
altogether evil. There was much good **done** ;
the preachers were **very zealous** ; and, although

cessive application of criminating **epithets** against the
Rev. Egerton Ryerson, when the primary original charge
of the London **Committee** against **him was,** not any
moral crime **or private delinquency, but an** alleged
official irregularity in his communication with the Govern-
ment in behalf of the Canada Connexion; yet the London
Committee applies epithets against Mr. E. Ryerson, which
are only applied to characters **of the** deepest moral tur-
pitude. Such an obvious **disproportion** between the original allegations of **the** London Committee and the vitu-
perative epithets which they employ against the individual,
appears to this Committee inconsistent **with** the **calm**-
ness, dignity, and propriety which **ought to characterize**
the proceedings **of** ecclesiasitical **bodies, and to have**
little affinity with **that** charity **which is recommended**
and portrayed by St. Paul in the **1**3th **Chapter of the First**
Epistle to the Corinthians."

"**VII.** That the assertion **of the** London Wesleyan
Committee, that the resolutions **of the** Canada Conference adopted at Belleville, June, 1840, were **a virtual**
dissolution **of the Union, is** a most unjust misrepresenta-
tion **of** the motives **and** feelings **of that** body. For, 1.
In each **of those** resolutions the **Canada** Conference
expressed its **determined** adherence to the **Articles**
of Union. 2. That **the** English **Conference** representatives should possess and **exercise all the powers**
for which the Articles of Union **provided.** 3. **That**
the Canadian Conference **claimed** nothing **more** than
was explicitly secured **by the** Articles of Union. The

in many instances, Christ was doubtless, preached
through envy and strife, yet *Christ was preached,*
and many souls were saved. The preachers were
devoted to the one great work of spreading

London **Wesleyan Committee** have specified no single
Article of the Union which has **ever** been infringed
by the Canada **Conference, or by any** member of it.
The allegation **of the** London Committee is, therefore,
as groundless **as it is hasty and** uncharitable.

"VIII. That, notwithstanding the London Wesleyan
Committee propose, in **their** 10th and 11th resolutions,
not to interfere with the societies of **the** Canada Conference, **but to extend their** operations amongst the destitute **settlers and heathen** tribes, **yet the** operations of
their **agents** and missionaries **in Upper** Canada are, for
the **most** part, of **an** opposite **character, as,** out of from
fifteen to twenty missionaries **here, only** *five* **of them are**
labouring in fields which are not **occupied by preachers**
of the Canada Conference ; the other fifteen **are labour-**
ing as missionaries *within the bounds of regular circuits,*
dividing neighbourhoods, societies, and families, and
producing all the other **evils of** schism, strife, and
divisions.

"IX. That, it **is much to be lamented that whilst the**
London Wesleyan Committee **have** pressed into **their**
service almost every circumstance **which was** calculated
to excite recrimination and hostilities, and justify the aggressions of **their** missionaries upon **our societies in**
Upper Canada, they **seem to have passed over,** with little
or no notice, those considerations which might tend to
promote **the unity** of Methodism **in** Canada. They do
not deny that the representatives of the Canada Conference had expressed a readiness to agree to every demand

holiness over the land, and God was manifestly with them. During the six years the aggregate increase in the Church membership connected with the Canada Conference was 6,622. The increase in the Missionary District I do not know. But during one of the six years,

on the score of non-interference in politics—to drop the Church establishment question in silence—to disclaim to the Secretary of State, having made any application for the disputed grant—to allow the English Conferences all the power over the Canada Connexion provided for by the Articles of Union, to grant them all the control in Upper Canada they possess in other British provinces, provided they would assume the same responsibility in supporting the preachers in Upper Canada they do in other British provinces. The only two practical points on which the Representatives of the Canada Conference seem to have opposed the demands made upon them were, their refusal to make the *Guardian* the advocate of Church and state union, and the refusal of one of them to *turn advocate* in behalf of the London Committee to a Government grant, even in case of its transfer to the Clergy Reserve Fund.

"X. That on review of the whole matter, this Committee is of opinion that no sufficient or justifiable ground of hostility, division, or disunion between the English and Canada Conferences exists; that for the honour of Christianity and the character of Methodism, a speedy end should be put to these unnatural scenes of schism and contention; and that every possible means should be employed to restore to Methodism that *unity* which, for a hundred years, has been its boast and its glory."

1845, there was a decrease of 803—a diminution in members which was very saddening to the hearts of preachers who met in Conference that year. But dark and gloomy as these times were, I never lost the hope, and I may say the belief, that Providence, often duly chastising us, would in some way terminate these calamities. Under this impression I kept up a correspondence with Messrs. Lord and Stinson, also with Dr. Alder, during the whole of the disruption, and a few letters were written to Dr. Richey. At the Kingston Conference of 1846, a constant and strong conviction was upon my soul, that the time had come for some steps to be taken towards conciliation and effecting a re-union in some way.

This thought was made the subject of consultation with a number of the preachers, and was finally brought under the consideration of the Conference. After much discussion a Committee was appointed to consider it, and directed to report the result of their deliberations to the Conference. The Committee after several meetings and viewing completely the subject in all its bearings, adopted and reported resolutions favourable to seeking reconciliation, by correcting the misunderstandings between the two bodies. The Committee also recommended the appointment of a deputation to the British

Conference. The report was adopted by a large majority of the Conference, and the Rev. J. Ryerson, and the Rev. A. Green were chosen representatives.

On arriving in London, we obtained interviews with the Missionary Secretaries and other leading ministers, but these interviews elicited nothing favourable or encouraging respecting the object of our mission. We were treated as strangers, or parties in whom no one had any interest. Many a sorrowful and anxious hour did the deputation pass during these dark days of discouragement. Yet we were not entirely despondent, but resolved to go forward and meet the Conference which was to commence at Bristol, the 27th of July, 1848. On the second day of the session, Messrs. Ryerson and Green were respectfully received and requested to take seats on the platform; but they were not requested to address the Conference on the subject of their mission, or any other subject; indeed they were virtual'y disallowed doing so throughout the whole session of the Conference. However, they sought every possible opportunity for private conversation with the ministers, especially the leading ones. After being in Bristol ten or twelve days, I sent a note to Dr. Alder, requesting an interview with him; this was granted. I then embraced this opportunity of laying before him **all** the troubles in Canada, in *every* point of view, their causes, origin, progress, results, &c., &c., and most earnestly and affectionately **pressed** on his consideration the terrible magnitude of the evil, and the indispensable duty of those **who** possessed the power to terminate the strife ; that he (Dr. Alder) should **at** once undertake the pacification of the contending parties; that **as he had the** power to restore peace, on him would rest the responsibility **if this wicked** and ruinous warfare continued. **Dr. Alder was** greatly affected and gave me **his promise** and **his** hand to use his utmost **exertions to end** the discord, and have the questions **of dispute settled by such** arrangements as would **most** probably prove beneficial to both parties.

As I have **already said, the** questions at **issue** were not discussed **in the** British Conference ; **but a large** Committee of most **of its** leading **members** was appointed, **to** whom **was** referred **the whole subject,** with **full power to** act in **behalf of the** Conference.

This Committee **met in** London, four or five **weeks after the** Conference, and immediately **entered upon the** business **for** which they were **convened. The** consideration **of** this business engaged their most earnest attention for several **days,** during which time all the troubles in

Canada were impartially and prayerfully investigated—nothing set down in anger **or** malice—
nothing kept **back on** either side.   **Dr.** Richey,
from the Canada District Meeting, **was present**
and took part **in** all **the** discussions, [but against
the Canada Conference.]   The final result was,
the adoption and passing, **by a unanimous vote,**
the resolutions which *now* constitute **the** Articles
of Union between the British and Canadian
Conferences and which are published **in the**
Book of Discipline **of the** Wesleyan Methodist
Church in Canada.   **Dr.** Alder was sent out to
the Canadian Conference, appointed to **be held
at** Toronto, **June,** 1847.   The Canada **District**
assembled in Richmond Street Church **at the**
same time.   The Rev. E. Wood, (now Dr. **Wood)**
from New Brunswick, **accompanied** Dr. **Alder,**
and was made **a** great **instrument of good in**
assisting to adjust **differences.   Several** members of the Canadian Conference **were opposed**
to any settlement **or** re-union **with the British**
Conference.   A pamphlet was published, **signed**
by four **of** the ministers, professing **to review the**
revised Articles of Union, which had been laid
before the **public** on the return **of** the representatives from England. This pamphlet **was a**
fallacious and shallow production which **was**
fully proved in the **course** of **the** discussions
in Conference.   The **great and good** measure

was at length unanimously sanctioned by the Conference, with one, or two, or three exceptions.

The Canada Missionary District was not so well agreed for the restoration of peace, or for the adoption of the resolutions which had been passed to promote it. Their discussions were long and vigorous; but Dr. Alder succeeded ultimately in bringing the meeting to a satisfactory acquiescence, although several of the preachers requested to be removed from the Province to Lower Canada, or elsewhere—a request which was immediately granted.

Thus ended the unnatural strife which had agitated the Church in every part of the country during six long, dark, and painful years. The foundation was laid for union on broad, just, and catholic principles, which have proved so effective in promoting the unity, harmony, and prospects of the Church, and which we trust will for all time bind the two branches of the same family together as long as the militant church is destined to exist.

THE END.

www.ingramcontent.com/pod-product-compliance
Lightning Source LLC
Chambersburg PA
CBHW031348290326
41932CB00044B/565

9 7 8 3 3 3 7 1 8 6 8 8 3